EVERY

OTHER

WEEKEND

Other Books in the Minirth-Meier Clinic Series

The Anger Workbook
Dr. Les Carter, Dr. Frank Minirth
A Circle of Love
Guy Chandler, Laura A. Brown,
Jane Swindell
Don't Let Jerks Get the Best of You
Dr. Paul Meier
The Father Book
Dr. Frank Minirth, Dr. Brian Newman,
Dr. Paul Warren
Imperative People
Dr. Les Carter
In Search of the Heart
Dr. David Allen
The Intimacy Factor
Dr. David Stoop, Jan Stoop
Intimate Moments
David & Teresa Ferguson,
Chris & Holly Thurman
The Lies We Believe
Dr. Chris Thurman
Love Hunger: Recovery from Food Addiction
Dr. Frank Minirth, Dr. Paul Meier,
Dr. Robert Hemfelt, Dr. Sharon Sneed
Love Hunger Weight-Loss Workbook
Dr. Frank Minirth, Dr. Paul Meier,
Dr. Robert Hemfelt, Dr. Sharon Sneed
The Love Hunger Action Plan
Dr. Sharon Sneed
Love Is a Choice
Dr. Robert Hemfelt, Dr. Frank Minirth,
Dr. Paul Meier, Don Hawkins
Love Is a Choice Workbook
Dr. Robert Hemfelt, Dr. Frank Minirth,
Dr. Paul Meier, Dr. Brian Newman,
Dr. Debi Newman
Passages of Marriage
Dr. Frank Minirth, Mary Alice Minirth,
Dr. Brian Newman, Dr. Deborah
Newman, Dr. Robert Hemfelt,
Susan Hemfelt

Passages of Marriage Series
  New Love
  New Love Study Guide
  Realistic Love
  Realistic Love Study Guide
  Steadfast Love
  Steadfast Love Study Guide
  Renewing Love
  Renewing Love Study Guide
  Transcendent Love
  Transcendent Love Study Guide
  Dr. Frank & Mary Alice Minirth,
  Drs. Brian & Deborah Newman,
  Dr. Robert & Susan Hemfelt
The Path to Serenity
  Dr. Robert Hemfelt, Dr. Frank Minirth,
  Dr. Richard Fowler, Dr. Paul Meier
Please Let Me Know You, God
  Dr. Larry D. Stephens
The Quest
  Kevin Brown, Ray Mitsch
Reclaiming Your Inner Child Workbook
  Ken Parker
Steps to a New Beginning
  Sam Shoemaker, Dr. Frank Minirth,
  Dr. Richard Fowler, Dr. Brian
  Newman, Dave Carder
The Thin Disguise
  Pam Vredevelt, Dr. Deborah Newman,
  Harry Beverly, Dr. Frank Minirth
Things that Go Bump in the Night
  Dr. Paul Warren, Dr. Frank Minirth
The Twelve Best Kept Secrets for Living
an Emotionally Healthy Life
  Dr. Chris Thurman
What They Didn't Teach You in Seminary
  Dr. Paul Meier, Dr. Frank Minirth,
  Dr. David Congo, Dr. Brian Newman,
  Dr. Richard Meier, Dr. Allen Doran

For general information about other Minirth-Meier Clinic branch offices, counseling services, educational resources and hospital programs, call toll-free 1-800-545-1819. National Headquarters: 214-669-1733 or 800-229-3000.

EVERY OTHER WEEKEND

Kenneth Parker and Van Jones

A
JANET
THOMA
BOOK

THOMAS NELSON PUBLISHERS
NASHVILLE

Published in Nashville, Tennessee, by Janet Thoma Books, a division of Thomas Nelson, Inc., Publishers, and distributed in Canada by Word Communications, Ltd., Richmond, British Columbia, and in the United Kingdom by Word (UK), Ltd., Milton Keynes, England.

Scripture quotations are from the NEW KING JAMES VERSION of the Bible. Copyright © 1979, 1980, 1982, Thomas Nelson, Inc., Publishers.

Except for those stories clearly identified as the personal experiences of the authors or stories credited to other published sources, all the stories contained in this book are based on composite case studies. Names, places, events, and dialogue have been altered for dramatic and illustrative purposes.

Library of Congress Cataloging-in-Publication Data

Parker, Kenneth F.
    Every other weekend / by Kenneth Parker, Van Jones.
      p. cm.
    ISBN 0-8407-7803-1
    1. Divorced fathers—United States. 2. Father and child—United States. I.
Jones, Van. II. Title
    HQ756.P383 1993
    306.874'2—dc20   93-15276
                                                      CIP

Printed in the United States of America
97 96 95 94 93 — 7 6 5 4 3 2 1

Contents

Acknowledgments

My thanks to my wife, Mary Jo, and my children: Wayne Shoquist, Laurie McConnell, and Mandi Parker—it has been a real adventure that is ever unfolding.

To my parents, Gerald and Tommie Lou Parker, it has been quite a trip, but thank God we took it.

To my Lord who gave me the purpose and the means to achieve it— I'm eternally grateful.

Finally, to my patients, you were my greatest teachers, and I love you all.

—Kenneth F. Parker

To my children, Libby and Benjamin, thank you for so richly enhancing my life, and encouraging me in my "absent" fathering role.

To my stepchildren, Amy, Kevin, and Katie, thank you for allowing me to be a part of your lives.

To my wife, Ibby, thank you so much for the love, support, and wisdom you have shared with me.

Thanks to Kenneth Parker for including me in this project.

To all the families who have experienced the trauma of divorce yet shared your stories so that others may benefit from your experiences—thank you.

—Van Jones

Finally, both authors would like to thank Jim Denney for his professionalism and creativity in putting their ideas into words.

Part One

YOUR PERSPECTIVE

Chapter/1

FATHERING FROM AFAR

The book you hold in your hands didn't just come out of clinical research or psychology textbooks. We have *lived* the issues and experiences in this book. And we are still living them. We have also counseled scores of men who have gone through the same experiences you are going through.

We know what divorce feels like. We know what it means to squeeze your entire fathering role into an every-other-weekend time frame. We know about the anger, the grief, and the fear—especially the fear of losing your children—that surrounds the divorce process.

You'll find our own stories—the personal stories of Kenneth Parker and Van Jones—woven throughout these chapters. We want you to know about the mistakes we have made and the truths we have learned from those mistakes. We want you to know about the hurts we have endured and how we overcame them. We want to show you how we have learned to make the fathering role work, even in the aftermath of divorce.

Here are our stories.

VAN'S STORY

"I slipped the card into the envelope and sealed the flap," recalls Van Jones, "then I wrote my wife's name on the front. The card said, 'Have a great flight and a successful trip! Love, Van.'

"I went into the bedroom. My wife's suitcase was on the bed, packed and shut. In another hour, she would be on a plane for New York, representing her business at a trade show.

"I opened the suitcase and slipped the card between a couple of blouses so she would find it when she unpacked. I had started to shut the lid when I glimpsed the title of a book: *How to Tell Your Children About Divorce*. When I pulled that book out of the pocket, I found two more books in there, both on divorce.

"A wave of cold fear went through me, and for a long moment I felt detached from reality. Why would my wife be reading books about divorce? We had been married seventeen years. We had two beautiful children. We were still in the process of remodeling our dream house. We were doing well financially. Sure, I knew we were both dissatisfied with the state of our marriage. A lot of people are unhappy in their marriages.

"But *divorce!*

"After all, I'm a counselor. When people are having trouble with their marriages, I'm the one they come to for help. How could *my* marriage end in divorce?

"Moments later, I found my wife in the kitchen, a glass of ice water raised to her lips. The shock of my discovery must have shown on my face. For a few long seconds, neither of us said anything. My mind was whirling rapidly, trying to find the words to begin. The only sound was the faint tinkling of ice in her glass.

"'We have to talk,' I said at last, fighting to keep my voice steady.

"'What about?'

"'I was leaving a card in your suitcase . . . I found some books in there. Books about divorce.'

"'Oh.' Her expression was unreadable.

"'Are you planning to get a divorce?' I asked.

"'I'm considering it,' she said. 'We've discussed it before, you know.'

"'Are you serious?'

"She was. We agreed to talk about it when she got back from New York.

"I had denied this could happen to me, and to our family. I didn't believe in divorce. We had two kids, for crying out loud! What would happen to them? And what about the in-laws and extended family members who were so deeply involved with our family?

"Somehow, I knew we would work this thing out. Okay, we had grown apart and no longer had as much in common as we once had. But whatever the problem was, we could fix it. We just needed to talk it out, and things would get better. As soon as she got back from New York, we would get this thing patched up and get on with our marriage.

"But it didn't work out that way."

A Blow to the Solar Plexus

In the fall of 1984, Van Jones and his wife decided to separate.

"My wife had prepared our fourteen-year-old daughter, Libby, for this," Van remembers. "We decided that we would tell our nine-year-old son, Benjamin, together.

"'Benj,' I said, 'we need to talk to you.'

"He looked up at me with an expression that said, *Uh-oh, what did I do now?* He followed my wife and me into the den, with no idea what was coming.

"Our den, with its beamed ceiling and large raised hearth and fireplace, had always been the warmest, most comfortable room in the house. Since that day I've always associated that room with sadness and grief. I couldn't help thinking, *I don't even want this! Why do I have to tell him? Will Benjamin and Libby think this was all my idea? Will my kids hate me for this?*

"I sat down in the big, wooden rocking chair in front of the fireplace, and my wife seated herself a little ways away. I lifted Benjamin into my lap and said, 'Your mother and I are going to get a divorce.'

"His reaction was one of total surprise and innocence. He couldn't understand why his mom and dad would want to do something like this. And then he did what every child *should* do when confronted with news like this: he fell apart. He grieved. He threw his arms around me and wept openly and bitterly. I hugged him tightly to myself as though he might be ripped away from me at any second.

"It was at that point that the divorce first became real to me. As I clutched my son and absorbed his grief into my own soul, I knew at last that my family was being dissolved. Like a blow to the solar plexus, it hit me that my life with my kids was changing forever, and there wasn't anything I could do about it.

" 'Why?' he asked. 'Why are you and Mom getting a divorce?'

" 'Because we don't love each other anymore,' I answered. 'Your mother and I think it's best we don't continue to live together. But no matter what happens between your mother and me, we will always love you.'

"I looked over my shoulder and caught my wife's eye. I don't remember if there were tears in her eyes, but I know there were tears in mine. I thought, *I can't believe you're doing this to us.* I hoped she could read my mind.

"In the next few weeks, I packed up, moved into an apartment, and began finding out what it was like to be single again. What it was mostly was horrible—horribly sad and horribly lonely.

"The divorce proceedings were fairly straightforward. We worked out a decent financial and visitation arrangement. I chose not to fight for custody of my children. I just didn't want to drag them through something as nasty as a custody fight, and we had ruled out joint custody.

"During the two months of our separation, I isolated myself. I grieved. I read books. I jogged a lot. I got a lot of support from good friends and family. I remember a strange sense of unreality during that time, a sense of feeling like this couldn't really be happening. In January 1985, however, when I signed the final divorce decree, I knew it was real.

"A divorce decree is supposed to signify closure, the end of a chapter, the beginning of a new phase in life. In a legal sense, this is true. In an emotional and experiential sense, a divorce decree is just a piece of paper. Divorce is not an event; it is a process. And the process goes on for years.

"For me, the divorce process has been a difficult experience. It's been a period of isolation and loneliness, a period of tough challenges and deep disappointments. But it has also been an experience of personal growth, filled with unexpected joys and dividends. I've been able to build a new quality of relationship with my son and daughter from my first marriage. I've discovered a fulfilling new role as husband and father in my second marriage. I've grown in the challenges that stepfathering presents. And I've also encountered emotional strengths and spiritual resources that I never before knew existed.

"I would never wish the hurt of divorce on anyone," Van concludes. "But for any man who has chosen divorce, or who has had divorce thrust on him, my wish is that he would eventually find the same sense of peace that I've found."

KEN'S STORY

Like Van Jones, Kenneth Parker is a marriage and family counselor. Ken's story is different from Van's, but he, too, is a man who knows the issues of divorce and fathering from the inside. His parents were divorced when he was a child, and today he is the stepfather of two children.

"When I married my present wife, Mary Jo," Ken recalls, "her children, Wayne and Laurie, were both in grade school. Technically, they became my stepchildren, although I quickly grew to love them and to think of them as *my* own kids. Two years after we were married, Mary Jo and I had a daughter, Mandi.

"When Wayne was in high school, he played quick back on the football team. He was a fine young man, a good student, and a good athlete. I was very proud of him. So was Wayne's biological father.

"Wayne's father and I have always gotten along well. We would sit side by side in the stands and cheer Wayne on throughout his high school football career. During one game, Wayne won an award for his achievements on the field: a football painted in the school colors. After receiving the football, Wayne's girlfriend dashed up into the stands and handed it to me. 'Hold this for me, okay?' she said. 'I'll get it after the game.'

"The game started, and Wayne's father and I sat watching.

" 'Hey, Ken!' called a voice below me. I looked and there, climbing up the bleachers toward me, was an acquaintance of mine, a fellow named Tom. 'What do you have there?' Tom asked.

" 'Oh, this?' I asked, holding up Wayne's football. I started to answer—then stopped.

"Should I say, '*My* son won it'? No, not with Wayne's biological father sitting right next to me. I didn't want to be rude to him.

"Then should I point to Wayne's father next to me and say, '*His* son won it'? Absolutely not! Wayne was my son too.

"I thought for a moment. Pointing to both of us, I said, '*Our* son won it!'

"Tom just stood there for a moment with the funniest look on his face. Then he shook his head and walked away.

"Divorce creates situations and relationships that can be difficult, sometimes awkward to explain, sometimes funny to think back on. But divorce doesn't have to result in lifelong pain and bitterness for the parents or indelible emotional scars for the kids. Divorce doesn't mean that we as fathers have to lose our kids or our role as fathers. Genuine fatherhood—a rich, rewarding, effective fathering role—is still possible, even after divorce.

"I bring a little different perspective to the subject of fathering from afar than Van does. Unlike Van, I have not been separated from my own biological child by divorce. Rather, my perspective is that of the child of divorce (my parents divorced when I was six) and of the stepfather. I also have firsthand experience of divorce and remarriage. By pooling the insights of our life experience and counseling experience, Van and I have assembled a comprehensive picture of the feelings, issues, and problems of fathering from afar, and we deliver an arsenal of practical strategies for dealing with those feelings, issues, and problems."

Calling It Quits

Ken recalls his experience with divorce. It's an experience which has given him an understanding of the problems of divorced men.

"I joined the Navy fresh out of high school in 1965. During my four years in the service, I did two tours of the Gulf of Tonkin aboard a destroyer, the USS *Preston*. After my discharge, I settled briefly in Long Beach, California. There I fell in love and married a divorcée with a child of her own. Like a lot of ex-servicemen in their early twenties, I had been around the world and I thought I knew what life was all about.

"The truth is, I didn't know the first thing about responsibility and relationships, and I had no business getting married. To me, getting married was not a lifetime commitment, nor was it just a temporary fling. It was simply something I wanted to do. I was living for the moment, without any thoughts of the future.

"We moved from Southern California, where she had been living, to Wichita Falls, Texas. And for a California girl, Wichita Falls takes some getting used to. To be truthful, I was a guy who also took some getting used to. I liked my bars, my drinking, and my night life. After a few years, I figured out that the only thing I didn't like about my life was being married.

"My wife hadn't done anything wrong. We didn't have an extraordinary amount of conflict. It was just that there was not much of a relationship between us, and I was too self-centered to try to make things work. My attitude was: it was fun while it lasted, but being married just doesn't suit me. I thought nothing of just calling it quits and shedding my responsibilities like a snake shedding its skin.

The divorce was my idea, and even though my wife didn't really want a divorce, she didn't fight it either. I put her and her child on an airplane, and they went back to California. I never saw either of them again, and I only heard from her once after that (a short phone call about a tax matter).

"Looking back, I regret the ease with which I bailed out on a commitment and a relationship. I continue to be astonished at the casual way that I just put my wife on a plane and sent her out of my life without a single twinge of conscience. I was immature, to say the least.

"I remained unmarried for the next five years, working on a degree in counseling during the day while enjoying my wild life at night. Finally, in 1977, I met and married my present wife, Mary Jo. She was working as a secretary at the mental health center where I worked. Like my first wife, Mary Jo was a divorcée, and she had two children. Our decision to marry was impulsive—no long courtship, no careful planning, no long-term thinking about the future. We simply fell in love and got married.

"Ever since my discharge from the Navy, I had been a heavy drinker. After four years of putting up with my lifestyle, Mary Jo sat me down for a serious talk. In her quiet but firm way, she told me, 'You can continue drinking if you want to. But if you do, then there are some choices I will have to make.' I didn't like the sound of that. But she was right. I had to honestly confront the effect my drinking was having on my wife, my stepkids, my biological daughter, and myself.

"Ironically, I had been a therapist for years and had already counseled scores of alcoholics. (Often while I was hung over myself!) But until Mary Jo confronted me, I had denied the obvious fact that I was as much an alcoholic as many of the people I counseled. Once I came to terms with my own addictive behavior, my choices became crystal clear. I immediately stopped drinking. In fact, I became as compulsive about my abstinence as I had previously been about my drinking. It was, at least, a healthy compulsion.

"At about that time, I started reading the *Big Book of Alcoholics Anonymous*. This is the book that first formulated A.A.'s famous 'Twelve Steps.' Those Steps make frequent reference to 'God as we understand Him' or 'a Power greater than ourselves.' The Twelve Steps forced me to take a serious look at the spiritual dimension of life and to confront a number of questions: Is God real? Is He relevant to my life? Should I make a decision to turn my will and my life over to this higher Power?

"Today," Ken concludes, "the spiritual dimension of my life is an essential factor in the decisions I make in my relationships and in my lifestyle. Later in this book, we will show how the spiritual component has a profound effect on our role as fathers—particularly as men who want to be effective, *involved* fathers to our kids, despite the geographical distance that separates us from them."

WE'VE BEEN DOWN THAT ROAD

We have spent hundreds of hours as students of psychology, as clinical counselors, and as observers of the human condition. Yet, even with all our academic study and clinical practice, we believe it is our life experience that has truly shaped our approaches to the issues in this book. The principles you will encounter in the following chapters are real because we know what you are going through. If your parents were divorced during your childhood, if you are feeling your way through the wilderness of divorce right now, if you are a stepfather trying to fit into a new family, if you are afraid you may be losing your kids, if you are seeing relationships damaged because of your addiction to alcohol or some other substance—we really do understand. We've been down those roads.

The journey hasn't been easy for either of us. And neither has yours. We know that. We've all made mistakes; we've been hurt; and we've hurt others, including those we love the most. The key is to take stock of where we are, admit our mistakes, learn from them, and start making the changes that will help make us better fathers and better human beings. It is never too late to change.

THE GOOD NEWS

We have written a practical, personal, nontechnical guide for *absent* fathers who still want to be *effective* fathers. This book is for men who have been divorced and who do not have custody of their children, but who still want to maintain a good relationship with their kids. In these pages, we will show you that it really is possible to maintain a positive, involved fathering role with your kids—even on an every-other-weekend basis.

From the outset, we want you to know that, even though you are going through one of the toughest experiences you will ever have to face, you're going to be okay. One of the most painful aspects of divorce for any man is the sense of powerlessness it creates—the feeling that life is spinning out of his control. That is why we have included a number of specific strategies that will *enable* you to regain control of your fathering role and *empower* you to be the kind of father you want to be.

It really doesn't matter who initiated the divorce. It doesn't matter who did what to whom, whether the breakup was "your fault" or "her fault." That's history. It does no good to endlessly ask ourselves, "Why did this happen?" It's much more crucial to decide, "This is what I can do about it right now." It's normal to feel angry in the aftermath of a divorce, but it's important to try to move beyond blaming and bitterness. Blaming hinders recovery. Our goal is to give you the practical tools you need, so that you can work effectively within the system as it exists today.

In this book, you will get straight talk, practical counsel, and realistic, experience-based insights. This is men talking to men, so we can talk freely about the problems men face during a separation and divorce. We're not going to try to sell you a lot of empty platitudes or psycho-jargon. We're not going to preach to you and tell you this is what you "ought" to do. We're here to talk about *what works*.

In the next few pages, we will examine what happens to Dad, Mom, and the kids when their family splits up. We'll talk about what the divorce experience is like for children, so you can better understand and respond to what your kids are going through. We'll explore ways to close the books on unfinished emotional business so you can get on with the business of living. We'll also discover some of the surprising (and often hidden) legal ramifications of divorce and absent fathering, including what your rights and responsibilities may be.

Because you're reading this book, it's clear that you want to succeed as a father, despite your divorce. The good news is that you *can* succeed. You can make your fathering role work, both for you and your children, even if you only see them every other weekend.

Let's not fool each other. Fathering from afar is not an easy job. It's tough. *Man, is it tough!* But the rewards are enormous: the life-long friendship and respect of your children and the pleasure of seeing them grow into happy, secure adults.

You *can* do it. You can build that kind of lifelong relationship with your children. And you will.

You've already taken the first step.

Chapter 2

WHEN FAMILIES SPLIT

Carl is a stockbroker, a member of the Chamber of Commerce and the Golden Lakes Country Club. He's a real button-down kind of guy. He wears Italian three-piece suits, his tie is just the right width, and his hair is just the right length. His manners, his speech, and his behavior have always been perfectly proper . . . that is, until his divorce. Since he and Katy split up, he's been acting a little crazy.

Take the time he got his nose broken.

He pulled in the driveway of the house that used to be *his* house. When Katy married the dirty so-and-so who broke up their happy home, the dirty so-and-so elected to move into the house with Katy and the kids. The rationale was that it would be less stressful for the kids if they could stay in their own environment.

Carl knew the *real* reason the guy moved into the house Carl was still making payments on. It was Katy's idea—just one more vicious way to grind her spike heels into Carl's face!

Carl got out of the car and stamped up the front walk. He pounded on the expensive solid-oak front door (which he had hung on the hinges with his own hands six years ago during a mad frenzy of do-it-yourself home improvement). By now, Carl had worked

himself into a pretty good lather. He was so angry that he had virtually forgotten that his reason for being there was to pick up his kids
for their every-other-weekend visit at his one-bedroom apartment.

It didn't help Carl's disposition any when the door opened and
there stood Brad, Katy's new husband (the dirty so-and-so himself).
"Oh," said Brad, "it's you." Barring the doorway with his body to
make it clear that Carl wasn't welcome inside, he turned and called
over his shoulder, "Kids, your dad is here!"

Then Brad and Carl stood and faced each other for a few long,
awkward moments. Finally, Carl sighed and said, "You should've
had them ready when I got here. You knew I was going to be here at
nine."

Brad gave one of his smug, superior grins. "You know, those kids
are late all the time. I've been trying to break them of that, but you
know how it is with kids and bad habits—"

"What's that supposed to mean?" asked Carl defensively. "When
my kids lived with me, they were *never* late. If you're saying it's my
fault that they—"

"Hey, chill out, Carl," said Brad, with that patented smirk of his.
Carl would have just loved to wipe that smirk off his face. "Don't
take everything so personally. The kids will be out in a minute, and
you can be on your way, okay?"

"Just put a lid on the small talk, Brad, and we'll get along just
fine."

"You're gonna wear a hole in your gut carrying around all that
hostility, Carl."

"You just keep your nose out of my gut, *Bradley*." Carl knew Brad
hated to be called Bradley. He liked the way the guy stiffened whenever anyone called him that.

Just then, Katy appeared at the door. "Oh, hi, Carl," she said
cheerily (a little *too* cheerily, thought Carl; it was obviously put on
for his benefit). She wrapped her arms around Brad and clung to
him like a teenager clinging to her steady boyfriend. This was getting downright nauseating!

"Kids!" Carl shouted, his blood simmering, heading for a full,
rolling boil. "Will you get out here now!"

"That vein's standing out on your forehead again, Carl," Katy observed. Indeed, Carl's blood pressure could have blown the gauge right off a sphygmomanometer, and Katy's remark didn't help any.

Brad cupped one hand over his mouth and whispered something in Katy's ear. Both laughed at the private joke. It was more than Carl could stand. Something snapped inside him. Before he realized what was happening, his right hand balled into a fist and pulled back like the piston of an old-time steam engine.

All three kids, Rex, Jill, and Kami, appeared just in time to see their father land a haymaker right in their stepfather's breadbasket. Unfortunately for Carl, Brad had been working out on the Nautilus machine lately. He absorbed Carl's haymaker without flinching, then returned a shot of his own. It found Carl's nose like a Cruise missile homing on a Scud launcher. In full view of his ex-wife and three kids, Carl got his nose broken and bloodied.

Five minutes later, the police arrived and found Carl kneeling on the sidewalk, bleeding onto the lantanas. Katy's lawyer showed up too. So did half the neighborhood. It was the worst humiliation of Carl's entire adult life.

Today, a court order prevents Carl (solid-citizen, button-down stockbroker Carl) from setting foot on the property he still makes mortgage payments on. Every other Saturday, his ex-wife brings the children to her attorney's office and leaves. Then Carl picks the kids up at the office and takes them home. The kids call this process "the prisoner of war exchange."

When families split, human behavior can get pretty crazy.

AN INSIGHT-ORIENTED APPROACH

What made Carl behave the way he did? In his business life, he is careful, considerate, and prudent in all his decisions. Under pressure, he is as cool as the center seed of a cucumber. Why, then, in the aftermath of divorce, does he relate to his ex-wife and her new husband like some sort of hairy primate? Different counselors and therapists would give you different answers to these questions.

A behavioral therapist might say to Carl, "Let's take a look at your behavior. What you have learned from this situation is that when you go to your ex-wife's house and encounter her new husband, conflict arises. Therefore, what changes can you make in your behavior that would keep this problem from happening again in the future?"

The behavioral approach imposes external controls or limits on what a person does, so that he can make better choices in the future. In Carl's case, the court imposed exactly that sort of remedy on Carl when it ordered him to stay away from the house where his ex-wife, his children, and his muscular rival lived. The court created controls on Carl's behavior by arranging for him to meet his kids on comparatively neutral territory—an attorney's office.

A cognitive therapist would take a different approach. The word "cognitive" comes from the Latin *cognoscere*, which means "to know, to think, to perceive." A cognitive therapist would ask Carl, "What are you thinking and telling yourself when you go to your ex-wife's house? What kinds of things are you saying to yourself that are causing conflict to arise?"

A lot of Carl's anger could be traced to the bitter, resentful thoughts he had as he drove over to the house, as he pulled into the driveway, as he knocked on the door: "Why do I have to make payments on a house this guy is living in? Why do I have to live in a crummy, one-bedroom apartment? Katy just loves grinding her spike heels into my face! And that dirty so-and-so she married! Boy, would I love to wipe that smirk right off his face!" And on and on. Psychologists call this kind of thinking *negative self-talk*.

The cognitive therapist would say, "Let's change your self-talk. Let's substitute positive for negative self-talk, so that your thinking no longer leads you into conflict."

Behavioral therapy and cognitive therapy: these are two good, productive approaches. From the examples above, you can see how Carl could have been helped by either of these approaches.

We, however, take a slightly different approach, what we call an "insight-oriented" approach. If Carl would come to either Van or Ken with this problem, we would say, "Carl, let's see if we can find out what is going on inside you that is setting you up for conflict. What are the unconscious messages and emotional forces operating beneath the surface of your behavior, beneath the surface of your thinking?"

Those unconscious messages and emotional forces deep inside us drive both our thinking and our behavior. Because they come from hidden sources within us, such as repressed traumas or emotional wounds in childhood, those messages are the hardest to uncover and reveal. They lurk, hidden yet powerful, beneath the surface of our awareness.

What we do in our counseling practices, and what we are seeking to accomplish in this book, is to raise your level of understanding and insight. Our goal is to help you discover *why* you do and think in certain unproductive ways, so that you can make productive changes. Our goal is to help you come to a place where you can say, "So *that's* why I do that!"

Insight-oriented therapy can also help us to better understand why the other players in the drama of our lives do the things they do. Another goal of this book is to help you come to a place where you can say, "So *that's* why she does those things! That's why she says those things! That's why my kids act the way they do!"

If we can better understand our own hidden motivations, and those of the people around us, we can learn to interact more productively and to do the things that are in our own best interests and in the best interests of our children.

UNDERSTANDING THE FAMILY SYSTEM

One of the best tools we have for revealing and understanding hidden motivations is a concept called *systems theory*. It may sound complex, but it is actually a very simple concept. With just a brief introduction to systems theory, we believe you will gain a much clearer understanding of what happens when families split, why various people in the family do the things they do, and why you do the things you do.

According to systems theory, a system may be defined as "a collection of several parts which work together in a cooperative way." The efficient functioning of the system depends on each of the parts fulfilling certain roles and working in certain ways. In organizations such as corporations and bureaucracies, the parts of the system could be departments, offices, or individual people in the organization. In a family system, those parts are the people in the family. Each family member has an assigned role and certain assigned duties within that role. These roles are not assigned in a conscious way. Seldom does anyone in the family system say, "I'll do such and such, and you do this, and she'll do that." People tend to settle into their roles without consciously examining them, and these roles become interactive and interdependent. Each family member depends on all the other family members to function within their roles.

In the family system, Dad has certain responsibilities, duties, and roles. Mom has her responsibilities, duties, and roles, which complement Dad's. The children also have their roles. All of these prescribed roles are interlocking and interdependent. Because the family is a system made up of parts that function together in a cooperative way, families will tend to follow certain predictable patterns of behavior and interaction.

Here is a diagram of a typical family system prior to a divorce. Let's use the Cleaver family from the TV series *Leave It To Beaver* to illustrate the point:

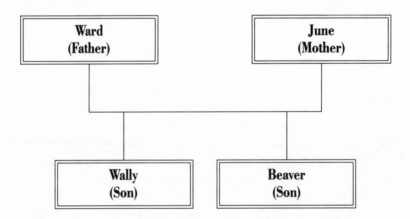

When families split, regardless of whose idea the divorce or separation was, the result is *two new systems,* each with vestiges of the former system superimposed. Here's what the Cleaver family might look like after divorce:

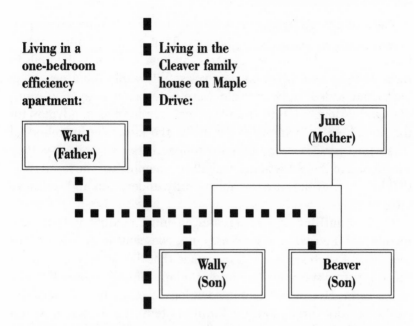

Notice, first of all, the geographical arrangement of the Cleaver family following the breakup between Ward and June. Ward lives by himself in an efficiency apartment near his office. June, Wally, and the Beav still live in the two-story house on Maple Drive. This raises an important subject: even today, with changing legal and social attitudes toward custody arrangements, it is still almost always the case that when a family splits, Dad ends up by himself and the kids end up with Mom. (We will look at custody and living arrangements in greater detail in later chapters.)

Next, notice that there are now *two* overlapping systems. Each new system contains one biological parent. One system consists of Ward, Wally, and the Beav. The other system consists of June, Wally, and the Beav. Each parent has a vested interest in the children; each has parental responsibilities and duties; each has history and memories built up with those children; each has certain patterns of relating to the other parent. These two new systems, which were once part of a single family system, now function in geographically different places—and the children have one foot in each system.

The original family system was made up of individuals with pre-scribed roles and expected behaviors. That original family system has now split into two new systems, and each of the individuals in those systems now takes on new roles. Yet, while some new roles have been added, some old roles have been taken away. For exam-ple, Dad no longer has the role of carpenter-plumber-handyman for the household or homework coach for the kids. The members of these two new systems can no longer function the way they functioned in the old system. And all the members of the family feel that loss, even if they are not able to fully understand and verbalize what they feel.

This re-shuffling of roles creates an inner conflict within each member of the two new systems. On a conscious level, the various members of each system will recognize that the old system is gone, this is a new system, and each must adapt himself or herself to the new system. However, on an unconscious level, there is a strong dy-namic at work throughout the family system: the old system strug-gles to right itself and restore itself.

We hasten to add, however, that the fact that many family mem-bers want to restore the old system does *not* mean that Mom is eager for reconciliation. What she longs for is stability, a sense of order in her family life. And she may feel that the best way to set the system right is by excluding you.

What Happens to Mom in the New System?

She is dealing with a new role. In the vast majority of divorce cases, she becomes what is called *the custodial parent* (that is, she is awarded custody of the children). In their book, *Second Chances: Men, Women and Children a Decade after Divorce* (New York: Ticknor & Fields, 1990), authors Wallerstein and Blakeslee report that close to 90 percent of children remain in their mother's primary custody after divorce. Even in situations where there is joint cus-tody, the kids usually live most of the year with Mom. (Joint custody is a concept that is not well understood by most people. Even when Mom and Dad share custodial responsibility, the kids usually live primarily with Mom. For a complete discussion of custody issues, see Chapter 5: The Absent Father and the Law.)

She is now the sole authority figure in her new family system, which means she assumes a lot of added responsibility. She must fulfill the role of both parents. She is required to transact business—particularly visitation and child support business—with a person who used to be her partner and who is now (in an unfortunate majority of cases) her adversary.

In some respects, Mom's role may not change that much. She is still parenting the kids on a daily basis, just as before. In most cases, she continues living in the same home. And although she may now have to take on an additional responsibility as breadwinner, roughly two-thirds of American households are two-income households to begin with. Therefore if Mom was already working outside the home, that aspect of her role may remain largely unchanged.

Her lifestyle, however, has changed. Her responsibilities are greater than before. In many cases, she has to make a dollar go further now. She must now see to many of the decisions and household duties (bill-paying, car repair, home maintenance) that may have been Dad's responsibility in the past. On the average, women with young children experience a 73 percent decline in their standard of living during the first year after divorce (Wallerstein & Blakeslee, 1990). Even in the best and most amicable of divorces, Mom acquires a lot of added stresses and problems. Her life becomes more complicated.

What Happens to the Children in the New System?

The children are usually more strongly impacted by divorce than Mom. They now have only one custodial parent. Whereas they used to be part of one system, they now have membership in *two* family systems. They suddenly have to deal with issues of divided loyalty: *Mom and Dad are at odds. I love them both. How can I be loyal to one without being disloyal to the other?*

Roles become confused. The role of a six-year-old child, for example, may become that of a "supporter" of a grieving or angry parent. Instead of being cared *for*—as a six-year-old child is supposed to be—the child may find himself or herself in a "care-*giving*" role toward one or both parents. The child's energies are consumed by the effort of having to assume roles that are not appropriate to the maturity-level of a six-year-old.

They find themselves having to answer to two separate parents, often with separate sets of rules for each household (or family system). Whereas the two parents used to function as a joint parental unit, they have now become two separate units. Each parent has different values, and these differences will be reflected in the two new family systems.

Mom may not let the children watch PG-rated movies; Dad may draw the line at R. Mom may impose a school-night bedtime of 8:30; Dad may say 10:00. Mom may give each child a set of chores and duties; Dad's household may be leisure-land. (Of course, it could be the other way around, with Mom being the easy-going parent and Dad playing the role of General Patton.)

Prior to the divorce, both parents had their individual values, beliefs, and parenting styles, just as they do after the divorce. The difference is that Mom and Dad were able to sort through all the parenting decisions together when they lived under the same roof. Now they can't, and the differences between Mom and Dad—and between their respective family systems—have become much more pronounced.

The children experience the greatest changes in their relationship with absent Dad. He used to live at home. If the kids needed him to help with problems, answer questions, or pal around with, he was usually there. Now time with Dad is intermittent, and must be scheduled well in advance.

Life becomes even more complicated for children if one or both of their parents remarry. Just about the time everyone has figured out his or her new role in the new system and things begin to settle down, Mom or Dad remarries. This upsets everything! The kids are really divided now. We have Mom, we have Dad, we have a stepparent—and suddenly there is all this *tension* again!

Confusion sets in. The child started out with just one system. Then that system split in two. Now the number of systems is compounding at an exponential rate. There are new in-laws, new siblings, and new grandparents to relate to. It is not unusual for such children to have four parents and six or more grandparents showing up at their school plays, sporting events, and graduation exercises.

Life gets even more complicated if the stepparent brings children into the relationship. Now the child must fit these new siblings into his or her world.

Let's say that at the same time Ward and June Cleaver split up, there is another TV divorce. Shortly after the cancellation of *Father Knows Best*, Jim and Margaret Anderson's marriage hits the rocks. Jim meets June Cleaver at a singles mixer, they fall in love, and get married. Just look at the resulting systems:

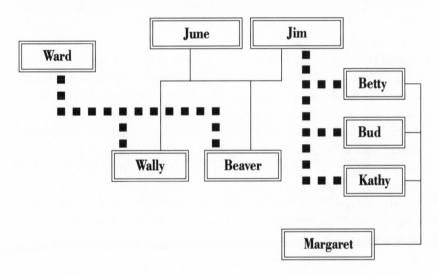

How many systems can you count in the above diagram? Ward and his sons, Wally and the Beav, are a system. June, Jim, Wally, and Beaver are another. Jim and his three kids, Betty, Bud, and Kathy, are another. So are Margaret, Betty, Bud, and Kathy. During the summer, Jim's three kids come to live with him, June, and her two boys (it's a big house); that's another system.

Oh, we almost forgot to mention that Margaret Anderson has been dating Sheriff Andy Taylor of Mayberry, and if *they* get married . . .

Well, if you're getting confused, think how the kids must feel!

What Happens to Dad in the New System?

Let's take a look at the systems involved: even though Mom and the kids have formed a new system, it is not all that different from the old system. Often, they still live in the same house. The kids usually continue going to the same school. The routines and roles change somewhat, but not all that much.

Now look at Dad's new circumstances: He has become a system of one. Sure, he is still the children's father, but he no longer has daily contact with them, and this fact often creates an enormous sense of loss, grief, and sadness for the absent Dad. Usually he is the one who moves out, so he must now adjust to a smaller, more modest living space (and often a starkly silent and lonely living space at that).

Dad has experienced a shattering revision in his role. Many men tend to derive their sense of worth and identity from their work and family roles. Divorce, then, has the effect of stripping away about two-thirds of Dad's identity. Many of the roles that defined him as a man: husband, father, provider, advisor, fix-it man, maintenance supervisor, and so forth have been suddenly wiped out. He has moved out of his house and into an efficiency apartment. He is stunned and disoriented.

"My divorce," recalls Ken, "was entirely my idea. I thought that once I was on my own again, I would be 'free.' I was totally unprepared for the impact that divorce—a divorce I asked for and wanted—would have on me.

"I remember the day I took my first wife and her child to the airport, put them on the plane, and sent them out of my life. After they left, I drove back home and walked into an empty house. All at once, it hit me: What do I do now? It was amazing how those hours stretched endlessly ahead of me.

"No matter whose idea it is, divorce is hard on a man."

Now, we are *not* saying that anybody has it easy in a divorce. Please don't shove this book in your ex-wife's face and say, "See there? These guys are counselors, and they say you women have it easy and we men have it tough!" That's not what we're saying at all. Divorce is devastating to everyone involved. We are not minimizing the wife's pain, which is certainly considerable. Rather, we are underscoring the fact that the male partner to a divorce has specific areas of hurt and trauma that result from his displacement from the family system. For decades, the father's special hurts have been discounted, under-addressed, and even ignored by society. We want to correct that deficiency in this book.

There are so many features of the fathering role which, taken one by one, seem minor. Yet the sudden removal of all of these responsibilities, chores, and pleasures of fathering can have a profound psychological impact on Dad. He no longer gives guidance, help, and discipline to his children. He no longer tucks them into bed, reads them a story, or receives their hugs around his neck. He's no longer there to fix the slipped chain on his son's bicycle or drive his daughter to her dance class. If Dad wants to teach his kids how to dribble a basketball or swing a bat, he has to squeeze it into his two allotted weekends a month. He is no longer simply a father, but an *absent father*.

The drastic impact of divorce upon Dad becomes even more apparent when we look at his role from the perspective of systems theory:

The original family system has split in two. Absent father becomes a system of one. Mother and the children start a new system of their own. Within a few weeks or months, this new system develops its own rhythms and routines. It finds its own equilibrium and is soon functioning without Dad. Before long, it has actually built up a tendency to *exclude* Dad.

The System Hates Change

"Exclude Dad?" you might ask. "How can that be? Sure, my ex-wife isn't particularly fond of me these days, but my *kids?* They *love* me!"

Sure they do. But the system is powerful. *And the system abhors change.*

In his 1963 book *The Ordeal of Change*, the American longshoreman-turned-philosopher, Eric Hoffer, tells a story that shows how strongly we human beings fear change. The story takes place during the Great Depression of the 1930s, when Hoffer was struggling to survive as a migrant farm laborer. Hoffer was part of a group of laborers who worked in the fields picking peas.

One day, the road boss came into the field and told the laborers that they would be put on a train and shipped to another state. There, they would be put to work picking green beans.

Hoffer immediately saw a change of mood come over his fellow workers—a deep gloom, a sense of foreboding. At the same time, Hoffer noted a real feeling of fear within himself. This gloomy mood persisted among the men as they climbed aboard the train and began their trek to the new fields. Throughout the trip, Hoffer pondered why there was such a sense of apprehension within himself and these other men. *This is ridiculous,* he thought. *We're all far from home, whether we pick peas or green beans. The work is hard, whether we pick peas or green beans. The money is terrible, whether we pick peas or green beans. What is the difference whether we pick one vegetable or another?*

Then an insight occurred to Hoffer: *We know we can pick peas. We don't know yet if we can pick green beans.*

Change scares us. Even a seemingly insignificant change can be threatening to us. As individual human beings and as systems (organized collections of human beings) we like consistency, familiarity, and routine. Most of all, *we hate change!*

Family systems, too, are threatened by change. Whenever some aspect of the system becomes disrupted or out of balance, the system will always attempt to right itself and return to its original state. Once Mom and the kids have become a system of their own, once they have started functioning with their own rhythms and routines, Dad is no longer part of the system. In fact, he may even be treated as an intruder.

When the System Wobbles

The functioning of the new system of Mom and the kids could be compared to balancing an automobile tire. To balance the tire, you add or subtract lead weights to different parts of the wheel rim. You keep making adjustments to the weights until the tire can spin without wobbling.

During the first few weeks and months without Dad, Mom and the kids are making those same kinds of adjustments, changing this or that aspect of their lives to try to get their family system to function efficiently and stop wobbling. Finally they get their system balanced and functioning smoothly without Dad. So if Dad re-enters the system—for example, when he shows up at the house on visitation days—it is like adding a weight to the rim of an already-balanced wheel. Their family system begins to wobble, and struggles to restore its balance. And it frequently does so by excluding Dad.

It is natural in a situation like this for Dad to feel anger, bitterness, and hurt. Though he doesn't understand *why* he has been excluded by the system, he knows that he has come to feel like an intruder instead of a father. He may respond by taking an adversarial stance toward his ex-wife. The children may then become pawns in a battle which nobody wins.

This is the dynamic that was being played out in the life of Carl, the somewhat out-of-control stockbroker we met at the beginning of this chapter. He didn't know anything about systems theory. All he knew was that he felt like an outsider in the house he once lived in and was still paying for—and he was boiling mad.

At a conscious level, he knew he had been excluded by the system, which had once been *his* family system. He had lost his wife, his home, and a huge chunk of his finances. He no longer had the kind of contact with his kids he once enjoyed. And another guy was sleeping with his ex-wife and playing father to his kids. (Brad, the other guy in Carl's case, happened to be a jerk—but the same hurt and angry feelings Carl felt can occur in an absent father even if the other guy is a decent and likeable fellow.)

On an unconscious level, his self-esteem had taken a bruising. He felt inferior and ineffectual as a human being. "I'm not much of a man," he told himself. "If I were, I would still have my family."

How did Carl respond to these feelings? By *working against the system*—violently. He threw an ill-advised punch at his ex-wife's husband and got his nose flattened in return. He was humiliated before his ex-wife, his kids, and his former neighbors.

But Carl has since learned that there is a better way. A way of working not against the system, but *within* the system. A way that is best for everyone involved: best for his ex-wife, best for his children, and yes, best for himself as well.

In the coming chapters, we are going to show how an absent father can operate effectively and positively in the new system, and continue to be the kind of father he wants to be. We will explore the functioning of the entire system, and we will learn how to see the world through the eyes of each player in the system. When you turn the page, we will begin by taking a closer look at the emotional price a man pays when he goes through a divorce.

Chapter/3

HOW IT FEELS

I made a last-ditch effort," recalls Van Jones, "to get my marriage and my family back together again. I was sure that if we could just start talking, we could work it out. So I talked my wife into going with me to a marriage counselor. 'Just one counseling session,' I said. 'Just one hour with a counselor. Is that too much to ask after seventeen years of marriage?'

"Well, she agreed to go with me—just for one session. So we got into the counselor's office. It's hard to remember clearly what all my motives were, but I suspect that on some level I felt the therapist would side with me. In the back of my mind, I was probably thinking, 'This guy will certainly see how hard I'm trying to work things out, and he'll see how unreasonable my wife is being. He'll help me find some way to maneuver her back in line.' I was really in denial at that point. I could not accept that this was really happening, and that our marriage had been deteriorating for a long time.

"When we arrived at the counselor's office, my wife was very reserved, very polite. I, on the other hand, came in with my agenda all planned, and I launched right into it. For the next forty-five minutes, I talked about how I was going to really work on our issues, how I was going to be a changed man, how I was going to be a better listener and a better husband. It was the most eloquent speech of my entire life.

"When I had finished, the counselor turned to my wife and asked, 'Would you like to work with your husband on these issues?'

"She said, 'No. I don't want to work on these issues. I simply want a divorce. There is nothing else to discuss.'

"My wife had prepared herself for the decisions we were about to make. She knew where she was and what she wanted. I had been thinking that my forty-five-minute monologue was somehow going to shake her determination, but that wasn't going to happen. My wife had faced the fact that our marriage was not working, I had not. I had been in denial for quite a long time.

"The counselor looked at me and asked, 'What do you want to do now?'

"I spread my hands and said, 'I dunno. What can we do?'

"He said, 'Okay. It appears that things will just follow their course.' Meaning: divorce was inevitable. So the session ended, and things did indeed follow their course.

"I've seen denial from both sides. I saw it from the inside prior to and during my separation and divorce. And I've seen it from the outside as a therapist. Every now and then, a couple comes to me for counseling and it's obvious what's going on: one spouse has filed for divorce, and the other has dragged the spouse into my office in a last-ditch attempt to save their marriage. And I look at these people and I see myself and my ex-wife sitting in those chairs. One of them says to me, 'We're getting close to a divorce. Can you help us?' And the other replies, 'We're not just close to divorce. We're there.' It's like deja vu, a replay of that period in my own life. Once you see this pattern unfolding, you know how it's going to end."

Denial is one of a number of stages people go through during the divorce process. Other stages in the process include bargaining, anger, and acceptance. If these emotional stages of the divorce process sound familiar, it is because these are also the emotional stages of the dying process.

In 1969, the Swiss psychiatrist Elisabeth Kubler-Ross wrote a book called *On Death and Dying* (New York: Macmillan, 1970) in which she identified five stages people go through when they realize they are about to die. What many psychologists and psychiatrists have found, however, is that these stages are not only associated with facing the loss of one's life but accompany *any* major loss. The loss of a career. The loss of one's health. A major financial loss. The loss of a loved one. The loss of a marriage. The loss of daily contact with one's children.

In the next few pages, we have added two stages to the five Kubler-Ross stages, adapting those stages to the specific emotional issues of the divorce process. People who are dying have to accommodate themselves to the fact that their lives are about to end. People who are going through divorce have to accommodate themselves to the fact that their lives are going to go on but in a fundamentally different way than before. When a marriage disintegrates, the father goes through a grief-like path that is very personal and individual yet also fairly predictable in its stages. The first stage of that path is *denial*.

DENIAL

Denial usually begins when the problems in the marriage begin. One or both parties in the marriage says, "Sure, we've got problems. Doesn't everybody? All we need to do is work harder. If things become too much for us to work out ourselves, we'll talk to a friend or to our pastor. I'll change. She'll change. Somebody will change. But therapy? Professional counseling? No, that's for people with *real* marriage problems, not for people like us."

This couple will drift along for a while, denying the issues that are pulling them apart. Eventually things will become so bad that one party finds the marriage unbearable. There's one silent treatment too many. Or one fight too many. Or one hurt too many. And one side or the other says, "Enough is enough. I'm getting out." Now things have come to a head. A crisis has been provoked. Sometimes the shock of that crisis is enough to jar the denying party out of his or her denial. Sometimes a bad situation is still reversible, even at the point of crisis.

But all too often, as Van experienced, the crisis point merely sets the stage for another level of denial: "Okay, I admit I've let our relationship deteriorate. I admit I had a lot to do with the problems in our marriage. All right, so maybe I don't win the prize for 'Husband of the Year.' But we can still turn this thing around. She won't really leave me. I'm going to change, and we're going into counseling, and everything's going to be just fine."

In many (if not most) cases, by the time the relationship reaches the crisis stage, it is too late for things to be "just fine." A ship whose course might have been corrected at an early part of the voyage is now headed straight for the rocks, and there's no time to turn her around. It's time to hit the lifeboats.

"Some couples come into my office," says Ken, "and they are clearly headed for divorce, yet one of them just can't see it. The wife may say to me, 'I want a divorce. I never want to live near this man again. I refuse to even go home with him tonight. I'm leaving him the moment we walk out of this office. I just came to your office today because I want you to make him understand that I'm absolutely serious about this divorce.'

"There's not much to misunderstand in a statement like that. Yet the husband will turn right around and say, 'Well, I think if we're patient and work hard at our relationship, we can make a go of this.'

"So the wife gets exasperated and says, 'Don't you even hear what I'm saying? It's over. The end. That's all she wrote. I don't love you, and I am not going to live with you anymore.'

"And the husband says, 'Hey, I really hear you. I can see you feel real strongly about this. I'm not saying this is going to be easy. I'm just saying it'll take time, but we can work this out.'

"I have actually seen communication like this, where the denial is so thick you can cut it with a knife."

From the examples we've cited, you might think that only men experience denial. To prevent any misunderstanding, we want to point out that women are just as good at denial as men are. However, this is a book for men, about the process that men go through during a divorce. So we are primarily dealing with the denial that men experience. And we've seen denial take many different forms.

Sometimes the guy in denial says, "Just give me one more chance," or, "We can work it out." Sometimes denial takes the form of blaming the other person: "If she would just change, everything would be okay." Sometimes denial takes the form of minimizing the seriousness of the problem: "She just needs to get this out of her system," or, "I don't know what's gotten into her, but as soon as she comes to her senses everything will be okay," or, "You know how women get sometimes." Denial is usually the first emotional issue men encounter in separation: denial that there is a problem, denial that the problem may be out of our control, even denial that the breakup is really happening.

Denial is usually followed by *bargaining*.

BARGAINING

The marriage may be horrible. There may be conflict, misery, and pain all the time. Still, our unconscious self is driving us, compelling us to restore the system. So we keep trying to put the marriage, the system, back together. We keep applying bailing wire and Band-Aids in a desperate attempt to keep the system from rattling apart.

Why? Because, deep down, we like consistency and we don't like change. Sure, we consciously like to think of ourselves as dedicated to change and improvement and progress. We are fascinated with the latest innovations in business, or computers, or cuisine. But that's at the conscious level. Unconsciously, we are willing to bargain like crazy, to give away the whole candy store, if only we can preserve the status quo.

There are both *overt* and *covert* forms of bargaining. To put it another way, there is "outright" bargaining and there is "sneaky" bargaining.

When you engage in overt or outright bargaining, you are trying to cut a deal to save your marriage and your family. "Honey, I was wrong," you might say, which, of course is a good bargaining ploy. "If you don't like something about me, I'll change it. If you want me to do something differently, I'll do it. Anything you say, just give me another chance. But please don't leave me."

Then there is covert bargaining. That is where you manipulate other people to intercede for you. It may be a mutual friend. It may be one of your wife's relatives. It may be a counselor or pastor. Worst of all, it may even be your kids.

Here's how it works: You are separated and your kids come to visit you. During their visit, you put on your funeral face, you mope around the house, you show the kids how unhappy you are, and maybe even cry in front of them. "I don't know why your mother is doing this," you moan. "Kids, all I want is to be your daddy again. My place is back home with you." The idea is that they will go home and tell Mom how badly she has hurt Daddy, and Mom will relent and take Daddy back.

If you have been involved in manipulating your children's emotions, please think about this: you may give an Academy Award performance, producing more sappy tears than the death scene in *Love Story*—but this is a cruel and destructive thing to do to your kids. It harms their self-esteem and emotional well-being. It creates conflict within them, forcing them into a dilemma over their loyalty toward you versus their loyalty toward Mom. If you manipulate your children into bargaining for you, then you are emotionally abusing your children.

Though the emotional stage of bargaining often drives us to engage in embarrassing and even damaging behavior, there is nothing pathological or shameful about going through a time of bargaining. Stages such as denial and bargaining are simply a natural part of the process of grieving for a lost relationship. These defense mechanisms act as shields. They prevent us from having to deal with the full emotional impact of a tragedy until we are ready. They help us to get through a very difficult time.

Defense mechanisms such as denial and bargaining are like strong painkillers. They help you survive a trauma so that the healing can begin. Like many strong painkillers, these defense mechanisms can also become habit-forming. But if you determine to squarely face and work through your issues and your hurt, you will get past your denial and bargaining.

The bargaining stage is usually followed by *anger*.

ANGER

Ray had gone through the denial stage: "She'll come back. She gets mad like this, but it always blows over." Then Ray went through bargaining: "Honey, please come back! Tell me what you're sore about and I'll make it up to you!"

Ray went through anger the night his wife, Carly, tried to leave him. She had told him many times before that she would leave him. But this time she actually bundled their three-year-old son into the car, along with as many of her belongings as would fit. That's when Ray went ballistic.

He picked Carly up, carried her back into the apartment, and tossed her into the living room. She hit a lamp, gashed her arm, and received twelve stitches. Ray received thirty days probation on a domestic assault charge. Three months later, he also received a divorce decree.

Different guys handle anger in different ways. Nate slashed his wife's tires. Kurt ordered his wife to leave town. Tyler broke into his wife's house, slashed the furniture, kicked in the TV screen, and ransacked the bedroom. Eric hung around his wife's office, harassing her, getting her rattled, and creating trouble with her employer.

It would be safe to say that a guy who is in the anger phase of a divorce does not always behave like Prince Charming. In fact, anger can lead us into very illogical forms of behavior, as Ken can personally attest.

"When I was in the Navy," he recalls, "I was engaged to a girl in California. We had set the date for the wedding and were making plans for a life together. But while I was overseas, she broke our engagement. It was bad enough that she broke up with me, but what *really* hurt was that she started going with a *Marine!*

"I got back to the States at Christmastime and went straight to her house as soon as I got off the ship. We had a fairly heated verbal exchange, and it ended with her giving me back all the wedding gifts. These were the gifts my mother had shipped out from Texas. It was a whole table full of presents, a ton of stuff. They were from all my relatives who couldn't come out to California for the wedding.

Now, of course, there wasn't going to be any wedding. So my ex-fiancée gave them back to me, still in their shipping wrappers, and I put them in the car and drove off.

"I went to a bar to have a couple of drinks and calm down. In the bar, I met a woman who was recently divorced and a single parent. I bought her a drink and had a couple myself while she talked about how hard life was for her and her child.

"After listening for a while, I said, 'Wait right here.' I went out to my car and came back with an arm load of presents. I dumped them in front of her and said, 'There you go! Merry Christmas!' Well, her eyes got as big as saucers. She just couldn't believe I was giving her all this stuff. After I convinced her I was on the level, I said, 'There's more in the car. You can have it all.' So we went out and loaded all the packages into her car.

"The presents really should have gone back to the people who gave them, but I was so mad I wasn't thinking clearly. It actually made some kind of bizarre sense at the time. It seemed to me that giving those presents to a strange woman in a bar was a logical way to get even with my ex-fiancée!"

Few of us do our best thinking when we are angry. In fact, most of us can point to some very embarrassing things we have done while angry. But is it *wrong* to feel angry? No! It's *natural* to feel angry when people or circumstances hurt us. Anger is a natural, even healthy, part of the healing process. The problem with anger is that most of us have never learned how to express our anger appropriately and constructively. When we express our anger in inappropriate, destructive ways, other people get hurt, and so do we! Our own self-esteem and personal dignity suffers when we allow anger to drive our behavior in unproductive or explosive directions.

When a marriage breaks down, you can count on one thing: there is going to be anger. And if we don't learn how to handle and express our anger in productive ways, we will create conditions in which we will not be able to work effectively in the system. That means it will be a lot harder for us to maintain effective and satisfying contact with our children. To be an effective father after a separation and divorce, you must work within the system—not the system as you would like it to be, but the system that is. Working within the system requires learning to express anger in an appropriate and productive way.

Dr. Chris Thurman, author and psychologist at the Minirth-Meier Tunnell and Wilson Clinic in Austin, Texas, suggests that there are four approaches to expressing anger:

1. Passive
2. Aggressive
3. Passive-Aggressive
4. Assertive

Let's take a close look at each of these four ways of handling anger:

The Passive Approach

We make no response, even though we are angry, and this makes us angry with ourselves. When anger turns inward and eats away at our vitals, it becomes depression. The mind-set of the passive person is, "I don't count. Therefore my feelings don't count enough to be expressed."

The Aggressive Approach

We explode; we rage; we ventilate; we let someone have it with our words, our fists, or our weapons. The mind-set of the aggressive person is, "You don't count. Your feelings don't count. Therefore, if I hurt you with my words or actions, it doesn't matter. All that matters is that I get to express my anger."

The Passive-Aggressive Approach

We express anger in a sneaky, subtle way; we try to get even without getting caught. The mind-set of the passive-aggressive person is, "I don't count, but you don't count, either. I am angry, but I don't feel competent to assert my anger. I want to hurt you, but I don't want to get blamed for it."

The aggressive approach is familiar to most: threats, physical abuse, destruction of property, and physical intimidation—your basic cave-man behavior. Passive-aggressive anger is a little trickier. We can be passive-aggressive without even realizing it. When we express our anger in a passive-aggressive way, we are acting aggressively but in such a way that we *appear* to be passive.

For example, when John divorced Sally, he figured that putting geographical distance between the two of them would help him get over the anger he carried toward her. Two years later, he's as angry as he ever was—and he displays it through passive-aggressive behavior. Every other Saturday, he is supposed to pick up the children at 9 A.M, keep them overnight, and return them to Sally's house by 7 P.M. on Sunday.

Not long ago, John learned that Sally likes to play tennis on Saturday mornings. So now he delays his arrival until 10 or 11, which ruins Sally's morning. John always has an excuse: he overslept, or an old college buddy called him up just as he was going out the door, or the car was making a funny sound and he thought he ought to check it out. And the excuses are technically accurate: he *did* decide not to set his alarm Friday night, and he *did* manage to keep his buddy on the phone for an extra hour or so, and he *did* finally decide to do something about that squeaky suspension after letting it go for five months.

On Sunday nights, he likes to take the kids to Dairy Queen on the way back to their mother's house. They usually stop at DQ around quarter to 7 (plenty of time for a quick cone and still get them home on time). Of course, he ends up buying them each a three-scoop sundae, which has the double advantage of taking a long time to eat (they don't get to Sally's until 8:30 P.M.) *and* getting them all sugared up (Sally can't get them calmed down until at least 10 P.M.).

In frustration, Sally finally confronts him. "John," she says, "why are you doing this? Can't you see that you're not just hurting me, but you're hurting your own kids?"

John shrugs, a look of surprised innocence on his face. "Why am I doing what? I told you why I was late—"

"You're late every single week! You're late picking them up and you're late bringing them back, and you deliberately get them all hyped up before you bring them home! I know you're angry with me, but do you have to use the kids to get at me?"

"What are you talking about?" asks John with eyes as wide as

Bambi's. "I'm not angry! I'm just showing my kids a good time. What's wrong with that?"

The sad thing is that, on one level, John actually believes what he is saying. Passive-aggressive anger is often *denied* anger. Though passive-aggressive anger can be a conscious, deliberate tactic for getting even, as often as not the passive-aggressive person is actually fooling himself into believing he is not really angry at all.

Passive-aggressive anger is behavior with a hidden agenda. For example, the man who is chronically late making child support payments may say, "Well, I had a lot going on," or, "It slipped my mind," or, "She doesn't really need the money that badly." But the real agenda, the *hidden* agenda, is to be late enough so that she has to call, so that she has to be dependent on him, so that he can control and inconvenience her.

The difference between *aggressive anger* and *passive-aggressive anger* is like the difference between a battleship and a submarine. When a battleship launches a naval attack, it turns broadside to the target and lets go with a twenty-round salvo of 16-inch shells. A battleship offensive creates a lot of racket, chaos, and turmoil—but at least everything happens on the surface, in plain sight. That's what aggressive anger is like: destructive, but out in the open.

Passive-aggressive behavior is like a sneak attack by submarine. A submarine strikes from under the surface. It comes up to periscope depth, launches a couple of torpedoes, then dives for the bottom before the torpedoes even hit their target. When the torpedoes hit, the people on the ship are looking around saying, "What happened? Where did that come from?"

The problem with passive-aggressive anger from the absent father's point of view is that, while it may offer a short-lived sense of triumph ("Torpedoes one and two . . . direct hit amid ships!"), passive-aggressive anger always works against you in the long term. It clouds your goals. It creates friction in the business relationship between you and your ex-wife, which can make it more difficult to transact such matters as visitation and child support. It can even drive your ex-wife away to another city or state, and that would cause you to lose much of the contact with your children you now enjoy.

Clearly, when you are in the anger stage of a divorce, it is critically important to find productive rather than destructive ways of handling anger. Passive, aggressive, and passive-aggressive approaches work against the system and against your goals. There is only one healthy, productive approach to dealing with anger: the *assertive* approach.

The Assertive Approach

Using the assertive approach, we express our anger with a mature and genuine respect for the other person's feelings. The mind-set of the assertive person is, "I count, and you count too. I have a right to tell you I am angry, but I don't have a right to hurt you with my anger."

Here are some tips on the assertive expression of anger:

- Assertive statements of anger usually begin with the word "I"—"I feel angry over what has happened," or, "I feel angry with you." Aggressive anger usually blames and begins with the word "you"—"You really make me mad!" or, "You really messed up our entire family! I hope you're happy!"
- Assertive statements of anger reflect the distinction between subjective feelings and objective fact. Assertive statements say, "This is what is going on inside me." They do not claim to have a corner on the entire truth or on objective reality. Assertive statements often begin with, "I feel . . ." or, "My opinion is . . ."
- Assertive anger is willing to listen to and respect the feelings of the other person. Assertiveness says, "My feelings count, but so do yours. Listen to how I feel, then let me hear how you feel. I won't interrupt you. I won't plan my rebuttal. I will just listen."

"When I am counseling people who are in conflict and having trouble communicating," says Ken, "I will often make them begin their statements with the words, 'You may not agree with me, but I feel. . . .' These words set the tone for assertive expression of anger. They make the point that the feelings expressed here are purely internal emotions and thoughts and are not meant to be a description of reality. These words recognize that the other person may have a totally different point of view and defuse the need people often feel to jump in with rebuttal and argument and shouting, all of which gets in the way of working within the system."

As long as the assertive mind-set is before us, we will never go wrong with our anger.

SADNESS

Sadness is a bleak, discouraged mood that accompanies a loss, and it may last a few weeks or a few months. It may come and go as different events or milestones force you to feel your loss all over again. A communication from your ex-wife, the unmarked passage of an anniversary, or encountering a photo album in a trunk may trigger sadness.

The sadness stage can be a very deceptive and painful phase of your recovery. When you are experiencing sadness, there is a tendency to think it will always be this way. If you are experiencing such feelings now, remember that this is a natural part of the recovery process. It will pass.

"After my divorce," says Van, "I lost a lot of weight. I call it 'The Divorce Diet.' It's just normal when you are going through a period of sadness to experience a loss of appetite and a loss of sleep. But some men will go exactly the opposite direction. They may sleep all the time because it is too painful to be conscious and to feel the sadness. Some will actually gain weight because they are compulsively over-eating, trying to stuff the emptiness inside with food. Temporary imbalances in sleeping and eating patterns during a time of sadness are nothing to be overly concerned about. These imbalances only become a concern if they become chronic."

It is easy to understand why sadness is a predictable component of the divorce process. Even if the man initiated the divorce, even if he can no longer stand to be around his ex-wife, there is an enormous loss that comes with his divorce. He is used to coming home to a house with kids, a wife, maybe dogs and cats. Now he comes home to an empty apartment. He is unprepared for the loneliness he now feels.

"Probably *the* most difficult thing I had to face in my divorce," Van recalls, "was that terrible thought, 'I'm losing my kids.' I was certainly losing the day to day contact with them I had once enjoyed. I was losing the privilege of raising them, of coming home to them every night, of putting them to bed, of sharing their daily ups and downs. To me, that was what 'family' was all about, and so I felt I was losing my family. For me, that was the worst. That was my emotional abyss."

Loneliness and sense of loss are natural and unavoidable aspects of the divorce process. If that is what you are feeling right now, we can assure you on the authority of our own experience that it will pass.

"The feelings of loss are real," says Van, "and there are real losses that an absent father suffers. Your time with your kids is restricted, and you miss a lot of the joy and satisfaction of parenting you might have had if there had been no divorce. But in time you gain a new perspective. You realize that your relationship with your kids has changed, but it hasn't ended. There are still plenty of joys and good times ahead. They still love you, and you still have a significant role to play in their lives. Once you start to gain that perspective, your sadness begins to lift."

Some people confuse sadness with depression. But there is a major distinction between sadness and true clinical depression. Sadness is a comparatively short-term problem; depression is a chronic, long-term problem. Sadness is usually the result of a specific event or events in our lives; depression is sometimes linked to specific events but is usually rooted in physiological processes (such as chemical imbalances in the brain) or deep psychological issues (such as a childhood trauma or the post-traumatic stress syndrome experienced by many war veterans).

Clinical depression can be identified when a number of accompanying symptoms become fairly pronounced. A partial list of these symptoms includes:

- Prolonged sleep and appetite disturbance.
- Periods of crying.
- Lower energy level.

- Lower motivation.
- Listlessness and apathy.
- Feelings of hopelessness and helplessness.
- Ruminating thinking (that is, going back over the same gloomy thoughts, or replaying certain bleak memories over and over in your mind).
- Recurring thoughts of suicide.

If a person experiences several of the above symptoms on a regular basis, this may indicate that the person is suffering from clinical depression. It is important to understand, however, that many of these symptoms will occur in people who are not clinically depressed. They may simply be the temporary signs of the stage of sadness in the aftermath of divorce or some other painful event.

If, however, these symptoms tend to be present and unabating over a period of time, or if you are experiencing thoughts of suicide or causing harm to someone else, then we strongly encourage you to seek professional counseling. While sadness is a stage we all go through from time to time, true clinical depression rarely goes away by itself; it must be professionally treated. Please understand that this book is not intended to be a substitute for psychotherapy or other professional treatment.

DESPAIR

The next phase a man often encounters in the divorce process is *despair*. Not all people go through this stage. It is common, but it is not inevitable.

Despair is a point where we accept our situation, but we tell ourselves it is a terrible situation which we can't possibly endure. Despair is a kind of negative, gloomy acceptance. It is the stage in our recovery process where all denial ends, where all bargaining ends, where anger is recognized as impotent and ineffectual. We are face to face with the reality that we are single again.

Despair looks endless, like a tunnel with no light at the end. But despair does pass. It may pass like a kidney stone, but it will pass. In our many years as therapists, we have seen hundreds of individuals enter our offices in states of despair. *All* of those individuals who were willing to endure the recovery process, one day at a time, were able to get better and move on. We have seen and counseled people at every stage in the divorce process, and we have heard many of them say, "It won't get better; it's hopeless." But they *did* get better.

"I know what despair feels like," says Van. "There was a period following my divorce where I felt absolutely without hope. The future was like a blank wall. I had lost my family, and there was nothing I could do to restore what I had lost. The pain would last forever. At least, that's what I thought—but I was wrong. If there is one ray of hope I could pull out of my own experience and give to the reader, it would be this: despair feels like the end, but it is not the end. It is one more stage in the healing process."

The Spiritual Dimension of Despair

The despair stage also has a spiritual dimension. Many men in a state of despair find it hard to experience the love of God. It is normal, even for men who have had a deep, lifelong religious faith, to feel very un-spiritual at this point in their lives, and to wonder if they have been abandoned or rejected by God. This is true no matter who initiated the divorce. If Jack left his wife, he may feel cut off from God by feelings of guilt. If Jack's wife left him, he may wonder why God allowed this to happen. He may feel that God has forgotten him or is mad at him and is punishing him by taking away his family.

The authors of this book don't claim to be theologians. We are not seminary-trained; we were trained in secular graduate schools. But we want to be frank about the fact that we both read the Bible and try to order our lives by what it teaches. The views we share on the spiritual aspects of divorce are personal opinions and are not necessarily the views of any church or denomination or of the Minirth-Meier Clinic. We feel it is only fair for you to know what our opinions are based on.

There is a passage from the Old Testament that we believe has been misconstrued and wrongly used against divorced people. Some will say, "The Bible says, 'God hates divorce,' so if you're divorced then God can't have anything to do with you." Hogwash! What that verse (Malachi 2:16) says is, "For the LORD God of Israel says that He hates divorce,/For it covers one's garment with violence." It's clear when you read this passage in context that God does hate divorce, but he hates divorce *because he loves people!* And that includes *divorced* people. He hates divorce because "it covers one's garment with violence"; it produces suffering and brokenness in many lives.

Throughout the Bible, we see that God loves people who suffer, he loves people who sin, he loves people who make mistakes. In John 8, we see that Jesus Christ showed love to a woman who was caught in the act of adultery. He forgave her. Yes, he told her clearly not to commit adultery again, but he just as clearly forgave her and restored her.

Divorce does not mean God is through with you. God hates divorce, but then so does practically everybody else (except, perhaps, some divorce lawyers). Van hates divorce. Ken hates divorce. So do you. But that is because divorce is painful, it hurts us, it hurts our ex-wives, and it hurts our children. No one loves divorce, least of all the people who have to go through it. So don't ever let anyone make you feel unworthy because you are divorced. Tell that person to go back and read the Bible more carefully!

If you are in the despair stage of the divorce process, you may not be able to perceive God's love as clearly as when your life was stable and functioning smoothly. This does not mean God loves you less or has abandoned you. It simply means that your perception has been clouded by the emotional hurt of divorce. If you read the Bible through, as we have, you will find that God's love never changes. No matter what has happened in your life or what you have done, you are still okay, God still loves you, and you are going to get through this.

"What If I Don't Get Better?"

The symptoms of despair can be very similar to the symptoms of clinical depression. These symptoms include:

- Missing work, either because of a lack of energy, a series of physical aliments, or a general feeling that work has lost its sig-

nificance as a priority: "Who cares? What's the use? Why make money just to pay alimony and child support?"
- Increased substance abuse; drinking or drug use to numb the pain of living.
- Chronic sleep disturbance.
- Chronic appetite disturbance.
- Decreased attention paid to personal appearance, such as shaving and attire.
- Unrelenting feelings of guilt, shame, worthlessness, uselessness, or hopelessness.

People who are going through a stage of despair may experience one or more of the above symptoms for a period of weeks or even months. But they will get better in time. If people don't get better in time, then they are not merely sad or merely in despair; they are clinically depressed. This is a clinical condition superimposed on their situation, and that condition needs treatment. The person who is depressed may need therapy and even medical treatment with antidepressant medication. Clinical depression is a state of being or a process operating within them that is not allowing them to improve.

There is also another possible explanation for people who do not seem to be able to get past the stage of despair. There are some people who learn to despair from childhood. Such people, in effect, were taught by their parents to despair. They were raised to be victims and will likely see themselves as victims for the rest of their lives. In their minds, everything that happens to them is just another sign that they are being continually victimized.

When people are raised to see themselves as victims, they may go on despairing forever, but there is a secondary advantage to seeing themselves as victims. They derive a perverse kind of satisfaction or comfort from being a perpetual victim. "People always treat me this way; the fact that my wife treated me this way is just one more example. Therefore, I don't have to change anything about myself. The problem is not me but what other people always do to me." Or, "Look at me, I'm a victim. Help me, pity me, pay attention to me. Whenever I mope around and cry and carry on, I get attention and sympathy." This kind of despair is not a short-term problem; it is a personality disorder. It also should be treated by a professional therapist.

We want to be very honest with you about this issue. Frankly, despair is a point where we psychotherapists get a little anxious. This is a stage where people who are prone to suicide may take that route rather than waiting for things to get better. They think, "My life is never going to get better. My choice is to go on feeling this way for forty years or end it now." Many choose the latter.

That is why we want you to understand that things *will* get better. These feelings are temporary, but death is permanent. If you give life a chance, these feelings *will* pass. Don't yield your life to feelings which, simply put, are not true. Yes, your feelings are real, but they are not necessarily indicators of reality. Your life is not hopeless.

We're not trying to pump you up with Pollyanna-like false optimism. This is a clinical fact: if you choose to live and grow through this experience, you will get better, period. If you have entertained thoughts of suicide, please believe these words, even if you believe nothing else we say in this book.

How to Get Back on Top

Despair is the bottom. If you've hit despair, you've gone as low as you can go. It doesn't get any worse than this. If you don't believe us when we say it will get better from now on, that's okay. Sometimes it's hard to really believe this at a feelings level. Still, we think it helps for you to hear it from someone who knows the process and has experienced it. Sometimes it helps just to hear it and know it intellectually, even though you don't experience any hope at the feelings level right now. In time, it'll come. Believe us, hope will come.

Once you get to the bottom, there's only one way left to go. It's time to start moving up. You're at the bottom now, but you *can* get back on top. And there are some positive actions you can take to help you get back on top *faster*.

Recovery begins with how you look at yourself, with what you tell yourself, with how you define yourself. In the former system—

your cozy little family comprised of yourself, your wife, and your 2.3 children—you defined yourself by your roles: husband, lover, father, provider, guide, advisor, fixer, problem solver, guardian, and the like. These roles are gone now. That means you are forced to redefine yourself. You have to find meaning for being on this planet—a meaning that is different and separate from your previous roles in the former family system.

You are now a business partner with the woman who used to be your bed partner. She is no longer your wife; she is a person with whom you negotiate and transact business, and the goal of that business is to seek the highest welfare for your children. You have logistical concerns to work out. You must arrange a mutually beneficial visitation schedule. You must make sure that child support payments are made so that your children can be well cared for.

There are certainly other roles which can help you redefine yourself in a meaningful way. But one of the most important ways is to take a close look at the needs of your children. They need the love, guidance, and wise involvement of their father.

We know of no better way to get beyond the stage of despair than to move your focus out of yourself and on to your children.

ACCEPTANCE

When we were in despair, we told ourselves, "This is the way my life is now, and even though I am not okay, this is the way my life will always be." In the acceptance stage, we tell ourselves, "This is the way my life is now—and that's okay, and I'm okay." Despair and acceptance are very similar in that both grief stages are based on essentially the same set of facts, but each puts a completely different spin on those facts. Despair takes a negative, hopeless attitude; acceptance is positive and hopeful.

Despair looks at the ruins of a marriage and says, "I've lost everything. It's all over. I had love once, but now it's gone. I had a family once, but now it's gone." Acceptance looks at those same ruins and says, "That marriage is over, but I am going to be okay. I may even love again. I still have my children, even though I don't live with them. I will always have their love, and I will always be their dad;

and I am determined to be the best father I can possibly be under these less-than-ideal circumstances."

When you get to acceptance, you will know it. It has a distinctly different feel than all the other stages of the divorce recovery process. More than anything else, acceptance feels like *hope*. It's like taking a deep breath and saying, "This is how it is—and it's okay."

Ironically, we may experience anger again at this stage, just as we did earlier in the grieving process. That's normal. The recurrence of anger at this point is not a setback, but a sign of recovery. Whereas the emotions of sadness and despair are directed inward, the emotion of anger is directed outward. We take sadness and despair into ourselves, often in the form of self-blame and self-pity. Anger, however, is something we direct away from ourselves. This can often be very healthy.

Take Bill, for example. When Bill went through a period of despair, he often made statements such as, "If only I had done this or done that, we would still be together. I should have done something sooner. I only have myself to blame." In time, he came to a place of acceptance, and he began to make such statements as, "Well, I made it through this, and I'm okay. Now I see that I was wrong to take all the blame for the breakup. She hurt me, manipulated me, and made me feel like dirt. I won't ever let anyone do that to me again." This is anger—healthy, constructive anger. Bill's later statements went something like, "Sure it was half my fault, but it was half her fault as well," and show that he has learned and grown from this experience.

We often counsel people (both men and women) who take total responsibility for the breakdown of their marriage. Rarely, if ever, are these feelings justified. Certainly, we are each 100 percent responsible for our own actions. That is, if a man abuses his wife, commits adultery, lies, or commits some other harmful act against his wife, he cannot say, "It's partly her fault." He is completely responsible for his own actions. But if a marriage breaks down, there are not one but two people involved. It is a partnership, and *no one person can be responsible for the failure of a partnership*.

There is a short, anonymous poem that packs a wallop of practical insight. It reads:

> When life seems disconnected,
> Your thinking may be misdirected,
> For life, you see, is as it should be—
> It's just not what you expected.

When you get to the point that you can say, "Life has not turned out the way I expected, but that's okay; everything is as it should be," you have reached acceptance.

Acceptance doesn't mean everything is okay. Acceptance doesn't mean the pain is gone, or the anger is gone. It doesn't mean that you don't occasionally, temporarily slide back into a little bargaining or a brief wallow in self-pity. It doesn't mean the issues are resolved, and life is now a bed of roses. Life may still be a bed of fertilizer. And let's face it: fertilizer doesn't smell very pretty, but it sure promotes growth! Acceptance means you have made a decision not to stay mired in the fertilizer of the past. You are going to live in the now, shovel in hand, and try to get through *today's* fertilizer as best as you can. You have accepted the reality of your divorce; you have accepted the emotions you feel as a result of the divorce; and you have accepted that the divorce was not an event in your past, but a process you continue to move through, and that's okay. You're going to get through it!

Acceptance is a good place to be. It's a healthy, liberating stage of the divorce process. In the grief process model of Elisabeth Kubler-Ross, acceptance is the final destination; there is no stage beyond acceptance. You accept your death, and then you do your death.

But divorce is not as final as death. You still have a life to live beyond the divorce decree. More than that, you still have children to parent and business to transact. And you have one more stage to negotiate in the divorce process. That stage is called *forgiveness*.

FORGIVENESS

What we mean by forgiveness is very simple. Forgiveness is the decision we make that we will no longer blame, judge, or condemn another person. When you reach the forgiveness stage (and not everyone reaches this stage by a long shot), you forgive your ex-wife, and you forgive yourself.

There are a lot of people who only get it half-right. They can forgive others; but they forget to forgive themselves! They don't give themselves latitude for being fallible and human. Forgiving ourselves is a kind of gracious honesty. It doesn't mean minimizing or excusing things we have done. It doesn't mean saying, "Well, what I did wasn't so bad," or, "What I did wasn't as bad as what she did." No, when we forgive ourselves, we look squarely at our mistakes and we say, "I did this. It was a lousy thing to do. I admit it and confess it. But I'm not going to beat myself down about it any longer. I'm not going to blame or condemn myself any longer. That's the past. I'm going to live in the now."

Here again, we come to an issue that cannot be adequately addressed without taking the spiritual dimension into account. As Christian therapists, we believe that the key to true self-forgiveness is that we must have Someone to confess our sins and faults to; Someone who will receive that guilt, and remove it from ourselves; Someone who will then offer us His total unconditional forgiveness. The Someone we refer to is God, who offers us forgiveness through Jesus Christ.

Forgiveness toward your ex-wife (or toward others who have hurt you) works the same way as forgiving yourself. You don't have to deny, excuse, or minimize what that person has done to you. You can look squarely at that person's mistakes and sins and say, "She did this to me. It was a lousy thing to do. But that was then, and this is now. I'm not going to hold it over her head, or try to get even, or dwell on it any more. Sure, it will pop into my mind from time to time, but I'm not going to roll it around in there and stew over it. I'm going to let it go. No more judgment. No more finger pointing. No more condemnation. I forgive and I am free."

It's hard. We know that. But forgiveness is the only way to freedom from the hurts of the past. And we want you to be *free*. Again, this chapter is not a substitute for professional treatment. If you feel you are stuck in any of these phases, you may want to contact a professional therapist or your pastor for help in moving through the grief process of your divorce.

ARE YOU OUT OF PHASE?

What we have done in this chapter is to draw a model of the divorce recovery process that looks good on paper:

Stage 1: Denial
Stage 2: Bargaining
Stage 3: Anger
Stage 4: Sadness
Stage 5: Despair
Stage 6: Acceptance
Stage 7: Forgiveness

The problem with a neat little model like this is that human beings are rarely as precise and predictable as models on paper. You may not proceed through these phases in exactly this way. You may find some phases easy, others difficult. You may not experience these stages in exactly the same order as we've listed them. You may swing from Anger to Acceptance to Denial to Anger again—all on the same day! You may not be able to tell when you move from one stage to the next. And that's okay.

These seven stages of the divorce process are fluid and frequently ambiguous in real life. Don't expect to reach a point at 3:47 P.M. next Tuesday where you can say, "Yes, I've stopped my anger and started my sadness at this point." There may, in fact, be times when you're not sure what you're feeling, or what stage you are in. There may be times when it seems you are experiencing two or three phases at the same time. There may even be times when you think you are completely out of phase!

There's probably some compulsive guy out there reading this book who is thinking to himself, "I've got it! I'll just take a day off work tomorrow and get through all these stages in a hurry. I'll do my denial at 8 o'clock, start my bargaining at 9, do anger at 10, sadness at 11, knock off for lunch at noon, then I'll hit despair, acceptance, and forgiveness in the afternoon!"

Be patient with yourself. You can't cycle through these stages on a schedule, and there will even be days when you slip backwards a notch or two. Take your time. Remember that divorce, like any loss, is a process. Just let yourself go through the process at your own pace, and you'll be fine.

The reason we have explored these seven stages of the divorce process is to help you identify where you are; to help you understand what you are feeling; and to give you an overview of the entire healing process, so that you can see where you've been, and where you are going. When you go through a tough experience like divorce, it helps to know that there is a process to it and that the process is leading you toward a destination. The hurt you have suffered as a result of this divorce is not meaningless. The life you are now living is not hopeless. You're going to make it. You're going to be okay.

In the next chapter, we will examine practical ways to bring closure to old issues and healing to old wounds.

Chapter/4

TAKING CARE OF BUSINESS

I'm not angry," said Phil. "I'm past that. Even though the divorce was my idea, it's been hard to get Elyse out of my system. But everything is finally coming together. It's been hard, but I've learned a lot through this experience."

"What have you learned?" asked Phil's therapist.

"I've learned you can't trust women," Phil replied. "They're devious, selfish, and sneaky. I've learned that if you never trust a woman, you'll never get hurt."

"Are you saying that *all* women—"

"Yep, liars and cheats, every one."

"I understand that you're hurt because your wife had an affair. But do you think it's logical to generalize about half of the human race from one experience?"

"Look," Phil replied defensively, "you asked me what I learned, and that's what I learned."

"Let me just leave you with a thought," Phil's therapist said. "Many people find it easier and safer to generalize about 'all men' or 'all women' than to admit, 'I'm angry with this one person.' I would encourage you to think about who you are really angry with and then deal openly with those feelings of anger."

Phil's face darkened. "I'm *not* angry! How many times do I have to say it before you believe me?"

"It doesn't matter if I believe you or not," said the therapist. "What's important is what you truly feel. I'm just offering a suggestion."

Phil left the therapist's office, feeling vaguely dissatisfied with the way the session had gone.

A few days later, Phil had his fifteen-year-old daughter, Keri, over for a weekend visit. During the past year, Phil had always looked forward to these biweekly visits. But lately, these visits made him feel like he was in the Land of Oz. During one visit, Keri would be as sweet and innocent as little Dorothy Gale of Kansas, and the next week she would be the Wicked Witch of the West—irritable, hot-tempered, moody, and downright frightening. At first, Phil was bewildered. Then it occurred to him that Keri's "witchy" moods seemed to occur on every other visit (that is, in 28-day cycles). His gentle, affectionate, doe-eyed daughter had become a *woman!* She had joined the enemy!

The more he thought about it, the more convinced he became that Keri was becoming more and more like her mother. He could see his ex-wife in her facial expressions, in her voice, in her mannerisms. The more like Elyse she became, the harder it was for Phil to get along with her.

Sometimes when Keri was in one of her dark moods, she would say hurtful things such as accusing Phil of destroying their home. On one such weekend, Keri started in on him while they were in the car, driving to his house. "Daddy, I just *hate* this," she growled. "I hate bouncing *back* and *forth,* from *Mom's* house to *your* house. If you weren't so *stubborn* and *pig-headed,* we'd still be a *family* and I wouldn't have to *do* this!"

Phil's knuckles whitened as he clutched the steering wheel. He hated that vocal mannerism Keri had of emphasizing every third or fourth word in a sentence (just like Elyse did when she was in a snotty mood). "What do you mean? How was I stubborn and pig-headed?"

"Mom didn't *want* a divorce! It was all *your* idea!"

"Well, having an affair was her idea!"

"She *said* she was *sorry!*"

"Oh, well, that fixes everything, doesn't it?"

"She *said* she'd stop! Why couldn't you just *forgive* her and let things be the way they *used* to?"

"I couldn't trust her anymore, Keri! Can't you see that? When you're married to someone, you have to be able to trust that person."

"You *see?* Stubborn and pig-headed! And *selfish* too! All you care about is *your* feelings!" She made a face and mocked him in a jeering voice. " 'I can't *trust* her, I can't *trust* her!' What about *my* feelings, Daddy? What about *Mom's* feelings? Did you ever consider that maybe she had a good *reason* for having an *affair?*"

Phil's teeth ground until they hurt. He slammed on the brakes and whipped the car to the side of the road. The driver behind him honked and passed him. Phil's hands and jaw muscles clenched and unclenched. Keri looked back at him with fury—almost daring him to reach out and strike her. Several seconds passed in silence as they stared each other down. Then Phil's anger was replaced by sadness as a huge wave of depression swept over him. In that instant, it felt like he had completely lost everything he had once called "family." First he had lost his wife; now his daughter.

He swung the car around and, without another word, returned to Elyse's home and left Keri and her suitcase on the doorstep. Two weeks later, Keri again came to visit, and neither Phil nor Keri apologized or mentioned the hurtful argument in the car. As always, the emotional debris of their conflict was swept under the rug like so much lint and dust.

A couple of months later, Phil brought Keri over for the weekend, and she was again in one of her "witchy" moods. She came into the kitchen while Phil was fixing lunch. He was just putting the finishing touches on one of his specialties: two big sub sandwiches with lots of salami, pepperoni, Swiss cheese, and red onions.

"I'm going to meet some friends at the mall for lunch, Dad," she said casually.

Phil couldn't believe her thoughtlessness. "Why didn't you tell me that before I made lunch for the two of us?" he asked. "What am I supposed to do with two big sandwiches?"

"Save one for later. That's why God created refrigerators."

"And what about my plans? You can go to the mall anytime, but I only get to see you every two weeks. I was thinking we could go out to the Water Gardens or maybe take in a matinee—whatever you want."

Keri got a pouty look on her face. "I *want* to go to the *mall* with my *friends*," she insisted in her snottiest tone of voice. "I'll be *back* in a couple of *hours* and we can *do* something together *then*."

Phil felt his anger rising, yet he tried to stuff his annoyance and get along. "Okay," he said. "Just tell me who you're going with and when you'll be back."

Keri's voice was shrill and biting. "I *told* you!" she said. "I'll be *back* in a couple of *hours!* Why do you want to *know* who I'm *going* with? You don't *know* them, they're just *my* friends!"

He slapped her.

Keri looked stunned—but Phil was just as stunned. It was as if his hand reached out with a will of its own! He couldn't believe it! Yet there was the evidence: an angry red handprint on his daughter's wide-eyed face.

Keri turned and ran to the guest room. Phil stood for a long time, looking down at the two sandwiches, feeling cruel and stupid. Then he turned and went to the guest room. The door was shut and locked, but he could hear her clearly. She was sobbing.

"Keri, honey, I'm sorry! I don't know why—"

"Shut up! Go away! I hate you!"

A half-hour later, Keri's friends came by, picked Keri up, and took her away. Around six o'clock that evening, Elyse called and coldly informed Phil that she had picked Keri up at the mall, and Keri didn't want to go back to her father's house. Elyse's final words before hanging up were, "I *just* can't *believe* you *did* that!"

Phil hung up the phone, slumped into a chair, and muttered, "I can't believe it either."

THINKING → FEELING → BEHAVIOR

Anytime there is a separation or divorce, each side will have feelings, hurts, and issues that must be dealt with. This is true in even the most "civilized" divorces. After all, if there weren't feelings, hurts, and issues even in amicable divorces, there probably wouldn't have been a divorce; the couples probably would have remained married. If the divorce is explosive and bitter, these issues multiply exponentially.

The man who goes through a separation and divorce without adequately acknowledging and dealing with his feelings and his issues is headed for some serious pitfalls. As counselors, whenever we hear a divorced father say, "Hey, I'm fine, I'm not angry, I've gotten past all that," we see red warning lights flashing. One of our objectives is to help our clients get in conscious contact with their feelings, and to find closure for any unfinished business they are carrying around.

If we avoid resolving the unfinished emotional business of our separation and divorce, we may:

- Retard our own recovery and emotional growth.
- Get stuck in one of the stages of grief.
- Fall into illogical thinking (such as generalizing about "all women").
- Damage relationships (especially with our children).
- Create situations which might hinder our visitation rights and our fathering role.

Why do we behave the way we do? Why do we, like Phil, sometimes do things that are wrong and destructive? Often, it is because of the unfinished business that simmers on the back burner of our minds. Behavior doesn't just happen. Behavior is driven, powered, and channeled by forces within us, forces which few of us understand very well. Some of our behavior is driven by conscious, rational, logical thought. But much, perhaps most, of our behavior (certainly much more of our behavior than we generally wish to admit) is driven by our *emotions*.

There is a very simple model we therapists use to show our clients why they do the things they do. That model looks like this:

Thinking → Feeling → Behavior

Or to put it into other words, thinking affects feelings, and feelings affect behavior. Here's how it works in real life:

We experience an event. Is it a good event or a bad event? That depends on how we interpret that event, how we think about it, what we tell ourselves about it. If we tell ourselves, *This event is terrible, painful, unfair!*, then that self-talk will cause certain feelings to arise within us: fear, anxiety, anger, resentment, self-pity. Those feelings will, in turn, cause us to behave in certain ways: to lash out, to retreat into denial, to withdraw into depression, to act offensively or defensively.

There are many events which, at first glance, appear to be completely negative. Yet, if we learn how to re-interpret these events, to think about them differently, to change our self-talk regarding these events, then we can change our feelings and ultimately our behavior as well.

Ted, for example, looks at divorce as "The End," as the "Ultimate Calamity," as the "Absolute Worst." His negative thinking causes him to become depressed and resentful. His feelings lead to behavior toward his ex-wife that actually undermines and sabotages his desire to have close contact with his children.

By contrast, Alec has a positive outlook on crisis and change. He looks at life after divorce as a "New Beginning," a "Challenge," a "Growth Experience." Things are tough, no question about that. But Alec's attitude is upbeat and optimistic. His behavior toward his ex-wife and his children reflects his upbeat attitude. Alec is able to smoothly negotiate business with his ex-wife because there is not a lot of negative emotion and destructive behavior getting in the way. Alec's thinking, feelings, and behavior are coordinated to make this new system work in his favor and in his children's best interests.

The way we perceive and think about an event is often more important and profound than the event itself. You are divorced or separated, but that divorce or separation doesn't *make* you feel a certain way, such as sad or depressed. It is *how you perceive the divorce* and *what you tell yourself about the divorce* that drives your emotions in one direction or another.

Take ten men, put them through the identical divorce process, with identical problems to solve, and you will get ten different responses. You will have ten men at ten different places on the continuum of feelings. Why? Because each man is telling himself something different about his divorce than the next man.

The Thinking → Feeling → Behavior model holds true even when the feelings are repressed or denied. Our unconscious thoughts can lead to unacknowledged feelings, which drive our behavior along inappropriate pathways. That is why we sometimes engage in behavior that we are unable to logically, rationally explain. We act almost without thinking. And then we reflect, "Why in the world did I do *that*?!"

"If Only I Had Taken Care of Business . . ."

"Thinking affects feelings," said Phil. "Feelings affect behavior." He was rolling these new insights around in his mind. Phil was sitting in his therapist's office just a few days after the incident in which he struck his daughter across the face. "I think I understand what you were trying to tell me the last time I was here. The anger was there inside me, and saying it wasn't there didn't make it so. I need to deal with my resentment toward Elyse."

"So," said the counselor, "you've decided you are not past the anger after all?"

Phil shook his head. "I guess the anger is going to be there a while. But I don't ever want to misdirect my anger again—and certainly not against my daughter. I kept seeing and hearing Elyse in the things Keri did and said. But Keri is not Elyse. She is her own unique self. And no other woman is Elyse, either. Ever since I realized that my beef is really with Elyse, I've stopped being angry with all women."

"How did you come to see that?" asked the counselor.

"I did a lot of thinking after that incident with Keri. There was a kind of *deja vu* about that whole thing—like I had been through that same situation before. Then it came to me: it was a lot like the day I found out that Elyse had been unfaithful to me.

"It was a Saturday morning, about an hour before noon, and I had been out mowing the lawn. I came in for a glass of water. I stopped at the door, and I heard Elyse talking on the kitchen phone. She was arranging to meet this guy for lunch somewhere. When I walked in, she started stammering, and she got this startled, guilty look on her face.

"I said, 'Going someplace?' and she said, 'I'm meeting some girl friends for lunch.' I asked who, and she got real defensive and said something like, 'They're *my* friends and *you* don't know them,' then I called her a liar, and we had a short, but very loud argument, and she left. We divorced sometime after that, and Elyse began living with the guy.

"It's been more than a year since the divorce, and I've been stuffing my anger all this time. But you can't just stuff something like that. The awful thing is that when my anger finally erupted out into the open, it spilled all over Keri. It burned her like acid. That's a real hard thing for me to live with."

"If only I had taken care of business—my unfinished business with Elyse—instead of taking it out on Keri."

Unfinished business is like a land mine buried in the soul. All it takes is a little pressure in the wrong place and BOOM! It can go off with explosive results. Unfinished business can cause us to hurt the people we love. Or it can lead us into making disastrous life decisions. Or it can cause us to retreat and withdraw from life.

In the rest of this chapter, we will draw you a map of the post-divorce minefield. We will show you where much of your own unfinished business may lie buried. Our hope is that you will disarm those mines before they damage your life and your most important relationships.

So watch your step. The first mine is just ahead . . .

LAND MINE NO. 1: STUCK IN DENIAL

Denial is a wonderful self-defense mechanism for people in pain. It's one of the most powerful forces in the human emotional makeup. Denial can blind us to even the most obvious truths. Denial can move mountains. A man in denial will tend to say,

- "Divorce hasn't changed my life one bit," or
- "Divorce is just a minor inconvenience," or
- "Divorce is the best thing that ever happened to me!"

In the short term, denial serves as a Band-Aid on an emotional wound, protecting the psyche while healing takes place. But if denial persists over the long term, it stops the emotional healing process and stunts our emotional, spiritual, and relational growth. If we fail to take care of the unfinished business from our divorce, we run a serious risk of getting stuck in denial.

"The approach I took after my separation," recalls Van, "was one of severe denial. Outwardly, I acted as if my life was proceeding along unchanged. I didn't share myself and my feelings at all with my kids. During visitations, I tried to make everything seem like it was the same as always, but without Mom in the picture.

"I think my kids took their cues from me, because they acted out the same denial I was in. They pretended nothing had happened just as I did. What if I had just sat down with them and said, 'Kids, I have to be honest with you. This thing is really hurting me. How about you guys? Is it hurting you too?' Not to get their sympathy, but to pierce this silent envelope of denial we were all living in.

"What it was, was unfinished business. If I had taken the lead and opened up the subject with my kids, we could have finished that business and moved past the pain a lot faster.

"Part of the reason for my denial was that I was out to show my ex-wife I was continuing on as if nothing had happened, that I was in great shape. At one point, I even wrote a two-page letter to my ex-wife, telling her what a wonderful couple we could have been if we had only worked at it. This was after seventeen years of marriage! If that isn't denial, I don't know what is. Fortunately, I never mailed that letter."

Another form of denial is when a man engages in building a case against his ex-wife. He makes her totally responsible for the breakup. "I didn't do anything wrong," he says. "That woman was just a witch! I did everything I was supposed to do, and she just walked all over my face!" A man who is stuck in this form of denial is not strong enough to admit to himself and others, "I screwed up. I failed. The divorce was as much my fault as hers."

This man's unfinished business is his own pride, his own guilt, and his own sense of failure. For a lot of guys, blame-shifting and denial can become a way of life; and they get very good at hiding their own faults from others and from themselves. But until a man becomes strong enough to confront his own responsibility for the marital breakdown, he is going to remain forever stuck in denial.

Another form of denial is when a man rationalizes his separation and divorce as a good thing. "At last I'm free; I'm out of it; I'm rid of the old ball and chain, and does it ever feel great! I can do anything I want, come and go when I want; I can scratch, and belch, and drink milk right out of the carton. Boy, this is the life!"

A fellow who's in this form of denial will come into the office right after his divorce grinning and joking and saying, "Boy, don't you guys envy me!" Inside, he's choking on a big wad of hurt—a hurt he refuses to acknowledge even to himself. If he doesn't deal with the unfinished business of this inner pain, he may remain stuck in denial for many months to come.

There's a big irony in the fact that a lot of men who read these words are in denial and won't even recognize it. You may be sitting there thinking, "Well, divorce really *isn't* so bad," or, "The divorce really *was* all her fault," or, "I really *am* finally free of the old ball and chain." If that's what you're thinking, we urge you to be open to the possibility that denial may be clouding your vision.

But if you have begun to suspect that you may be stuck in denial, and you want to get unstuck, we have some practical suggestions for disarming the land mine of denial:

Disarming Denial

Being in denial is like wearing a pair of yellow-tinted sunglasses. The whole world looks yellow to you because the blues and reds and greens of the world can't even get through the filters of your colored lenses. Only when you take your yellow glasses off, will you see the *true* colors of reality. The best way, then, to guard against denial is to continually test your view of reality. Here are some suggested ways to do that:

Strategy No. 1: Take a reality check. Find a person you can trust to be objective and truthful. Ask that person, "What do you think about the way I've handled this situation? Do you think my attitude and my behavior are in line with the situation? Do I have a good handle on this situation?" Make sure you choose a wise friend, a pastor, or a counselor whom you can depend on to tell you the hard truths (not just a buddy who will stroke you). The goal of taking a reality check isn't to confirm your delusions but to puncture your denial.

If you sense feelings of defensiveness arising when your friend or counselor tells you some hard truth about yourself, recognize that these feelings are signs of unfinished emotional business that need to be uncovered and dealt with. Defensiveness is a symptom of denial. Once you recognize defensiveness for what it is, you can feel free to let your guard down. It feels so good when you can stop defending and denying, and you can say, "Yes, that's who I am, that's what I do, and now that I'm aware of it, I can start making changes."

Strategy No. 2: Take a "feelings check." Denial is a state of clouded perception, clouded emotion, and clouded thinking. Ask yourself, "What am I feeling about this crisis? Am I behaving in a way that is appropriate and proportionate to my circumstances? Or do I lose control over minor problems? Have I acted or reacted, then wondered, 'Why in the heck did I do *that*?!'"

Strategy No. 3: Pray. The most effective solutions to emotional and perceptual problems are solutions with a *spiritual* dynamic. Ask God for the strength to face the truth and the full emotional impact of your separation or divorce. For example: "God, show me the truth I need to see. If there is a 'blind spot' in my life, open my eyes and help me see it. I trust You to give me what I can bear and no more. Strengthen me so that I can take the truth like a man." Pray this prayer on a regular, daily basis.

Strategy No. 4: Give up the right to blame others. Learn to accept the situation as it is without hating, blaming, or building a case against your ex-wife.

Most of us think that when something goes wrong, the blame has to go somewhere. But the central fact of your divorce is that it has happened, it can't be reversed, and all the blaming in the world won't change that. The feelings you have don't have to point in any direction. They don't have to be explained. They don't have to be defended. You just have to experience them and get past them.

We all need to be able to say, "Okay, this is the way it is. I feel hurt, mistreated, abandoned, and rejected. I have to deal with this. But I will choose to go through this without hating, blaming, or replaying the whole mess in my mind again and again."

Strategy No. 5: Listen to your children's feelings. If you are pretending there is nothing going on in your emotional life, chances are your kids are doing the same. Ask them, "How do you think we're handling this? How are you feeling? Let's talk about it." Ask open-ended questions, not leading questions.

This can be tricky. You want to invite your children to share their feelings without pressuring them or alarming them. If they're not ready to talk, that's okay. Also, you need to be careful not to build a case of blame against your ex-wife (your children's mother) while you are inviting them to share their feelings. Be careful not to say something like, "Kids, I'm in a lot of pain right now because your Mom really did a number on me. I bet you're hurting because of what she did too."

Don't feel like you have to sit your kids down and have a therapy session with them. Learn to listen to them wherever they are, whenever they talk about something that's on their minds. As Ken observes, "My daughter and I do some of our best talking while playing Nintendo™."

Let's say you pick up Johnny at Mom's house and take him home for a visit. On the way, he starts to cry. Some father's might respond, "Stop crying! You don't have anything to cry about!" Some fathers act this way because by shutting off the child's tears, they hope to keep their own pain from surfacing.

If, instead, you respond to Johnny's crying by gently offering to listen to his feelings, you will learn something about his hurts and possibly about your own hurts as well. "It's okay to cry, pal," you might say. "Sometimes I feel that way myself. You want to talk about it?" The better you are able to tune in to your children's feelings, the better you will be able to tune in to your own feelings—and the less likely you will remain stuck in denial.

LAND MINE NO. 2: STUCK IN BARGAINING

Wade had it bad. He had been separated from his wife Karen for six months, and the divorce was just days from being final. Still, Wade couldn't keep himself from getting in the car and driving slowly past the house or calling Karen up and pleading with her to take him back. The unfinished business which kept Wade stuck in bargaining was an issue psychologists call a *reconciliation fantasy*. He clung to the completely unrealistic idea that he and Karen could somehow get back together.

"I feel like a real chump for doing this," Wade explained to his counselor, "but I can't help myself. I keep telling myself I'm not going to do it again, but after a while, I just give in."

"What happens when you call her?"

"We end up talking for two hours. I give her all the reasons why things will be different. I tell her I'm in counseling, and I promise to change."

"And she says?"

"She says she doesn't care, she doesn't love me, and not to call her again."

"It doesn't sound like Karen's trying to give you any encouragement at all."

"Well . . ." Wade's brow furrowed. "She doesn't hang up on me. Doesn't that mean something?"

"It means she's polite. Or she pities you. Or she needs some assertiveness training. If I were counseling her, I'd tell her she needs to practice saying goodbye and hanging up the phone."

Wade didn't like that. "It could mean she still loves me," he said defensively.

"Do you really believe that, Wade?"

Wade looked away. He didn't answer.

"You know what you sound like, Wade?" the counselor asked.

Wade shook his head.

"'Throw me a crumb! I'll grab at any morsel!'" the counselor said in a whiny voice.

Wade winced. "Gee, am I really that pathetic?"

"From where I'm sitting?" said the counselor. "Yeah, you're that pathetic."

Wade chuckled ruefully.

"Tell me, Wade," said the counselor, "how do you feel after you've spent a couple hours pleading with Karen to take you back?"

"Totally wasted. I feel humiliated, rejected, ashamed. My head hurts. I feel like crying."

"Tell you what," said the counselor. "Next time you're tempted to call, try doing something else instead."

"Like what?"

"Pick up the phone, lift it over your head . . . then *bash* yourself with it as hard as you can."

Wade's eyes widened, and then, when he realized he was being kidded, he grinned.

"It'll produce the same effect," the counselor continued. "You'll feel wasted, your head will hurt, and you'll feel like crying. But you'll have saved yourself two hours on the phone, *and* it will give you a real focus for your pain."

Wade rubbed the top of his head and grinned. "I get your point. She doesn't love me, and she's never going to take me back. I have to accept that and move on."

"Exactly."

Wade had plenty of tough times after that. There were many times when he wanted to pick up the phone and call Karen. But the mental image of picking up that phone and bashing his skull with it reminded him of the fact that Karen didn't love him and there would never be a reconciliation.

Another way men sometimes get stuck in bargaining is by using their children as "bargaining chips." That is, they use the children as an excuse for coming around, calling, trying to maintain contact with the ex-wife. Again, this kind of bargaining is based on a reconciliation fantasy.

Dale was stuck in this kind of bargaining. He would show up

unannounced at the house or phone five or six times a week, always with some excuse related to the children: "Kyle forgot his baseball mitt last weekend. I was in the neighborhood, so . . ." Or, "I just called to check on the kids. I saw on the news there was some strange kind of flu going around the schools, and I was concerned . . ." Or, "I dropped by to see if Laurie needed any help with her algebra. That was always my best subject, you know . . ."

Does this sort of behavior hurt the kids? Probably not. But it drives his ex-wife nuts; and it prevents Dale from getting on with his life. He's clinging to the fantasy that somehow he and his ex-wife will get back together again. He's not going through the grief process. He's not dealing with his unfinished business. He's just stuck.

Some people use their friends in the bargaining process. Some men manipulate in-laws or mutual friends into bargaining on their behalf with lines like, "Maybe you can talk some sense into her," or, "I know she'd listen to you."

Another form of bargaining is religious bargaining, using the Bible as a bargaining chip. Sometimes a husband will drag his wife into counseling and say, "My wife wants a divorce! You've got to tell her how wrong she is! After all, the Bible says, 'God hates divorce!'" That husband will often become very offended when we tell him we are not there to make his wife's decision for her.

As Christian counselors, we believe in the sanctity of marriage, and we would never encourage anyone to seek a divorce as a solution to marital problems. However, it is not our role to advise a person either to stay married or to divorce. The role of a therapist is not to impose a solution but to help the client clarify issues and find his or her own solutions. We may try to get a commitment from both the husband and the wife that they will postpone any decision until they have worked together on their issues. But if the wife says, "I'm leaving," we will not stand shoulder to shoulder with the husband, bar the door, and say, "You can't do that! The Bible says you can't!"

Another form of religious bargaining is bargaining with God: "If you'll only bring her back, God, I'll be the best Christian you ever saw! I'll go to church every Sunday! I'll give 50 percent of my income to the church!"

Whatever form of bargaining you may be stuck in, the root problem is unfinished business: you have not closed the books on your loss. You have not accepted the reality that your marriage is truly over. You are harboring a reconciliation fantasy.

Regardless of what may be keeping you stuck where you are, you can bring your unfinished business to a conclusion and get on with your life. If you think you may be stuck in bargaining, here are some suggestions:

Disarming Bargaining

Strategy No. 1: Stop your bargaining behavior. Just bite the bullet and *stop*. No more calling and pleading. No more sending flowers. No more driving by her house. Recognize that the bargaining behavior will never bring about a reconciliation. It will only further alienate your ex-wife while lowering your own self-esteem and dignity.

If you find that you are so addicted to this relationship that you are unable to stop the bargaining behavior on your own, then get the help of a counselor who can help you find the insight you need to control your behavior. Realize that your anxiety will *initially* increase when you stop the behaviors, but if you persevere your anxiety will gradually decrease.

Strategy No. 2: Pray. If you feel a compulsion to call or visit your ex-wife to plead for reconciliation, ask God to help you use your time more productively. Ask for insight into the thought patterns that drive your bargaining behavior. Ask for the strength to endure the separation and the courage to face the fact that this marriage is truly over and that all bargaining must cease. Ask God for the serenity to accept what cannot be changed, and thank Him for His never-ending, unconditional love for you.

Strategy No. 3: Recognize your limitations. One person can't fix both sides of a relationship. If you were not 100 percent responsible for your wife's decision to leave you, what makes you think that your behavior can control it or change it now? You cannot control your wife's feelings or behavior. You cannot control her half of the relationship. You cannot control the future. The sooner you recognize your limitations in a two-way relationship, the sooner you get on with your life.

Strategy No. 4: If necessary, write an "availability letter." This may help you to finally close the books on your unfinished business. An availability letter says, in effect, "I'm available if you want to reconsider this separation and divorce." In a typical availability letter, you would list the areas of *your* behavior that you feel contributed to the breakdown in your marriage. You would say, "If you have any inclination to reconsider, then get in touch with me. If you choose not to respond, that's okay."

A letter of this kind has more dignity than getting on the phone and pleading. It gives you a sense of control, a sense that there is something positive you can do. When you tell her it's okay if she doesn't respond, *mean it!* If she doesn't respond, then release her. You have done what you can, and it's time to close the books.

One of the drawbacks to an availability letter is that it will probably keep your reconciliation fantasies alive a little while longer. But we feel that, in many cases, this is an acceptable price to pay if you can finally get some closure on your unfinished emotional business.

A final warning: We have seen a lot of these letters over the years, and it's an easy task to do badly. Tom's letter, for example, started off in a contrite, conciliatory tone and ended by blasting his ex-wife with both barrels; as I read it, I could see Tom getting angrier and angrier as he went along. Fred's letter closes, "So if you decide that you don't want to sin against God any longer . . ." And when Steve wrote his letter, he began by listing the things he had done wrong: "I realize I was wrong to put up with you so long. I was wrong to let you walk all over me. I was wrong to apologize that time I . . ." You get the idea.

Don't dash off your availability letter and immediately drop it in the mail. Run your first draft past an objective friend. Listen carefully to his advice. Then *edit*—a lot.

LAND MINE NO. 3: STUCK IN ANGER

A man who is stuck in *aggressive* anger may engage in one or more of the following behaviors:

- "Bad-mouthing" (berating) his ex-wife to his children, friends, family, and others.
- Threatening his ex-wife.
- Destroying or damaging property.
- Harassing phone calls or writing letters.
- Threatening to file for custody (not out of genuine concern for the children, but to hurt the ex-wife).

This last behavior—threatening to fight for custody—is one of the most common and most destructive acts a man can commit against his family. It is destructive not only to Mom, but to the kids as well. We often see a father saying, "I'm going to take the kids away from her! I'm a better parent than she is!" What he is really saying is, "I'm really torqued off at her, and to get even I'm going to drag her into court, ruin her reputation, and make her children hate her! I'll show her she can't win!" If you have decided to fight for custody, please consider this action very carefully and objectively. Don't do something in anger that will hurt your kids forever.

(In some rare cases, the mother is genuinely unfit to have custody of her children. In such cases, it is totally appropriate to sue for custody. However, you should not undertake such action without consulting both your attorney and your therapist. Ask them to help you determine whether your concerns about the children's mother are serious enough to warrant embarking on a process that will be emotionally and financially costly for you, your ex-wife, and your children.)

A man who is stuck in *passive-aggressive* anger will engage in behaviors that are no less destructive, but they are sneakier. His behaviors may include:

- Being chronically late in picking up children and/or taking children home for visitation.

- Being chronically late on support payments.
- Spending lavish amounts of money on the children in order to outdo the ex-wife and make her seem like a Scrooge. (Not to be confused with spending lavish amounts of money on the children because of guilt.)
- Bringing children to meet the new girlfriend (with the intent of undermining the ex-wife's image in the children's eyes).

A good example of a man stuck in passive-aggressive anger was José. When José found out his ex-wife, Allison, was dating while the kids were visiting him, he came up with a fiendish tactic: he would just not show up for the kids. He would take a trip, or spend a day at the office, or unplug his phone. And Allison couldn't find him, couldn't reach him by phone, couldn't date, couldn't do anything but babysit the kids all weekend.

Cute trick, eh? Oh, yes, it made Allison *furious!* And it gave José control over her love life. Meanwhile, his children were left to wonder why their dad didn't want them anymore. Like most aggressive or passive-aggressive behavior, this sort of ploy is aimed at the ex, but *it is always more damaging to the children.*

Many stuck-in-anger fathers forget that their children are living, feeling human beings who are often in their most formative years and are not mindless pieces of furniture that one side won in the settlement. No matter how young they are, these children are forming concepts that will be the foundation for their future lives. Are they going to grow up feeling loved—or feeling used as pawns in a battle between Mom and Dad?

If you are stuck in anger, it's time to finish up your unfinished business and get on with your life. Here are some suggested solutions:

Strategy No. 1: Accept and acknowledge your anger. Own it. Confess it. Say, "Yes, I'm angry—and that's okay for now."

Many of us are taught that anger is not an appropriate emotion, that it is sinful. If that is how we view anger, then we will be more likely to deny our anger to others and to ourselves. The only honest and healthy way to approach anger is to accept it as part of our humanity and to find healthy ways to express it.

The purpose of anger is to *distance* you from the one who hurts you. But getting *stuck* in anger does just the opposite: It welds you to that person with an acetylene torch. You become locked in mortal combat. The behavior that results is destructive to you, your children, and your role as a father.

Feelings of anger are a natural stage of the grieving process. The anger many men hold on to comes from a need to feel in control. When they begin to think, "Someone is affecting my life. I don't have control, I'm not making the choices for my own life," they begin to feel they are losing control, and this feeling leads to rage.

It is helpful, if you are feeling angry because of a lack of control over the events in your life, to review in your own mind the situations and factors that you *do* have control over. You have control over your own reactions, your response to your children, and your attitude. Often, the sense of powerlessness we feel is actually a distortion of reality, and we have more control over our own lives than we realize. Avoid becoming obsessed with what you can't control; focus on what you can and do control.

Strategy No. 2: Keep a journal or write a letter to your spouse (a letter which you may or may not mail). Anger often involves unfinished business: the debris from your shattered marriage that has never been cleaned up and disposed of, the things you wish you had said, the things left undone, the things that have never been openly acknowledged or admitted. You might begin with "I'm angry with you because . . ." or, "I'm sad because . . ." Writing those feelings down in a journal or a letter can help you close the books on that unfinished business.

Once you write those feelings down, should you send that letter to your ex-wife? Should you tell her you are angry because she left you or because of other hurts you received from her? That's a tough question. We would counsel you to do so *only if:*

- You feel you need to; *and*
- You feel absolutely confident you can do so in an assertive, non-aggressive manner;

- You use "I feel" statements instead of "You" statements; *and*
- You feel absolutely certain that she won't be hurt in the process.

There is a very clear purpose in writing and sending such a letter: the purpose of finishing unfinished business—and your motives must be positive, not destructive.

Very few people can write and send such a letter with pure motives and positive results. Whenever one of our clients says he would like to send a letter to his ex-wife as a way of finishing unfinished business, we ask, "What would you say to your ex-wife if you had the chance?" The average guy starts out calmly and rationally, but within three or four sentences he has completely blown his game plan. He starts either blaming and accusing or pleading and groveling. It is a rare man who can go through the pain of divorce and then confront his ex-wife about specific hurts in an assertive, non-aggressive way.

Another point to consider is that, emotionally, you and your ex-wife may be at very different places. You may be at a very good place, having gained a lot of insight into your issues and why the breakup occurred and having learned how to express your anger assertively. Your ex-wife, however, may not be able to handle your anger, even if it is expressed in a mature and productive way. She may not have done the work you have done to understand her own issues and feelings. Even if your intent is positive and productive, a letter from you may not be received by her in this way.

The riskiest and least advisable way to finish unfinished business with your ex-wife would be to talk to her in person. In a face-to-face confrontation, it is easy for a conversation to escalate from assertive to aggressive to completely out of control. It is all too easy for the old system to reassert itself and for the two of you to pick up old conflict patterns right where you left off. Misunderstandings multiply; barbs fly; she pushes your buttons, just as she did before the breakup. You can have the best intentions in the world, but one sentence or even one look from her can hook you back into the old pattern of relating. Soon your objectivity is right out the window.

If you really feel you should attempt to close out your unfinished business in a face-to-face discussion, it's best to role-play the encounter in advance with a therapist. Your therapist can try out various scenarios, attempting to push your buttons just as she would, and can suggest various strategies for maintaining your cool, even if she attacks you out of her own anger. Just remember that very few people can do this successfully.

Our experience is that most men who record their anger either in a journal or a letter find the catharsis they need. In fact, many men start a letter with the intention of mailing it, only to change their minds once it's written. The finished letter either goes into a journal or the fireplace. Sometimes the words just need to be written; they don't need to be read.

Strategy No. 3: Design your own anger management plan. Ask yourself, "How do I handle anger? Passively, aggressively, passive-aggressively, or assertively?" Then plan to be more intentional, productive, and assertive in the way you deal with anger. If you can't control your anger without some outside help, check with your pastor or counselor for the location of an anger management class in your area. Or seek the help of a professional therapist.

Anger is not just an emotion. It is a physiological reaction, and the body reacts to it in a physiological way. Anger releases chemicals in the brain and the bloodstream, which are designed to help us meet a short-term, outward threat. This is called the "fight-or-flight response," and it means that when you are angry you actually have a sudden surplus of pent-up energy. That energy wants to go somewhere, which is why people who are angry so often put their fist through a wall, or drive 110 miles an hour, or punch someone. These, of course, are all wildly inappropriate ways to release the surplus energy of anger!

There are, however, appropriate ways. If you have an anger management plan, you can be ready to direct your feelings and your energy into constructive channels. Just think of the body you could have if you spent all that anger in the weight room or on the racquetball court. Or you could use it to finally get your office organized. Or to get that novel written. Or to build that clubhouse for your kids.

Another good anger management tool is positive self-talk. Many people are stuck in chronic anger because their self-esteem is low. They unconsciously reinforce a cycle of anger, defeat, and hopelessness by telling themselves, "I'm no good, I'm always losing control, things will never get better." Such people need to focus on positive affirmations that reinforce their strengths and bolster their hopes:

- "I am a good father."
- "I handle my anger well."
- "I am a positive person."
- "I have control over my life and my behavior."

One of the best tools you can have in managing your anger is understanding the underlying reasons for your anger. Remember that anger is a *defensive* emotion, designed to shield you, to keep you from being vulnerable to another person. When someone hurts you, you feel angry, but the anger is a secondary emotion. The primary emotion is the hurt you feel inside, often at an unconscious, unacknowledged level. The emotion of anger covers the hurt and keeps it buried. As long as you feel anger (an emotion that is directed outward), you are too busy raging to feel the hurt (an emotion that is directed inward).

"Some years back," says Ken, "I played guitar and sang with a band. For some reason, the band leader felt threatened by me and engaged in some childish games to get me out of the band. When I asked him what it was all about, he just unleashed on me. 'This is my band, not yours!' he said. 'You're not going to come in here and take over!'

"Well, obviously he had problems that I didn't understand, so I took my guitar and left the band. The whole next day I hung around the house, ranting and raving about how it didn't make any sense, how I'd never given the guy one reason to think I was threatening his leadership. I was really grinding my molars over it.

"And my wife, who had been quietly watching me rave, finally said, 'Ken, you know what you're saying? You're saying you feel hurt. This guy hurt your feelings.'

"I was astounded by this insight. I hadn't seen it until she pointed it out to me. 'Yes,' I said, 'I'm just feeling hurt. I'm a good musician, and I got shoved out for no good reason, and that hurts.' And after I understood what I was angry about, the anger just went away."

That's the power of insight and understanding. When you understand *why* you are feeling angry, very often the anger goes away. Why? Because it's no longer needed. The insight has replaced the need to cover our true feelings and to direct our feelings outward.

Another emotion anger often covers is fear. "After my divorce," recalls Van, "I experienced a lot of anger. It took me a long time to understand *why* I was so angry. Eventually I realized that my anger was secondary to my fear. I felt my life was out of control. Someone else was making decisions that were affecting my life, and there was nothing I could do about it.

"My biggest fear was the fear of loss. I had lost my marriage. I had lost my home. I wondered, 'What will I lose next? Will I lose my kids? Will I lose their love for me?' Once I recognized the highly charged fears at the base of my anger, then anger became less of an issue for me."

Strategy No. 4: Pray. Anger is an emotional issue with strong spiritual dynamics. Our prayer, if we get stuck in anger, should be, "God, I'm raging inside, and I can't seem to get past it in my own strength. I need Your strength and wisdom. Reveal to me the deeper emotions and issues inside me. Help me resolve my unfinished business so I can get past this anger and get on with my life."

The Bible does not condemn the emotion of anger; rather, the Bible teaches that anger is a natural part of our humanity. And in the life of Christ, we see that there are times when anger is perfectly appropriate (as when He overturned the tables of the people who defiled God's House).[1] The Bible allows for the expression of anger, as long as it is expressed appropriately and in a way that doesn't harm others.[2] "Be angry, and do not sin," (Ephesians 4:26).

LAND MINE NO. 4: EMOTIONAL NUMBING

Emotional numbing is a peril we are all prone to in different ways. None of us wants to feel pain. At the first sign of a headache, we reach for a bottle of pills. If we get a stomach ache, we take a couple of tablespoons of that pink stuff. And who would want to get their teeth drilled without a stiff shot of Novocain?

But there are situations in life where it is much more therapeutic to go through the pain than to avoid it. Physical conditioning is one ("no pain, no gain"). Divorce recovery is another. If we numb ourselves, instead of courageously going through the pain of the process, we will not grow, we will not recover.

Certainly, a little "numbing out" can be beneficial. That's what our natural defense mechanisms (such as denial and anger) are all about: protecting us from the pain until we are strong enough to heal. The damage comes when these short-term defense mechanisms become long-term patterns of repression, denial, and avoidance.

For example, an abused child could not emotionally survive if he was not able to seal off his feelings and dissociate himself from his pain. When that child grows to adulthood, however, he often cannot remember his childhood. He may go through extreme depression without understanding the root causes. If he is unable to bring his feelings to the surface, he will be emotionally unhealthy. He needs to feel his pain, work through it, and be set free of those hidden emotional chains that keep him in bondage.

The same is true for a survivor of divorce. The breakdown of a marriage is a traumatic experience. Certain defense mechanisms, such as denial and anger, kick in to help you cope with that trauma. But once the initial shock of the divorce has subsided, you need to work through the pain. You can't go under it, over it, or around it and still expect to grow and recover. You have to go through the pain.

What are some of the things men do to avoid the pain and numb themselves emotionally?

Some will become involved in *drinking or drug abuse*. Using chemicals to numb emotional pain is just an extension of our society's habit of using chemicals to numb physical pain. Besides the fact that alcohol and drugs are addictive and have a tendency to destroy people's lives, these chemicals have another downside that is seldom talked about: they numb *all* the emotions, even our joys and pleasures.

"Before I quit drinking," recalls Ken, "I didn't realize how little of life I was experiencing. I'd go through family events like birthdays, Thanksgiving, and Christmas in a kind of emotional haze. I remember one Christmas I bought a weight bench for my son, Wayne, and I had a few drinks while I assembled it in the bedroom. After I had it all put together, I discovered something any sober man would have figured out from the get-go: the assembled bench wouldn't fit through the door. So I had to take it apart again to get it into the living room where the Christmas tree was.

"After I quit drinking, my experience of life became richer, sharper, more real. Maybe the painful things hurt more, but the good things were so much better. I found out how much fun a family Christmas can be when you're sober."

Other men, to numb their feelings, will become involved in *compulsive overeating* and will completely let themselves go physically. Still others immerse themselves in *compulsive exercising, body building, and running*. While balanced physical conditioning is a good thing, many men throw themselves into sports, such as marathon running, in order to fill an emotional hole in their lives and numb their emotional pain. That's why some sports physicians refer to these compulsive runners as "male anorexics."

And other men numb their pain with *compulsive workaholism*. Their work becomes their drug and their addiction. The workaholic claims he can't rest because he is too swamped, too far behind, or simply more ambitious than anyone else. In reality, however, he is doping himself on hyperactivity to keep himself from feeling his pain. Activity shields him from those times of stillness and solitude when the truth might break through and confront him with his inner poverty. He works hard, plays hard, parties hard—but he is really just running, staying one step ahead of the pain that is always yapping at his heels.

Some men numb their pain by *over-involvement with their children*. They are always hanging around their ex-wife's house, absorbed in every area of their children's lives, driving both Mom and the children crazy. In many cases, these men are numbing the guilt and remorse they feel over the divorce. In their effort to make it up to their kids, they may actually be driving a wedge into that relationship.

For some men, *promiscuous sex* is the "drug of choice" for numbing emotional pain. Though the sex act itself may take only a few minutes, some men can plan an entire day around the sexual conquest. Their thoughts at the office are preoccupied with sex. After work, they hang out in bars or nightclubs, looking for action. They become addicted to the emotional tingle of sexual adventure. Many of these men are using the highly charged emotions of the libido to numb their feelings of pain or guilt or to cover the emptiness and despair they fear may be lurking at the core of their lives.

Still others try to numb the pain of their divorce by *jumping into another relationship* too quickly. They don't want to go through the stages of grieving their loss and dealing with their issues. So they go out and quickly find some other lonely person, rush through the euphoria of the romantic chase, ignore all the advice of friends who ask, "Don't you think you ought to slow down a bit?" all in a desperate attempt to obliterate their pain. When a man short-circuits the grief process, his unfinished business will inevitably resurface to plague his second marriage (and his third, his fourth, and on and on).

Some men numb themselves by *over-intellectualizing*. We see many over-intellectualizers in counseling. Take Dan, for example. He comes into the counselor's office and sits down. His face is expressionless. "My wife and I are living in separate households now," he says.

"How does that make you feel?" asks the counselor.

"Well, I'm able to see the kids every other weekend, and I continue to work at my job."

"Fine," says the counselor, "but how do you *feel?*"

"Oh, I think this was probably for the best," says Dan. "The kids are in a more stable environment, and they're doing well at school."

"That's good," says the counselor, "but that's not what I asked. I want to know *what you are feeling* as a result of this divorce. Dan, tell me, *how do you feel?*"

"I have more time to do the things I enjoy," Dan replies (although it is not really a reply at all). Dan never talks about how he really feels. He talks about circumstances and events and opinions. His conversation is entirely intellectual and non-emotional. He can't bring himself to say, "I feel lonely. I hurt all the time. I miss my children. Sometimes I cry at night."

Other men numb their feelings by *staying involved with their first wife*. Roger and Ellyn are separated, and their divorce will be final in about two months. Roger keeps finding excuses to drop by the house. One thing leads to another, and before either of them knows what has happened, they are in bed together. Or one thing leads to another, and they end up in a big shouting match, one of the biggest blowups ever. They are separated—but they are still sexually and emotionally linked. In some ways, their relationship actually seems to have improved since their separation, and Roger has suggested that they start dating again. Ellyn thinks she still wants a divorce, but she also has doubts that she's doing the right thing.

By staying involved with each other in this love-hate, approach-avoidance way, they don't have to face the painful finality of truly divorcing, once-and-for-all. What they need is to make an iron-clad decision: end it or make it work. Either way, a counselor can help them draw some boundaries in their lives.

As you can see, the emotional numbing land mine can ambush us in any one of a variety of ways. Perhaps you see yourself in one of these scenarios. Or perhaps you simply do not feel anything in the aftermath of your separation or divorce—and you wonder why. If so, we have some practical suggestions for disarming the land mine of emotional numbing:

Disarming Emotional Numbing

Strategy No. 1: Pray. Again, emotional and behavioral problems have a spiritual dimension and demand spiritual solutions. By drawing on the strength of that Power that is beyond ourselves, we can gain the insight and the courage we need to face our feelings squarely, to experience them fully, and to work through them to a healthy conclusion. We suggest the following prayer:

"God, I trust You with my feelings, including those feelings and thoughts that lie out of reach of my conscious awareness. If there is something I should be feeling but have repressed or numbed, then I ask You to bring it to the surface. Help me to get out of the way of my own recovery. I trust You not to expose any feelings I can't handle. God, help me to get on with my life."

We're not suggesting you should manufacture a feeling just because you feel you should have one. We don't want you to say, "Well, I guess I should feel angry, so I'll start raging now." But if there are buried feelings that are holding back your recovery, we hope you will express a willingness, to yourself and to God, to face those feelings and move beyond them.

Strategy No. 2: Make an appointment with yourself. Tell yourself, "Friday night at eight, I'm going to sit down and look inside and be honest with myself about what I'm feeling." When Friday night at eight rolls around (or whatever time works for you), sit down alone in a quiet place and think about the family you no longer live with. Go through a family picture album. Play back some family videos. What feelings surface? What hurts? What fears?

You may be tempted to put the album away or shut off the VCR. That's a defense mechanism. It's understandable because we all seek pleasure and avoid pain. Persevere. Keep remembering. Punch through that wall of resistance. Even if it hurts now, a time will come when you'll be glad you did.

"Our memories were on slides," says Van. "After our separation, all those slides went right into the closet, and they didn't come out for months. If I had it to do over again, I would take time during the first couple of months of the separation, pull out the slides, and get out all those feelings of hurt and loss the very first thing. Instead, I did a lot of numbing. I could have gotten through my grieving faster if I had just looked at myself in the mirror and said, 'I'm hurting, but I'm going to get through it.'"

Strategy No. 3: Keep a journal. It can be very cathartic to write down what you are feeling whenever you feel it. Don't just journal events: "I went to work today, had lunch with Jack, and watched the Cowboys stomp the Broncos." Instead, make sure you journal your honest *feelings:* "Life stinks. I feel angry today. I thought about what Jane said to me when she kicked me out of the house; what right did she have to say a lousy thing like that? I miss my kids. Is this ever going to end?"

Don't edit. Don't hold back. Set it all down, exactly as you feel it. When you finish writing and close your journal, you'll probably find you have released a lot of the poisonous emotions that have been burning a hole in your gut. Journaling is one of the best ways a man can literally "close the books" on unfinished business.

Strategy No. 4: Stop your compulsive behavior. Easier said than done? Of course it is. So if you need help dealing with your drinking or drug abuse or workaholism or sex addiction, whatever behavior you are using to numb out, then *get the help you need.* Find a support group or a therapist who can help you gain control over your compulsions. In the process of getting to the bottom of your compulsive behavior, you will probably get to the bottom of a lot of the unfinished business that has been hindering your recovery and growth.

If, in the process of getting in touch with your real feelings, you feel that these emotions are becoming too intense for you to handle—and especially if you feel any suicidal urges—get in touch with a therapist or counselor right away. Remember, this book is not a substitute for psychotherapy. Divorce is one of the most stressful, shattering losses any human being can go through, and many of the issues and feelings which arise may be bigger than you can handle by yourself. If that's the case, don't hesitate to get the help you need so you can continue your personal growth and recovery.

CLOSING THE BOOKS

The choices we make and the behaviors we act out are driven by powerful emotional forces within us that few of us really understand. If you make a courageous effort to get in touch with those emotions, to close the books on that unfinished business, you will be able to operate more effectively within the post-divorce systems you now inhabit. You will be more effective in transacting the business of parenthood with your children's mother. And you will be more effective in your role as a father.

This is what Phil had to learn. Phil (the father whose story opened this chapter) spent many hours in therapy, working on the unfinished business from his marriage and divorce and from his ex-wife's infidelity. The incident in which he suddenly struck his daughter, Keri, forced him to face the fact that there were significant emotional issues buried beneath the surface of his awareness. That kind of sudden, volcanic anger doesn't just boil up from nowhere. Even though he had long denied it, that anger had been percolating inside him for a long time.

Since gaining a better understanding of the emotional issues that drive his behavior, Phil has been able to mend fences with his daughter. "I had a long talk with Keri the other day," he explains. "We went out to the park and I told her how sorry I was. I explained to her that there were a lot of feelings going on inside me that I hadn't admitted, even to myself. I was careful not to run her mother down. I want to be real careful not to lay any of this off on Keri or Elyse or anyone else.

"I explained to Keri that when I struck her, I was really striking out at her mom. I told her it was because I had not admitted to myself how angry I was. It was my problem and I had to solve it. I said it was hard to forgive myself for letting my unfinished business hurt her. I didn't think Keri would understand all that—she's only fifteen. But she hugged me, and she said she knew I was hurting a lot. And she forgave me."

Closing the books. Taking care of business. Just one more step on the path to recovery, one more way we can become more effective as fathers—even if we only see our kids every other weekend.

In the next chapter, we will look at some of the important legal and financial issues that affect your role as a visiting father.

Chapter/5

THE ABSENT FATHER AND THE LAW

Paul and his wife, Dorothy, were divorced twenty years ago, when their daughter Julie was four years old. "It was a bitter divorce," Paul recalls. "Dorothy was vengeful beyond belief. Well, to be honest, I guess I wasn't any better. I took her to court to get custody, and my lawyer tried every trick in the book to prove she was an unfit mother. The truth is, she wasn't any great shakes as a mother, but she wasn't as evil as we painted her in court.

"Well, Dorothy came back at me with everything she had. By the time her attorney got through with me, my reputation was in ruins. It was horrible. In the end, Dorothy got custody anyway. She spent the rest of my daughter's growing years poisoning her mind against me.

"I maintained visitation for a few years and tried to rebuild trust between my daughter and myself. But it was clear she hated me, so I finally gave up and only saw her at Christmas and during summer vacations.

"About a year ago, Julie dropped by my house unannounced. I mean, it was really right out of the blue. She had just gotten a new job and she needed a car, but her mom wouldn't co-sign the car loan. She asked if I would co-sign for her. I put my name on the dotted line, and that was the last I ever heard from Julie. I don't know where she lives or where the car is, but I've had to pay a bunch of her tickets, and I've had to make the payments on the car in order to keep my credit rating.

"Julie was raised by her mother to hate me, and she was told, 'Get back at your father any way you can.' So she got back at me, all right. I've paid a very high price, both emotionally and financially."

Does Paul have any regrets? "Boy, do I have regrets!" he says. "I often wonder how my life—and my daughter's life—would have turned out if I had not tried to use the court to get even with Dorothy."

Whenever a marriage breaks down, the law has an important role to play. It protects the interests of individuals. It attempts to divide assets, liabilities, and obligations in a fair and impartial way. Unfortunately, many people who are going through a divorce choose to wield the law as a club. They use the courts to punish someone they are angry with. A father who tries to get revenge against his wife at the bang of a gavel runs the risk of ruining not only her but himself and his children as well.

Compare the regrets expressed by Paul with the grateful memories of Art, a businessman in his early thirties. "My parents were divorced when I was five," Art recalls. "I don't remember any conflict or name-calling or anything like that. They didn't drag each other through the courts and make me choose between them.

"I remember one time asking my mother why Dad had left our home, and she said that sometimes it's best for a Mom and Dad to live in separate houses. I accepted that. When I was growing up, my parents always encouraged me to love and respect the other parent. My memory of that time is that Mom and Dad parted as friends, and I hardly knew the breakup was happening. I look back on that, and I'm grateful."

The law can have a major impact—for better or worse—on your relationship with your children. Whenever a separation and divorce take place, the paramount issue on the table is the welfare of the children. In writing and interpreting the laws surrounding divorce, the legislatures and the courts have properly focused their attention on the interests of the child. That, of course, is the issue every divorcing couple should be focusing on as well, but sadly, there is often so much anger and vengefulness going on that the adults forget that the children are even there, except as pawns in the larger game of "Let's Get Even."

Parents divorce each other. They don't divorce their children. No matter who gets the car or the house, no matter who gets stuck with the credit-card debt, we should never forget that the children are innocent participants in this situation. They need to be protected from the deadly fallout when the nuclear family explodes.

In this chapter, we will examine how the law affects you as a visiting father and how the law can help to protect your own best interests and the best interests of your child. The authors of this book are not attorneys but psychotherapists. We have gathered the information in this chapter—which is intentionally very general in nature—from discussions with attorneys who are experienced in family law. None of this information is intended as legal advice or to take the place of the counsel of an attorney.

The laws relating to such issues as divorce, child custody, and visitation rights vary from state to state and change from year to year; so it is important that you be guided through the divorce process by your own attorney. This chapter is not a legal manual but a general guide to the kinds of issues that you, as an absent father, need to be aware of. Our goal is not to replace your attorney but to better equip you to ask your attorney the right questions.

WHO GETS THE KIDS?

"Some time ago, I was called for jury duty in a divorce case," says Ken Parker. "One of the attorneys in the case stated that he would rather handle a murder case than a child custody case because murder is cleaner and does less emotional damage." Many other attorneys, as well as judges and court reporters, agree. Child custody cases can often be tragic, offensive, and distasteful beyond imagining. The strategy used in many of these cases is to attack, discredit, and destroy the other side. (And both sides have lived together long enough to have gathered plenty of intimate ammunition.) Like an old purse, a family is turned inside out, and every embarrassing and shameful secret is poured out on the courtroom floor.

In the end, someone is awarded custody of the children. But in a real sense, no one truly wins, not even the parent who prevails. Of course, the biggest losers of all are the children. They generally do not have the maturity and emotional strength to witness the deterioration of their parents' marriage. Children know when they are being used, and they will carry that knowledge with them for the rest of their lives.

Fortunately, there are fewer custody battles these days than in times past. Part of the reason is that society, the laws, and the courts have changed. Divorcing couples are being encouraged to share parental responsibility instead of seeking a winner-takes-all solution.

Another change for the better is an increased emphasis on the fathering role in our society. In past generations, a father was essentially a breadwinner. This has changed, in part, because breadwinning has become a team effort in many households today. As a result, parenthood is seen in the same light. Many fathers now take an active role in the rearing of their children. Dad doesn't just tuck the kids in bed at night anymore. He also bathes, feeds, reads stories, counsels, and disciplines.

This new awareness of the fathering role has helped to make custody wars less likely than in the past. The trend today is for courts to encourage divorcing couples to set up an arrangement which is usually called *joint custody* or *joint managing conservatorship*. It's a more balanced custody arrangement than the old either/or arrangement.

Joint custodial arrangements are widely misunderstood by non-lawyers. At first glance, joint custody looks like a fifty-fifty arrangement. But there is no magical formula for splitting one household into two and dividing the children evenly between the two parents. In practice, one parent still ends up being custodial and the other (usually Dad) ends up being non-custodial. In a joint custody arrangement, however, the non-custodial parent generally has more rights and decision-making powers regarding the welfare and upbringing of the child than the old sole custody system.

Keep in mind that the laws governing custody arrangements will vary from state to state, and you should consult a local attorney in order to fully understand how the laws of your jurisdiction affect you and your children. But in general, it is fair to say that the laws of our society have moved (at least on paper) away from gender bias and at least attempt to assess parental qualifications without regard to the sex of the parent.

For example, in Texas (the state where the authors live) the usual roles of conservatorship are:

Managing conservator—This is the custodial parent role. The child lives with this parent most of the year. The managing conservator has the responsibility for day-to-day management of the life and welfare of the child. This parent may also have additional rights and responsibilities as determined by the court.

Possessory conservator—This is the non-custodial parent role. This parent is acknowledged by the court to have "possessory rights" equal to those of the managing conservator. In other words, the fact that this parent is a visiting parent rather than a custodial parent does not diminish his legal standing as a parent. Under Texas law, the possessory conservator has certain rights, including the right to a continuing parental relationship, the right to scheduled visitation times with the child, the right to bequeath an inheritance to the child, and other rights which the court may choose to award. Texas law also confers certain responsibilities on the possessory conservator, such as the responsibility to pay child support according to a standardized formula.

By using these terms, the State of Texas recognizes that both parents are conservators; that is, both parents have rights and responsibilities where the children are concerned. It is an attempt to level the roles as much as possible. As a practical matter, however, the roles can only be leveled so far. Obviously, a child cannot live in Mom's house on even weeks and in Dad's house on odd weeks. The child has to *live with* one parent and *visit* the other.

Though Texas law requires that the managing conservator (the custodial parent) be determined without regard to the sex of the parent, in practice it is still the mother who is usually given that role. The fact that there is gender-neutral language in Texas law does not always give the father a fifty-fifty shot at custody. While the phrase *joint managing conservatorship* sounds like an equal arrangement, in most respects it is little different from awarding the mother sole custody. There are, however, a few real advantages to the father in joint custody or joint conservatorship arrangements, and these advantages should not be ignored.

For example, a joint custodial role *may* give you more control over deciding the residence of the child. Remember, the court may give you the right to visit your child every other weekend, but that right will have little meaning if your child is moved 3,000 miles away. "If both parents stay in the same town," said one attorney we spoke with, "there is no problem. But if the mother is given the sole right to determine the child's residence, she could move the child away for any reason whatsoever, and under the law she hasn't done anything wrong." If you want to have a say in determining the residence of your child, you should make your wishes known to your attorney so that he or she can seek to have this provision made a part of the divorce decree.

A joint custodial role may give you a major role in deciding other matters regarding the child's welfare and upbringing, including issues such as education, religious training, and health care. There is always a psychological benefit to a joint custodial role. When the court places you and your ex-wife on an equal footing before the law (however unequal it may seem in actual practice), this gives you a greater feeling of control over the situation. Plus, this may also help to reduce your fear that you are losing your children.

Your state, remember, may use different legal terminology and may define these roles differently. The important principle to understand is that in today's custody arrangements, there are generally two distinct roles, and there are legally defined rights and responsibilities for each role. Through this legal language, the state demonstrates a recognition that both parents have parental rights, interests, and responsibilities that need to be protected.

In most states, the rules for custody have been made more clear and specific in recent years. The purpose is to level the playing field between the parties and to make the process more predictable. The more clearly these issues are codified in law, the less the process can be skewed one way or the other by inappropriate factors such as biased judges or high-powered lawyers.

Yet, even though the rules have been tightened in most states, there is still enormous flexibility available to divorcing parents. Virtually any arrangement you and your wife agree on can become a part of the divorce decree, as long as the judge thinks it is workable and in the best interests of the children. The key is that the two of you have to agree. However, if you both can't agree the judge *must* make a decision between adversarial parties.

VISITATION

Even though divorce inevitably creates physical distance in your relationship with your children, the goal of family law and the courts is to see that the relationship between parents and their children is disturbed as little as possible. So the laws of all states make some provision to enable you to maintain regular contact with your children. This contact is called *visitation*, and it is a right you have as a father.

A typical visitation arrangement permits the father to have the children visit in his home on alternating weekends, around certain holidays, and for a period of time during school vacation. The visitation schedule is often negotiable, and you should make your wishes known to your attorney as early as possible in the divorce process so that your attorney can negotiate a favorable visitation arrangement.

The law protects your right to see your children and maintain a relationship with them. The divorce decree spells out the boundaries of your visitation rights, stating where and when and for how long you can visit with your children. Of course, this rigid structure tends to make visitation seem forced and artificial—almost as if you are permitted to see your own children "by appointment only."

No matter how generous your visitation arrangement, you will feel that your parental role has been diminished. A certain degree of spontaneity will be lost. There will be a beautiful Saturday afternoon when you would like to take your kids to the zoo or the park, but it won't be your visitation day. Then the next Saturday (your scheduled day with the children) it will be raining, the kids will be grumpy, and you'll have a raging head-cold.

Yet, for all its limitations, visitation is the best possible compromise in a less than perfect situation. It is within the admittedly narrow confines of visitation that your fathering role must now take place. And there is much more you can do to make the most of the time your divorce decree allows you with your children (for ways to make the most of your visitation time, see Chapter 9: The Effective Absent Father).

Sometimes an ex-wife will attempt to hinder or withhold visitation in order to "punish" the father. In such situations, it is wise to avoid retaliation. If your ex-wife interferes with your court-ordered visitation rights, you have a remedy at your disposal: you can file an action for contempt of court. If she does not obey the court order, she is committing a punishable offense. And remember: Your position in court will be much stronger if your behavior toward your ex-wife conforms with the provisions of the divorce decree.

CHILD SUPPORT

One of the most important legal and moral responsibilities you have as a divorced father is the responsibility for *child support*. Even though your children live with their mother, you are still responsible (along with their mother) for their physical well-being: food, shelter, education, and other necessities of life.

In many states, the courts determine what the non-custodial parent will pay in child support, taking in account such individual factors as the parent's income, educational background, age, physical ability to work, and other factors presented to the court as evidence. But many other states have adopted standardized guidelines which direct that a given percentage of the non-custodial parent's net resources be paid as child support.

The formula for determining the exact amount of child support to be paid is a state-by-state proposition, so consult with your attorney. You should be prepared to pay whatever the court orders and to make sure that there is adequate health insurance coverage for the children.

Because of the growing problem of fathers who skip out on their responsibility to pay child support, many states have made it possible to withhold child support from wage earnings. The withheld funds are sent directly to the child support office, which then writes a check to the mother. In some cases, however, wage-earner withholding of child support is not imposed unless a dad becomes delinquent in his child support payments.

There is a good reason for the state taking this kind of action. When Tom and his wife Sally divorced and the court ordered Tom to pay $500 a month in child support payments, Tom rebelled. He grudgingly made the first few payments, then stopped. Tom quit his job, moved to another state, and left no forwarding address. Tom's new job paid $500 a month less than his old job, so in practical terms he might as well have made the payments as the court ordered—plus now he had a contempt citation following him. But, of course, Tom wasn't thinking in practical terms. All he wanted was to get back at Sally.

But who was really hurt by Tom's vengeful tactics? Well, Sally was inconvenienced a bit, but she wasn't really hurt. She still got $500 a month to feed, clothe, and shelter the children—only instead of getting it from Tom, she got it from the government in the form of public assistance. The ones who were really hurt by Tom's tactics were Tom's children, the innocent pawns in this battle between Tom and Sally.

What Tom failed to understand is that child support is a legal obligation. Child support arrangements are part of the divorce decree. A divorce decree is an order of the court, and it is enforceable by contempt. Nonpayment of child support can land a dad in jail.

But even more importantly, child support is a moral obligation, an obligation of love. If your kids go without school clothes or hot lunches or health care because you wanted to get even with their mother, what kind of message are you sending them?

Your support payment is the same money you would be spending on your children if you were still living in the house with them. That money is part of your connection to your children and one of the ways you continue to demonstrate your love for them.

Some Child Support Myths

Whenever word gets around that you and your wife are splitting up, there is always some guy at the office or at the racquet club who will take you aside and fill you in on what this divorce thing is all about. Either he's been divorced himself or his brother-in-law is an attorney or something like that. For whatever reason, this guy is an "authority" on divorce, and he will proceed to pump you full of myths and misinformation about such matters as visitation and child support.

One myth newly divorced dads sometimes fall for: "If I buy back-to-school clothes for all my kids, I can deduct that amount from my child support payments," or, "If I take my kids to Disneyland, I can deduct those expenses from my child support payments." Be cautious. You normally cannot use your own purchases or expenses to offset child support payments to your wife. The courts generally take the position that as the children's father, you should be willing to put out additional money for the sake of your children, above and beyond what the judge orders. And that is a hard position to argue with from any point of view.

Another common myth: let's say, for the sake of discussion, your ex-wife is using visitation to get back at you. The court has ordered that she let you see your children on a certain schedule, but she hides them every time you arrive to pick them up. You haven't seen your children in two months. Certainly, you have a right to stop paying child support to force her to meet her obligations under the divorce decree, right?

Wrong. If you stop paying child support, your ex-wife can take you to court for contempt.

Child support and visitation rights are two completely separate, mutually exclusive issues. Your wife's behavior may be completely wrong and even illegal, but that does not give you the legal right to withhold child support. This principle cuts both ways: your ex-wife can't say to you, "You're two weeks late with your child support, so I can't let you see Jimmy." You both have an obligation under the terms of the divorce decree, but your obligation does not hinge on hers or vice versa.

HOW TO BEHAVE WHILE YOUR DIVORCE IS PENDING

Your conduct during the pendency of the divorce (that is, during the time between the filing and the time the decree is final) can have a profound effect on your rights and your relationship with your children. So here are a few pointers to remember while you are waiting for the divorce to become final.

Avoid stirring up conflict. The more difficult and obnoxious your behavior, the more threatened your wife will feel—and the more determined she will become to make life difficult for you. Focus on the needs of your children, not on getting even. Use a little extra charm and good humor. If you have trouble controlling your emotions, obtain counseling and seek help from God through prayer. By learning to relate cordially and constructively with your wife, you may actually get more concessions at the negotiating table. It could even save you from costly litigation. Remember: The law steps in when common sense and common courtesy fail.

Avoid trying to control your wife. Let her live her own life. Let her make her own decisions. If she decides to take the kids to visit her parents in California, there's nothing you can do about it. If you try to control her life while she's trying to divorce you, it is likely to backfire on you in court.

Respect your wife's right to a peaceful existence. Don't harass her—not during the day, not during the night, not at work. If you cannot have a civil conversation with her, then avoid contact with her. If necessary, communicate with her only through your attorney.

And remember that you, too, have a right to a peaceful existence. You have a right to protect yourself, your children, and your property. If you are receiving harassing visits or phone calls from your wife at home or at work, especially during the pendency of a divorce, ask your attorney about obtaining a restraining order or injunctive relief to remedy the problem. Don't take the matter into your own hands.

Be discreet. Avoid behavior that will aggravate the other side into retaliating. Carrying on a romance during the pendency of a divorce suggests that you are out hunting a new mate while you are still married. Even if your wife initiated the divorce, even if she says she doesn't care what you do, the idea that you are out dating before you are divorced from her may trigger retaliation.

"When a client comes to me," said one attorney, "and complains that his wife is bringing men home in front of the children, I encourage him to talk to a therapist and deal with his own feelings. At the same time, I go to work and negotiate with the other side. I try to get a mutual no-dating agreement for the sake of the children. I find it's always best for the kids if neither side carries on a romantic life until the divorce is final."

Avoid negative comments about your wife. Speak dispassionately and as positively as possible about her in conversations with friends, in front of the children, and in court. Attempts to malign her character or to tear her down in the eyes of her children could jeopardize your interests in the courtroom.

Avoid open displays of anger at home or in the courtroom. Judges like to have the facts so they can decide matters rationally and logically. They tend to get irritated when husbands or wives act irrationally and emotionally, and this never helps your case. Avoid emotional displays at home or in public that could be used against you.

If at all possible, remain friends with your wife. Take this position with her: "You and I can't get along in the same house, but there's no reason we can't part as friends. There's no reason we can't both try to do what's right for the children. I want to be fair to you, and I want you to be okay when this is over. That's one last gift I can give you when we say goodbye."

Some marriages dissolve with best wishes and a touch of sadness. Others go down in flames and fireworks. Comparing those two kinds of divorces, one truth always holds true: the children best able to recover from their parents' divorce are those whose parents go their separate ways, cordially and graciously.

ARE THE COURTS FAIR?

"'Unfair! Unfair!' I hear that word a lot," one attorney told us. "Time after time, I see people coming out of the courtroom feeling they were treated unfairly. They claim that either the judge was biased or the laws were screwball or the other side lied. These are common complaints, and in fact, from time to time, some people do get treated unfairly in court. But if you take a close look at each case, you find that people often feel they were treated unfairly because they didn't get the outcome they wanted. Yet the outcome they wanted was often unfair.

"In my experience as a family law attorney, I have found that the courts are pretty fair. If people work within the system, if they walk in with a cooperative attitude instead of a combative attitude, the system tends to treat them fairly. In most court actions, one side wins and the other loses—or there is a compromise which leaves both sides feeling unhappy. But the court system was designed to protect rights and render fair decisions, and most judges are conscientious in their pursuit of those goals."

In the past ten years, there have been sweeping changes in family law. Most of these changes are a reflection of a growing desire in the legislatures and the courts to ensure greater fairness to both sides. Many of those changes are designed to make the law function in a more gender-neutral way. In our society and in our laws, we are trying to get away from the idea that men have some rights and women have other rights. Instead, today's family law tends to talk about the rights of spouses or the rights of individuals, regardless of gender. Many changes in the law, such as the joint custody arrangement, tend to work in favor of absent fathers, giving them a more significant and involved role in the lives of their children.

The attorneys we spoke with offered a number of suggestions to ensure the fairest possible treatment by the court system:

Be willing to compromise. When both sides go to court breathing fire, making threats, and determined to get their way, everyone loses—except the lawyers. Remember, attorneys often get a higher fee for litigation than negotiated settlements. Wouldn't the money you and your ex spend on litigation be better spent on your children's education? If you enter the courthouse in the attack mode, you and your children will lose, emotionally and financially, no matter who "wins" in court.

Exercise caution before opting for a jury trial. Many states allow jury trials in divorce cases—but if you want a trial by jury, be prepared to accept the consequences. "Jury decisions can be much less predictable than a judge's decisions," said one lawyer. "This is not to say that jury trials are inherently unfair or that they reach wrong conclusions. This is not a criticism of the jury process. I'm just saying that jury trials introduce an extra element of uncertainty. You cannot know all that goes through a juror's mind when he or she is listening to your testimony.

"Sometimes a jury trial is unavoidable. So if you must have a jury trial, make sure you have an attorney with plenty of courtroom experience, someone who knows how to size up a juror."

TAXES AND FINANCES

Alan sat down in his attorney's office, grinning from ear to ear. "Boy, have I had a great week!" he said. "I just landed a fat new account, and to celebrate I went out and bought myself a new car."

His attorney frowned. "You did what?"

"I snagged a sweet deal on a brand new Infiniti Q45. Two-seventy-eight horsepower, zero to sixty in seven seconds, four-wheel steering, Bose stereo. It's sitting in your parking lot. The metallic blue job."

The attorney looked out the window. The car was there, all right, gleaming like a sapphire. "What did it cost you, Alan?"

"I stole it from the dealer for a cool thirty grand."

"Don't you know what you did, Alan? You just created a thirty-thousand dollar community asset! Guess who owns half of that Q45?"

Unfortunately for Alan, he lives in a community property state, and property acquired before the divorce is final becomes a jointly-owned asset. (What Alan did may or may not be a problem in your state.) The point is that divorce complicates a man's life in many unforeseen ways. While your divorce is pending, you should approach all major financial activities with caution, and always seek the advice of your attorney. Remember, the filing doesn't dissolve the marriage; only the decree can accomplish that. Until you get a divorce decree from the court, you are still married to your wife. During the pendency of your divorce (the time between the filing and the issuance of the final decree) avoid making any moves that would complicate your financial picture.

In this section, we will examine some of the financial and tax implications of divorce. Remember, this is not intended to be a detailed guide to financial and tax matters—just a handy reference to help you ask the right questions of your attorney and your accountant.

Credit Cards

In some states, you are still creating community debt until the divorce decree is final, so as soon as your divorce is filed, you should begin separating your financial affairs from your wife's financial affairs. If you and your wife are filing for divorce, you may want to cancel your joint credit cards.

If you expect your wife to behave in a vindictive fashion, you might consider closing all credit accounts so that no additional charges can be made. That includes bank cards, travel and leisure cards, department store cards, oil company cards, the works. Otherwise, in some jurisdictions, you may be handing your wife a loaded gun, aimed right at your wallet. Sometimes, in the heat of a separation and divorce, a wife will run charge accounts to the sky with the rationalization, "He has it coming to him anyway."

(This is not an indictment of ex-wives, by the way. This sort of behavior is rare, but it does happen and sometimes must be guarded against. Husbands have been known to engage in such tactics too. We are assuming that you will not behave in such a self-defeating way.)

Income Tax

Here are some general tax facts to be aware of when you are recently divorced:

If your divorce is finalized by December 31, the Internal Revenue Service recognizes you as divorced for the entire year. When you were married, you could file *jointly* or *married, filing separately*. Once you are divorced, the IRS will only allow you to file *separate* returns.

As a general rule in divorce, the custodial parent (usually Mom) is granted all the exemptions for dependents in the family. A lot of people use the exemption for dependents as a negotiating tool. While the divorce is pending, the two sides may negotiate who gets the exemption. Compromise is possible in such cases: Dad may take the exemption for one child, while Mom takes the exemption for the other.

Your wife is not taxed on the money she receives from you for child support. You are not entitled to a deduction for what you pay in child support.

Payments made by one spouse to the other to equalize the division of property in a settlement do not incur tax liability. For example, if Joe and Mary are trying to equalize the division of a major estate, Joe might give Mary $20,000 in cash to offset her interest in the boat and car Joe is keeping. Mary does not pay taxes on that $20,000 because that is not income to her. That value was already hers in the form of equity in the boat and car.

Division of Property

The division of property between spouses is a state-by-state proposition. Many western states are community property states. Community property simply means that legally married spouses have equal or common ownership interests in property acquired during marriage because there was a supportive team effort in acquiring this property. Ask your attorney to explain how assets are divided according to the laws of your state. Remember that assets acquired before the marriage may be treated differently from assets acquired during the marriage. Special attention should be paid to such matters as valuable gifts, inheritances, personal injury awards, and so forth.

In the codification and philosophy of family law, there is always a reference to the rights and welfare of the children. In divorce, everything hinges on how it affects the children—and that's as it should be. As you are considering the division of property with your wife, the question that should be uppermost in your mind is not, "How can I keep her from robbing me blind?" but, "How can I best make sure my children will have everything they need?" Every decision about every piece of property should be examined through the lens of that question.

The more you are able to negotiate with your spouse, the less control you will hand over to the court. If you and your wife are unable to agree and you leave it to the court to decide, you will be subject to the court's dictates. Those dictates may be flavored by the judge's personal and cultural bias. It is usually better, and less expensive, to negotiate than to litigate.

Debts

The flip side of the division of property is the division of debts. This can be a real sticking point in a divorce action. In most states, every debt acquired during the marriage is presumed to be an obligation of both parties.

One of the most widely misunderstood aspects of a divorce decree is the allocation of debts. The court can order you to pay the mortgage company and GMAC, and your wife to pay MasterCard and Sears—but that court order is not binding on the mortgage company, GMAC, MasterCard, or Sears. Those companies didn't ask you and your wife to get a divorce, and they don't want to hear about your divorce. They just want their money. They often have contracts which bind *both* of you to pay, not just one or the other, and those contracts remain in force regardless of any divorce decree.

Many of the loan and credit agreements you and your wife have signed during your marriage contain a statement that the two of you are "jointly and severally responsible" for the debt. That means the debt is *not* divided up, half to you, half to your wife. Rather, you are responsible for 100 percent of the debt and so is your wife. In the event that your wife defaults on the debt, the creditor may have the legal right to come after you for the entire debt (and vice versa). The creditor will likely go after the deepest pockets.

HOW TO SELECT A LAWYER

How do you select the *right* attorney to handle your divorce?

Selecting an attorney is much like selecting any other professional. When you look for a good surgeon, a good dentist, or even a trustworthy plumber or mechanic, the first rule is *ask around*. Talk to friends, ask your business associates, seek the experience of people who have used family law attorneys in the past. If you turn up two or more good reports on the same attorney, that is a good indication in that attorney's favor. If you are unable to get any referrals from friends and associates, then call the local Bar Association in your area for a referral (see the Yellow Pages under "Attorney Referral Service").

Next, interview the attorney. Many attorneys will give you an interview (approximately thirty minutes) without charge. You are hiring a professional to protect your interests during one of the most crucial and difficult junctures of your entire life. You have a right to feel confident in your attorney's abilities and commitment to your case. You have a right to know what to expect in terms of fees and expenses.

If possible, choose an attorney who understands family law and one who practices in your local area and is familiar with your local court system. Choose an attorney who demonstrates a genuine interest in what is best for you and your family. We believe an attorney who suggests ways of "getting even" or "riling up" your wife is the *wrong* attorney.

Make sure you understand everything the attorney tells you. Have your attorney explain all terms. Your attorney works for you. You pay your attorney to guide you through the intricacies of the law, and you have a right to ask questions and expect clear answers. If you don't understand something the first time, don't hesitate to ask for clarification. If the attorney is uncomfortable or impatient with your questions, then you may have the *wrong* attorney.

There are divorce attorneys who create conflict and fan the flames. We have all heard the horror stories: a couple decides to part on agreeable terms, then falls into the hands of unscrupulous attorneys. The attorneys churn up the conflict and turn a friendly divorce into the trial of the century. Though such situations are not as common as the folklore suggests, they do happen.

Beware of any attorney who makes guarantees: "You want to be the custodial parent? No problem! I guarantee you'll be awarded custody." No attorney can absolutely guarantee any outcome—and any attorney who does may be working on the fringes of legal ethics. If an attorney makes such a guarantee, exercise caution. Consider interviewing another attorney or two before making a decision.

Throughout your relationship with the attorney, listen to your instincts. Do you trust this person? Do you feel your values parallel your attorney's values? Do you sense this attorney is concerned and understanding about what is best for you and your children?

Remember that you, not the attorney, are in charge. The attorney is there to guide and serve you, and that's why you pay him or her a fee. You have the right to say, "I'll follow your advice on this matter, but I think your other suggestion would not be productive." If it appears that your lawyer is making the litigation or negotiation more troublesome and antagonistic than need be, or if you feel your attorney is not representing your wishes, then speak frankly to your attorney. Be clear and be assertive. Don't be intimidated.

DO I REALLY NEED AN ATTORNEY?

There's no law that says you *must* have an attorney. Any person has a right to handle his or her legal matters without the help of an attorney. If you are so inclined, you can write your own will, draw your own contracts, and represent yourself in court. You can also perform dentistry on yourself, but most people would not consider that very prudent. It is our belief that practicing do-it-yourself law is much like practicing do-it-yourself dentistry.

Even lawyers, when they are going through a divorce, usually hire another attorney to represent them. Why? Because they know how important it is to be advised and represented by someone who is not only skilled and conversant with the latest changes in the law, but above all by someone who is *dispassionate and objective*. Divorce is an emotionally charged process, and if those emotions get tangled up in the legal process, you and your child could end up the losers.

Just in case you're not convinced that you need an attorney, here are just a few of the many services an attorney performs for you during the divorce process:

A lawyer informs you. Divorce law has changed dramatically in the past few decades, and it continues to evolve today. These changing laws can be very confusing to the layman.

One attorney told us, "People are always asking me, 'Isn't such-and-such true?' I have to tell them, 'No, it used to be true but not anymore.' The culture is constantly changing, and the law tends to lag behind the culture by a few years. People change, new ideas take hold in the community, new standards come into practice, then judges change the way they rule, and finally the legislatures change the laws. A good attorney tracks all these trends. He or she is aware of the changing attitudes of the community, of the courts, and of the latest updates in the law, in order to keep the client informed of his options and his rights."

A lawyer separates emotion from fact. Many of the aspects of the divorce that are intensely important to you are of little or no importance to the court. As you explain your situation to the attorney, he or she can assess and categorize facts, separate things that matter from things that don't, and place your situation into a framework that has meaning within the legal system. The attorney will tell you, "These are the things that matter, and these are the things that are not legally relevant. Let's leave this emotion or this fact out of the picture." He or she can then inject some rational, practical recommendations into a situation that is by its very nature irrational and emotionally charged.

A lawyer can help prepare you for what lies ahead. Because of his or her training and experience, an attorney can head off problems that you would never see and can prepare you procedurally and emotionally to deal with the legal process of divorce. A good attorney is a good listener who is sensitive to the trauma you are going through.

"When a client comes to me," one attorney told us, "he is often feeling a lot of apprehension. He simply doesn't know what he's in for, and he feels his life is spinning out of control. Part of my job is to calm the client down, help relieve his guilt and fear, and give him a sense of control. I say, 'Here's what we are going to do, here's what the process is like, here's what to expect.' Often, just knowing what lies ahead helps enormously."

A lawyer is a strong advocate. A lot is at stake in a divorce proceeding, and you need a rational and persuasive voice as your advocate. You need someone who has a deep understanding of the law, and a knowledge of those portions of the law that will benefit you and your child. Even though your goal should not be to defeat or punish your wife, you still need an advocate who can help protect your rights and the welfare of your child.

A lawyer gives you the benefit of his or her experience. Experienced attorneys have seen many situations which are similar to yours. They have seen how the law and human behavior interact in these situations. Knowledge of the lawbooks is important, but equally important is a knowledge of human nature. That kind of savvy only comes with experience.

Another area where an attorney's experience can be very valuable is knowledge of judges. Most attorneys with courtroom experience have a good sense of the attitudes, tendencies, and eccentricities of a given judge. They have a sense of how certain judges tend to interpret the law and whose interests those judges tend to protect.

A lawyer acts as a buffer between two opposing parties. In some divorces, the husband and wife cannot deal with each other rationally. Lawyers act as alter egos of the parties, emotionally distancing the parties from each other and enabling them to negotiate in a business-like and productive manner.

TIPS TO GET THE LEGAL SYSTEM TO WORK IN YOUR FAVOR

Here are some tips for working within the legal system so that your interests and your role as father can be protected:

Don't enter the divorce process as if you are going into mortal combat. Avoid the notion that the person with the most money to hire the meanest lawyer will win. You are not there to destroy an enemy but to dissolve a marriage. Avoid blaming. Take the position that it just didn't work out, and it's time to part as friends.

The more issues you can negotiate directly with your wife, the less expensive it will be to have your attorney negotiate for you. If the two of you can't communicate without World War III breaking out, that's one thing. But if the two of you can work together, you will both be way ahead, emotionally and financially.

"If a couple comes to me with an agreement all hammered out," one attorney told us, "then all I have to do is reduce it to writing and make sure it conforms with the law. If two people can do that, they have just smoothed their way to a divorce. Unfortunately, couples who can do that are rare."

The attorney offered a story from his own experience that underscores the point. "I once had to stand in my client's garage," he said, "and referee while they divided up the contents. They couldn't do the least little thing without breaking into a fight. I mean, they argued over every hand towel, every gardening tool, and every bottle of kitchen cleaner. Why should intelligent adults need to hire an attorney to help them with something like that?"

You may find that anger, bitterness, and unfinished business make it hard for you to deal with legal matters in a reasonable, business-like way. If so, we encourage you to see a therapist who can help you resolve your emotional issues. Then you will be better equipped to deal with your legal issues.

Don't compare your divorce with another person's divorce. It's a common practice, of course, to share stories back and forth with other people who have been through divorce. But understand that every divorce is an individual case, involving differences in personalities, families, backgrounds, children, judges, attorneys, and jurisdictions. The fact that your case was handled one way and your friend's case was handled differently doesn't mean that you were treated unfairly. There may have been factors in your friend's situation that you are not aware of.

Remember, there are very few absolutes and guarantees in the law. There are always qualifications, exceptions, and contingencies which make the law flexible enough to apply in a variety of situations. This somewhat "elastic" quality of the law may cause it to seem unfair at times, but it is really the flexibility of the law that enables you, your children, and your wife to be treated as fairly and compassionately as possible.

Once you are divorced, you have a document called a divorce decree, which is an official order of the court. Do you have to honor that decree? The answer: "Yes—but . . ."

Yes, the decree must be honored, but the decree cannot forsee all future events and contingencies. If you are on good terms with your ex-wife, there is room for flexibility. "Like I tell every client," says one family law attorney, "your circumstances are going to be fluid. A lot can change in six months or a year. The decree may say, 'Do this, do that,' but if the terms of the decree become unworkable *and if both sides agree*, changes can be made without the involvement of the court.

"But always be aware of the risks when you stray from the terms of the decree. You *can* be punished by contempt for disobeying a court order *if* your ex-wife takes you back to court.

"The court doesn't want you to come in every six months to relitigate your divorce. Once you've left the courtroom with your decree in hand, try to avoid having to go back."

For example, Jack was in medical school and his wife was working at the time of the divorce. He had no income at the time the decree was handed down. Two years later, Jack was making $200,000 a year. Obviously, it makes sense for Jack to be mature enough to say, "I'm making this much, so I should pay a larger amount of child support."

Of course, either Jack or his wife has the right to go back to court and have the original decree modified. But if they are both mature adults who love their children, they should be able to resolve the matter themselves rather than encumbering the court and trying their divorce all over again. By this time, much of that old anger and bitterness should have subsided. If they *can't* work this out, then they are doomed to relive the upheaval of divorce whenever Jack's situation (or his wife's) changes. It will never die down.

DO THE RIGHT THING

You loved her once. You asked her to marry you, and she did. She bore you some beautiful, precious children. You were with her, holding her hand, when those children were born. Something happened along the way. Something was lost. Now it's over.

But there is one last gift you can give this woman you once loved: the gift of your respect and your fairness. You can try to use the legal process to destroy her and to punish her—or you can use the process to legally affirm a fair and compassionate decision, which you have voluntarily helped to shape.

Forget, for a moment, the woman you are divorcing. Think for a moment of the woman you fell in love with. And if that isn't enough to motivate you to do the right thing, then think of your children.

In the next section, we will look at the divorce process through the eyes of the other players in the game: your child, your ex-wife, and your ex-wife's new husband. By understanding how these various players think and feel during the separation, the divorce, and the aftermath of the divorce, you will be able to work more effectively within the system to achieve your goals as a father.

Part Two

THEIR PERSPECTIVE

Chapter/6

THE CHILD'S PERSPECTIVE

My parents divorced when I was about six," recalls Ken Parker, one of the authors of this book. "I don't remember the divorce as a big, destructive blow-up, as so many divorces are. It was just a split, a parting of the ways. Still, it was a profoundly disorienting experience for me as a child. I recall a lot of unsettledness and insecurity, a lot of inner chaos. I remember a desperate sense of wanting my mom and dad to get back together again."

Ken Parker has experienced divorce not only as an adult stepparent and as a counselor, but as a *child* of divorce. In this chapter, Ken offers a perspective on divorce that is often overlooked: the child's perspective.

"When a divorce is going on," says Ken, "the grown-ups get very focused on grown-up issues. But there are these little people hanging around the edges of divorce, and they are listening and watching and feeling a whole range of emotions. Nobody hears them, nobody understands what they are going through because they are just three or four feet high. They're invisible people."

From his perspective as an absent father, Van Jones strongly agrees. "Many parents tend to see kids as just part of the package. We don't treat them as individuals. We don't think about their opinions and feelings because of our own pain. We don't listen to their needs. We shield them. We talk about our big-people issues behind their backs, and we think they don't know what's going on. They see and hear more than we realize, and they hurt more than we can imagine. Adults look at divorce as the breakdown of a marriage. Children look at divorce as the destruction of their world."

It's easy for Mom and Dad to forget how small and contained a child's entire world is. When a divorce occurs, that child's emotional foundation, his source of security, and yes, his entire *world* is split in two. This is the system that surrounded and supported the child, that set his limits, that taught him what was acceptable and not acceptable, that defined his identity, and told him he is loved and valued. In a divorce, that entire system crumbles beneath the child's feet. How can any child of six or eleven or fifteen process such a massive emotional upheaval alone?

Someone once said that "children are wet cement." Childhood is a time when personality is formed, when values are instilled, when ego-strength is being built, when the child is learning who he or she is and beginning to develop coping skills. As a result, the issues and feelings a child deals with, and how he or she deals with them during the divorce process have profound long-term effects on the child throughout his or her life. This is true of even the most friendly and civilized divorces. Divorce affects kids forever.

Does that mean children of divorce are doomed to be emotionally or psychologically scarred by divorce? Absolutely not! A child's way of perceiving the world *will be changed forever* by the divorce process, but that change does not have to be destructive. We can raise strong, secure, healthy children, even through the process of a divorce, *if* we take time to see the divorce process through our children's eyes.

Regardless of what has happened between you and your wife, you want to be effective and positive in your fathering role, *and you can be*. In this chapter, we will focus on what your children are experiencing and feeling so you can more effectively meet their needs. Building on Ken's childhood experience, our combined clinical experience, and our experience as fathers of children who have been through divorce, we will show you how to provide effective fathering and a strong sense of security and self-esteem for your children, even from afar.

A CASE OF JET LAG

The divorce process introduces enormous change into a child's life at a time when he or she is seeking stability and security. Some of the disorientation a child feels comes from having his or her world split into two parts—while having to keep one foot in each world.

"After my parents' divorce," Ken recalls, "my mother and I moved from Grand Prairie, Texas, to Wichita Falls, where she soon remarried. I lived with my mother and stepfather, and I visited my biological father from time to time. It's not easy to shuttle back and forth from one parenting system to another. Whenever I traveled from one household to the other, I experienced what I call 'jet lag,' a temporary difficulty in re-adjusting to the new environment.

"My parents were two different people, and each household had its own values and ways of doing things. Each household had different rules and different expectations, and sometimes it was hard to remember what the rules were at any given time. But gradually, I settled in and adapted to the new system I found myself in.

"I vividly remember the feelings I had when I was on the train going from one house to the other. My mother would put me on a train in Wichita Falls, and my father would meet me at the Fort Worth depot. After the visit, I'd take the train back home again. It was certainly an adventure for a little guy of eight or nine years old, but it was also bewildering.

"I compare it to the experiences of servicemen during the Vietnam War. When I was in the Navy, it would take two or three weeks to travel by ship from Nam to the States. That was long enough to decompress and adjust from a life of gunnery and artillery barrages and air strikes to a life of picking up with your family and your best girl again.

"But the ground combat troops had a much more radical adjustment to make. One day they were slogging through rice paddies, taking sniper fire, watching for mines, tripwires, and punji sticks. The next day, they were on a plane heading stateside. They might go from a rice paddy to a busy San Francisco street within 24 to 48 hours, without any time to decompress. In many ways, that's what it was like for me as a child, taking that train ride from one home to the other."

The feelings Ken recalls are feelings many young children are not old enough or sophisticated enough to articulate: disorientation, confusion, an inability to readjust, all of which he sums up in the phrase "jet lag." This is not to say that the transition of a divorce is completely a negative experience for a child. Ken recalls a mixture of both excitement and sadness.

"There was always a sense of anticipation when I went to visit my father," says Ken. "But going home often left me sad and let down, like you get when a great vacation comes to an end. It wasn't that my father's house was a better place to live than my mother's. It was just that staying with my father was a vacation, and staying with my mother was real life.

"That's the way it is with kids in transition. They *live* with Mom, but they *visit* Dad. Where you visit is always more glamorous than where you live. Living with Mom represents school and chores and dull routine. Visiting Dad means getting special "guest" treatment, living on a vacation schedule, a lot of festivities, and maybe even a trip to Disneyland or Six Flags. The problem is you can't always live in Disneyland. Eventually, you have to go home, and there is always a little sadness when you go home."

In the transition from one house to another, a child will often feel as though he or she has fallen through the cracks between two worlds.

"When I was on the train home from my father's house," Ken remembers, "I often thought, 'My dad's back in his car, going home to his life without me. His new family is continuing on without me. I'm not a part of their lives anymore.' I felt like I was in the twilight zone. At times, I would visualize what my father and his family were doing. I was afraid I would be forgotten.

"It wasn't that I was treated better in one home than the other. But whenever I was traveling between these two households, it was as though I wasn't sure which house was *home*. I wanted to belong to both households, and it's hard for a child to deal with a divided sense of belonging."

DIVIDED LOYALTIES

Jay is a high school teacher in his mid-thirties. His parents divorced when he was seven. "I used to visit my dad for a month every summer," he recalls. "When I arrived, my dad would pump me for information: 'What's your mother up to these days? Who is she dating? What is this guy like? Does she let him sleep over? I hope you don't marry someone like your mother.' That sort of thing.

"Then I'd go home and go through the same routine with my mom: 'Where is your dad working now? Oh, he's still selling used cars, is he? Well, I sure hope you make more of yourself than that man did. He never was very motivated. That's one of the reasons I left him.' I always felt caught in this competition between them.

"Whenever I went from one house to the other, I had to remind myself of the rules: 'Okay, I'm in Mom's house now. I have to start liking Mom and not liking Dad again. We don't like Dad here. We don't defend him, we don't say anything nice about him.' I learned real early how to be careful what I say, how to deflect a question, how to shift the mood, so I could get along with whichever parent I was with."

Jay has described one of the hardest issues a child of divorce has to face: the issue of *divided loyalties*. In their anger and bitterness toward their spouses, parents often paint their children into an emotional corner from which there is no escape. The child is left feeling confused, "I love Mom and I love Dad. But now they are at war with each other. How can I love both?" The child's entire world has been ripped in half, and that child does not have the emotional strength or psychological understanding to reconcile these inner conflicts.

The issue of divided loyalties becomes even more complex when one or both parents remarries. Now the child thinks, "There's a pseudo-dad who has taken the place of my real dad, a pseudo-mom in place of my real mom. If I like (or even tolerate) this pseudo-parent, then I am being disloyal to my biological parent." The child must struggle to fit himself or herself into this new, evolving system.

Even in the friendliest divorces, the child will feel the tension of divided loyalties. So imagine what happens to a child in a "down and dirty" divorce! That poor kid is going to feel like the wishbone after the turkey is carved.

Parents who are otherwise loving and well-meaning will sometimes do the most outrageous, hurtful things to their children in the attempt to get back at their ex-spouses. Here are some of the destructive behaviors we have seen people engage in—behaviors which attempt to influence and win a child's loyalties, but which often scar a child emotionally:

- "Bad-mouthing" (slandering) the other parent in front of the child.
- Asking the child to spy and report back on the other parent.
- Pumping the child for information about the other parent.
- Engaging in a destructive custody battle for the sake of revenge against the child's mother.
- Expressing hostile feelings through the child by saying, for example, "Your mother really hurt me. The reason we're not together is that your mother sinned. Your mother broke her marriage vows. Your mother had an affair, and she was unfaithful to me."
- Buying the child's loyalties through lavish spending.
- Using the child to get back at the spouse by purposely going against the spouse's wishes.
- Letting the child operate totally without limits during visitation. (We are not suggesting that you, as the father, need to totally re-create the environment of Mom's home; you can and should have your own environment, values, rules, and ways of doing things, but you should not undermine your ex-wife's parental role.)

Jay recalls some of the hurtful labels that were placed on him and the intense pressures that were inflicted on him by his parents and other family members. "There were times," he said, "when my mother would get angry with me and verbally lash out at me: 'You're just like your father, a bad seed!' I didn't know what a 'bad seed' was, but I knew that when she compared me to Dad, it was no compliment."

This is the kind of hurt a child can suffer when his parents force him to choose sides in the divorce. These pressures create conflicting feelings within the child that he or she cannot resolve. Frequently, the only way a child can respond to such intense inner conflict is to "numb out," to repress all feelings. Some children "numb out" for life. Others turn to various defense mechanisms which become life-long habits.

"I Learned to Be Self-Contained"

"I turned inward at an early age," Jay recalls. "I became very selfish. I adopted an attitude that said, 'Whatever makes me happy is what I'm going to do. I'll just look out for myself.' I learned to be very self-contained, very guarded. I figured, 'When a parent talks to you, say the least amount possible, be as noncommittal and vague as you can be, change the subject and get away from the conversation as fast as you can.' Once I mastered the art of ducking uncomfortable questions, I could do what I wanted. I learned the art of evasion at a very deliberate and conscious level.

"Today, I don't know any other way to operate. I wish I wasn't evasive and noncommittal with people, but it's like I can't help myself. In social relationships, I avoid any conversation that goes deeper than the surface. My wife often complains that I'm too private, and that there is a Jay she still doesn't know. It's an old survival mechanism, and I don't know how to get rid of it. I still catch myself being very guarded, even with close friends. I'm always thinking, 'If you say too much, they're gonna get you.'"

Clearly, divorcing parents have an enormous responsibility. The choices they make during this crucial intersection in the child's life will have a profound influence on his or her lifelong habits and patterns.

"Biting My Tongue and Biding My Time"

Young children cannot resolve the inner conflicts of divided loyalties because they have not developed the capacity for holding more than one emotion at a given time. A very young child cannot love and be angry at the same time. If a child becomes extremely angry with his parent, he may say, "I hate you!" In the same way, the young child cannot understand how a parent can love him and be angry with him at the same time. Learning to resolve these conflicts is part of the maturing process.

If a child must go through the divorce process before he is mature enough to differentiate between temporary anger and hate—say, before the age of about five to seven—then this child will tend to think, "I can't love both of my parents. Since they hate each other, I must love one and hate the other."

The child needs to be able to say, at some point, "Mom and Dad can't get along, and they can't stay married, but I can still love them both." In order to do that, the child needs to have parents who place his or her needs above their own hostility. The child needs parents who will make it their first priority to preserve that child's emotional wholeness, not rip the child to pieces in an emotional tug-of-war.

Once the child is of grade-school age or older—if he or she is emotionally healthy and if the parents are careful not to divide the child's loyalties—that child will likely learn that it's okay to be loyal to both parents. But what if you do all the right things (no bad-mouthing your ex, no manipulation of your kids to be your spies, no bribing of your kids to buy their loyalties), yet your ex-wife insists on tearing you down and making you look like the bad guy in your children's eyes?

That's the toughest situation of all. Ryan, a divorced father in his mid-forties, describes his own dilemma this way: "There were a lot of things about my divorce that just devastated me. But one of the worst was the way my wife tried to turn my own kids against me. For a while, she succeeded, especially with my oldest daughter, who was thirteen at the time of the divorce. I got a lot of anger from her because she believed everything her mother said about me.

"I made a decision early on that I wasn't going to play that game, I wasn't going to fight back. I decided that the only way to vindicate myself in my kids' eyes was by taking the high road, not getting down in the gutter. When my daughter would say to me, 'It's your fault we aren't a family anymore,' I would very calmly say, 'Your mother and I both did the best we could to work at this marriage, and we both made a lot of mistakes. We're all hurting because of this divorce. But even though we can't all be a family anymore, I hope you will always know how much I love you and how much your mother loves you and how sorry we both are that you have been hurt by our problems.'

"Even though I was furious with my ex-wife, I tried to affirm her in my children's eyes—not for her sake but for the kids' sake. At that point, I was so angry that I couldn't have cared less about her. I did it because I was scared of losing my kids, and I knew that if I became hostile, I would only drive them away. There were times when I felt like a doormat, but I stuck to my game plan, and eventually her attacks on me cooled down, and my relationship with the kids grew stronger.

"The real payoff didn't come until about five years after the divorce. It was in the fall, and I was driving my daughter to college. She was beginning her first semester at SMU. It was just the two of us, and we were reminiscing a bit. And she said, 'Daddy, I never told you this before, but I really appreciate what you did for us kids when you and Mom were going through the divorce. The whole time she was cutting you down and telling us how awful you were, you never struck back. I didn't understand it at the time, but that must have been very hard for you. And I really love you for it.'

"Now, I'm no saint. There were plenty of times I wanted to haul off and let that woman have it with both barrels. There were plenty of times I wondered, 'Does anybody see? Does anybody understand that I'm the one being slandered here?' That's instinctive—but if I had gone with my instincts, I wouldn't have the relationship with my kids that I now enjoy. I would have diminished myself in my daughter's eyes. Those years of biting my tongue and biding my time paid off."

We're not suggesting that you avoid bad-mouthing your ex and dividing your children's loyalties merely because it's the right thing to do or because it will make you a better person. We are urging you to do this because by doing so you will reap practical results: emotionally healthy kids who respect you and want to have a good relationship with you. There may not be immediate rewards in doing the right thing. It will be hard and it will be costly, at least for a while. But ultimately, it will be worth it.

A CHILD'S FEARS

"Around the time of my parents' divorce," says Ken, "I used to drive them both crazy by running away from kindergarten. The teacher would turn her back for a moment, and I would be out of there like a shot. Sometimes my mother would let me off at the school, and I would beat her home. I did this fairly regularly, and my parents never really understood why. The fact is, I was *scared*. I was afraid of being abandoned. I thought my parents might leave me at kindergarten and never pick me up again.

"Where did this fear come from? Looking back, I realize it was part of my struggle to understand what was happening to my world. We had always been a family, as long as I could remember: Mom, Dad, and me. Now Dad was leaving the picture. What guarantee did I have that I wouldn't get left out of the picture too?

"That fear of abandonment settled down a bit after kindergarten but never completely left me through my school years. There were times as late as the third grade when I ran away from school."

Where do such fears come from? They arise when a child's sense of security and safety is shaken. One of a child's most basic needs is the need to see his parents together as a unit. When he sees that unit threatened, his whole world is threatened.

Does that mean that divorce is the worst thing that can happen to a child? No. Divorce is a difficult and painful experience in a child's life, but it's not the worst thing that could happen to a child. The best news of all is that the harmful effects of divorce can be reduced by caring, insightful parents.

"Looking back," says Ken Parker, "I can honestly say I'm glad that my life has taken the direction it has, including my childhood, as hard as it sometimes was. I've grown up. I've worked through most of my issues. I've become a therapist, and now I can help other people through a process I myself have experienced. I take the position that what should have happened *did* happen."

A CHILD'S FANTASIES

"I remember a lot of fantasies in my childhood," Ken recalls. "Fantasies of our family being together as we were before. I wanted that a lot. But instead of my parents getting back together, my mother married a man I didn't know, and I was expected to relate to him as 'father.' It just wasn't going to happen as far as I was concerned.

"I don't think my stepfather was quite prepared for the fact that when he married my mother, he was marrying me too. I made life pretty hard for him. I was really bent on getting my biological parents back together.

"For a couple of years after my mother remarried, I got to visit my father in Grand Prairie. I really enjoyed that, and I began to think, 'Wouldn't it be great if I could just live with my dad all year 'round! It would be an endless vacation.' I agitated and made a big stink, and finally, when I was nine, the grown-ups gave in and let me live with my biological father for a year. I spent my third-grade year going to school in Grand Prairie, and I occasionally visited my mother and my adoptive father.

"That was the year that one of my biggest childhood fantasies went down in flames. I found out that wherever you live is *home*, and wherever you visit is *vacation*. A vacation is fun, but *home* means routine and school and chores. At the end of that year, I decided to live in my mother's house after all.

"A child will cling to fantasies of what it's like to live with the other parent. My fantasies were based on the vacation atmosphere I had always experienced at my dad's home during those visits. When I moved there for a year, I was treated well, I was loved, but it wasn't vacation anymore. I wasn't treated special anymore. It was just a different home with a different routine, and I went to a different school. I'll always be grateful that my parents let me live with my biological father for a year because that was one less illusion I had to grow up with."

Fantasies are a major part of a child's life, especially a child of divorce. The fantasy that life would be better at the other parent's house is a very common one. Sometimes, as in Ken's case, this fantasy can only be quashed by a dose of reality.

Another very common fantasy, which Ken recalled from his own childhood, is a reconciliation fantasy. This is the belief which says, "This is a temporary situation. Someday Mom and Dad will get together again." Reconciliation fantasies are the most stubborn and deeply entrenched of childhood beliefs.

"I have a friend named Bob who is a family therapist," says Van Jones. "He is divorced and remarried. Some time ago, Bob's stepson had a conversation with his mother (Bob's wife) and asked if she and her first husband would ever get back together. Now, there is nothing unusual about a boy asking this question of his divorced and remarried mother. Reconciliation fantasies are so common that it happens all the time. What is unusual about this particular conversation between a boy and his remarried mother is that the boy was *twenty years old*, and his mother had been remarried for *more than ten years!*"

Reconciliation fantasies die very hard. They are often at the root of baffling behavior problems in children. Larry Matthews's parents separated when he was eight years old. His schoolwork took a nose-dive within weeks after his dad moved out. A normally quiet and cooperative boy, he was suddenly having fights with other boys at school. The school counselor called Larry into his office and had a long talk with him. Then he made two phone calls and asked both parents to come to his office for a conference.

"I'm glad you could both come," said the counselor when the Matthews arrived. "Larry told me about the separation, and he told me more than once that I should call both of you, not just one parent."

"I just don't know what's gotten into Larry," said his mother. "I mean, I know the separation has been rough on him, and that might cause him to lose concentration on his schoolwork for a while. But why is he getting into all these fights?"

"Well," said the counselor, "I have some thoughts about that. Mrs. Matthews, let me ask you this: did Larry ask you any questions about our meeting today?"

"Yes," she said. "He asked a lot of questions. Was I sure his father was going to be here? Where were we meeting? Could he come too? He was extremely curious. Do you think that means something?"

"I think so," said the counselor. "When I talked to Larry, I asked him if he could have three wishes, what would he wish for? His first wish was for the two of you to get back together. Now, the three of us can accept that that's not going to happen, but not Larry. What Larry is doing is fairly common: he is trying to bring the two of you back together through his behavior. If he acts up and punches some boy or if he lets his schoolwork slide, then the two of you will have to come back together to meet with his counselor."

"Not very realistic," said Mr. Matthews, "but ingenious."

"Sure," said the counselor. "He figures if he acts bad enough, his parents will have to communicate. He thinks that in time, you will get back together as a family again. In my experience, these reconciliation fantasies can go on for years. But through counseling, I'm confident Larry can be brought to a point of acceptance."

As parents, we need to recognize that our children's behavior is often a form of communication. If we learn to read and understand their behavior, rather than simply trying to suppress it or change it, we will be more successful in getting to their root problems and emotions.

THE SELF-BLAMING CHILD

Divorce is a very complex event with complex causes, and no young child has the sophistication to understand what has taken place. The issues that caused Mom and Dad to split are beyond the child's comprehension—yet the child still has a need to *try* to comprehend this event and account for the major change that has taken place in his or her life. So the child will tend to rationalize the split, seeking a simple, concrete *Why:* "Why did my parents stop loving each other? Why can't things be the way they were? Why did Daddy have to move out of the house?"

The grown-ups are often too busy with the details and legalities of the divorce process to focus on the questions of the children. So the child is frequently left to his or her own devices to figure out why his or her world has rattled apart. Generally, that child has two conclusions to choose from:

Conclusion No. 1: "The reason my parents got a divorce is that they are two individuals with differing values and beliefs and personalities. Unfortunately, they were unable to reconcile these disagreements, so they have decided that they need to separate. Despite the differences between them, they both continue to love me, and I am free to love them both." That, of course, is a very healthy, logical, and reasonable position for the child to take. Unfortunately, it is virtually impossible for a child to be this logical and reasonable about the highly emotional and threatening issue of divorce.

Perhaps a being with all the unemotional logic of Mr. Spock of the planet Vulcan could come to this conclusion completely on his own. But in our experience, normal human children virtually *never* take this option. Yet with a great deal of insight, support, and affirmation, children can often be encouraged to adopt Conclusion No. 1. Without such parental help, however, the natural inclination of a child of divorce is to opt for the following conclusion:

Conclusion No. 2: "The simplest explanation is that the divorce is my fault." Most children lean toward what is called *self-referential thinking,* an assumption that everything that happens is somehow related to them or caused by them. The younger the child, the stronger the tendency to interpret events in terms of self-reference.

From an adult point of view, this is clearly absurd. "The causes of this divorce," we say, "don't have anything to do with the children! The reasons for this split are strictly between my wife and me! We made mistakes, and we can't get along, and that's that!" But children don't understand this kind of logical, adult reasoning. Children don't perceive the world from a logical, adult point of view.

A large part of the problem is the way children perceive their parents. When a child is born, he perceives his parents as god-like beings. They are incapable of making mistakes or being wrong, and they hold the key to the child's survival in their hands. The child is completely dependent on the parent for food, clothing, housing, and happiness. This perception of the parents as god-like beings gradually diminishes as the child matures, but vestiges of this perception can persist—particularly at an unconscious level—throughout childhood and early adolescence.

Younger children are simply not sophisticated enough to say, "My parents were wrong, they made a mistake in their relationship, and that's why they are getting a divorce." So the child will assume the blame for the separation because that's the only thing that makes sense to him. These god-representatives couldn't have made a mistake, so it must be because of me.

If the child feels responsible for the parents' separation or for conflict in the marriage, he or she may assume responsibility for keeping the parents together. The child may become anxious at school, thinking, "I've got to get home. If I'm not there, they're going to start fighting. I'm the only thing holding them together." That's a terrible burden for a child to shoulder.

Once the child begins to take on the blame for his parents' divorce, defense mechanisms take over to protect him or her from this enormously painful idea. These defense mechanisms include:

- Denial—deciding that the divorce doesn't really matter, it's not important, it doesn't really hurt.
- Withdrawal into apathy and listlessness.
- Rebelling and acting out. Young children tend to act out their feelings as opposed to expressing them because they have not yet attained the language sophistication to say, "I'm hurting." The way the child says "I'm hurting" is through disapproved behavior.

It's important for the long-term emotional health of the child that he or she finds ways of expressing feelings about the divorce. "When I told my son that his mother and I were getting a divorce," recalls

Van, "he did exactly what he should have done. He fell apart. He wept. He grieved. Some kids give no visible reaction for months. Some never express their feelings. I've known parents who express worry when their kids cry or who seem pleased when their kids seem to accept their divorce in a stoic, unemotional way. Those parents have it all backwards. It's the kids who have retreated into denial or withdrawal that you have to worry about over the long haul. Those patterns of avoidance and denial which begin in childhood usually persist and can create major problems in adulthood.

"In the Children's Home where I work, I see many kids who are there because of an out-of-home placement. These kids often seem hardened on the outside because they deny the loss they feel—but they act it out later. The inability of many children (and adults) to admit, express, and work through their feelings of loss is a big issue in our society today."

When our children act out, rebel, destroy things, or cause problems at school, our tendency is to try to stop and punish that behavior. And it's true that we cannot simply allow that sort of behavior to continue and hurt other people. However, at the same time we are curbing the child's destructive actions, we must listen to what the child is trying to tell us through those actions. When a child acts out, we should:

Set limits on the behavior. We should say, "I can't allow you to destroy this," or, "I can't allow you to talk that way," or, "I can't allow you to hurt other people." Then:

Understand what the child is saying through that behavior. Draw the child's feelings out into the open. Help the child feel safe to *verbally* express what he or she has been trying to say through inappropriate behavior. Show the child you identify with his or her hurts; say, "These past few months have been hard for me, and sometimes I've felt very sad or very angry. So I know it's been hard for you too. Would you like to tell me how you've been feeling?"

The more the child is encouraged to verbalize his or her feelings, the less the child will need to express feelings through behavior—

and the less likely the child will retreat into habits of denial, withdrawal, or other defense mechanisms.

One way to help a young child express his or her emotions is by allowing the child to play those emotions out. A child who is too young to put feelings into words will often act out those feelings by playing with stuffed animals, dolls, or other toys. Just get down on the floor with your child, put yourself on his or her level, join in the play—and observe. It can be a very therapeutic experience for your child, and you will learn a lot.

EASING A CHILD THROUGH
THE DIVORCE PROCESS

Divorce is an imperfect solution to a problem between imperfect people living in an imperfect world. But if we were to design a "perfect" way for parents to approach this subject with their children, we would have both parents sit down with the children and say:

"It's not going to be possible for us to live together anymore. We are going to split up and live in separate households. But you need to understand, first of all, that this divorce is not your fault. It is a decision we're making as adults, and adults sometimes make decisions that don't have happy consequences. We know this decision hurts you, and we're very sorry about this, but the reasons for this decision have to do with problems between the two of us, and none of it is your fault.

"Second, we want you to know that we both love you, and we will always be your parents. You may be living with one parent and visiting the other, but we are both still your parents. We will continue to be involved with you. Neither of us will love you any less. Even though your dad won't live here anymore, he will always be your dad, and he will always love you the same as before.

"Third, we want you to know that you can love both of us at the same time, even if we're not living together, even if we sometimes get mad at each other, even though we sometimes say things we wish we hadn't said. That's what adults do sometimes, and we're sorry that we've hurt you. But please know that you are free to love both of us, even if we are not living together."

If parents would have a conversation like this with their children early in the divorce process and reinforce it from time to time, the children would grow up much healthier and happier than they usually do. Will a conversation like this solve the emotional problems that divorce brings on? Of course not. Will your children believe the divorce is not their fault simply because you have told them so? Perhaps not. They may have to hear this message again and again before it finally penetrates their unconscious mind. But as you continue to listen to their feelings, to gently correct their distorted perceptions, and to reinforce your love for them through actions as well as words, the message will reverberate within them, not only now but in years to come.

Divorce complicates life and makes it harder for us to raise emotionally healthy children. Harder—but not impossible. Here are some "Do's" and "Don'ts" for raising emotionally healthy children, even in the wake of divorce:

Don'ts:

- Don't slander the child's mother, especially in the child's presence.
- Don't use your child to get even with your ex-wife by going against her wishes or undermining her authority.
- Don't use your child as a spy. Don't pump your child for information about your ex-wife.
- Don't express your hostile feelings through the child.

Do's:

- Do set appropriate limits on the child. You can have your own rules and values, but try to cooperate with your ex-wife in arriving at reasonably consistent boundaries for the child in both households.
- Do special things with the children, let them know you missed them—but do not convey to them that it's their mother's fault you do not live at home (even if it is). Remember, someday it may be important for the child to better understand what happened between you and your ex-wife, but right now your children are not equipped to grasp the complexities of adult

problems. They don't need blaming or explanations. They need support and security. You can give your children a sense of stability, even after a divorce, if you will show them you love them, that you will always be available to them, and that the divorce doesn't change the father-child relationship.

- Do be aware of your children's attempts at "splitting." It's common for children to try to swing the divorce system to their advantage. A favorite technique is to "split" one parent against the other.

  Janie visits Dad and says, "Mom won't let me go to the park with my friends." Dad says, "Well, why is that?" Janie says, "Oh, you know how Mom is, she's so overprotective." Dad responds, "Well, then while you're here at my house, you can go to the park with your friends."

  What Janie neglected to mention is that her friends are drug-crazed bikers, and the park they are going to is Yosemite. Okay, an exaggerated example, but you get the picture. Kids will take advantage of the antagonism between Mom and Dad and try to make it work for their own ends. You can't blame them. You just have to stay a jump ahead of them.

  If your child paints one of Mom's decisions as unreasonable or unfair, get Mom's side of it before you jump in and undermine her authority. There are plenty of natural battlegrounds between you and your ex. Try not to make a battleground out of your children. Even though you no longer live together, you still need to find ways to support each other as parents—if not for the sake of your ex, then at least for the sake of your children!

- Do stay actively involved with your kids, especially in their school and sporting events. In order to do this, you may occasionally make some logistical adjustments (such as sitting in the back of the auditorium if your ex-wife and her new husband are sitting in the front). Avoid power struggles with your ex-wife.

  You will always, forever and ever, be the biological father of your child. There will never be another person who can fill your shoes, no matter who your child's stepfather is. One of the biggest fears fathers experience in a divorce is, "I'm going to lose my children." No, you won't. That role is yours for life, and from your children's perspective it is not even an issue. So relax. Feel free to take a back seat at that graduation or school play. If you show consideration to your ex-wife, feel good about it. You're not being a victim, you're being a *man*.

Certainly, not all divorces are antagonistic, and not all ex-wives are vindictive. This book uses extreme case examples for the purpose of helping absent fathers cope with difficult situations.

In this chapter, we have attempted to give you a glimpse of the divorce process through the eyes of a child. As you tune in more closely to your children's needs, their feelings, and their behavior, you will be able to more effectively meet their truest needs. You *can* be an effective father, even when you no longer live in the same house with your children.

In the next chapter, we will look at the divorce process from the perspective of the mother of your children, so that you can more effectively build a business-like relationship with her for your children's sake, and your own.

Chapter/7

THE MOTHER'S PERSPECTIVE

Oliver sat in the therapist's office, a very unhappy man. "This is so hard," he complained. "It's worse than when we were married! Sophie just keeps walking all over me! You won't believe what she said on the phone last week!"

"What was that?" asked the therapist.

"She said I could come to my daughter's school play, *but* I have to sit in the back row. She said she didn't want me making Steve feel uncomfortable."

"Steve?"

"The guy she's dating," Oliver replied bitterly. "Steve's bringing his camcorder, and Sophie wants to make sure I don't show up in any of the movies."

"I see. So what did you say to that?"

"I said Carrie's my daughter and I can sit any place I please. Where does she get off telling me where I can and can't sit at my own daughter's play?"

"And what did Sophie say to that?"

"Nothing." Oliver shrugged.

"Nothing?"

"Well . . . she sorta hung up on me."

"I see."

"Man, this divorce thing is just not working out at all. If Sophie would just be reasonable, things could go so much smoother."

"How do you intend to get Sophie to behave in a more reasonable way?"

Oliver looked up sharply. "What are you talking about? Sophie's not going to change! She's just gonna keep walking all over me! And there isn't a thing I can do about it!"

"I'm glad to hear you say that, Oliver," said the counselor. "I think that's a very realistic assessment. She's probably not going to change. Now, given the fact that Sophie will likely continue to operate in the way she chooses, what is it going to take to make this situation run more smoothly?"

Oliver frowned and thought. Then he looked up sharply. "Well, you won't believe what she's been telling our friends about me!"

"Okay, we've established that she's unfair, unreasonable, hostile, and generally not acting in your best interests. But you told me when you came in that the most important thing right now is your relationship with your children. What does this have to do with your relationship with your children?"

"Well . . . nothing, I guess."

"Okay. So what is it going to take to make this situation run more smoothly?"

"Well, she's not going to change."

"Right."

Oliver grimaced. "Are you saying *I* have to change?"

"I think you came to that conclusion on your own."

"But why do *I* have to change? She left me! She has another man sleeping in my house, in my bed! Why do I have to change?"

"Because you're here."

"What's that supposed to mean?"

"You're in this office, sitting in that chair. Sophie's not."

"But I didn't do anything wrong!"

"I never said you did. All I said is that you are here. You are my client. If Sophie was my client, I'd tell her some things she ought to do to make the system work. But she's not here. If somebody's going to make the changes necessary to make this system work, I guess it'll have to be you."

Oliver practically came out of his chair. "But that's not fair!"

"I know. But we're not talking about what's fair. We're talking about what makes the system run more smoothly."

Oliver sagged in his chair. It was clear he didn't like what he was hearing. But then he said something which proved to be the turning point in his attitude and in his post-divorce relationship with his children. "Tell me what I have to do," he said in a voice filled with resignation, "to keep a good relationship with my kids. I'll stuff it down. I'll do whatever I have to do. There's nothing more important to me than those kids."

The therapist smiled inwardly. He had just witnessed one of the most satisfying events anyone in his profession ever encounters: his client had reached an emotional barrier—and he had hurdled it. Oliver still had a long way to go, but he had just passed a difficult test.

"Sophie's the gate you have to pass through to get to your children," observed the therapist. "She has custody. You have to negotiate visitation with her. She could take the kids out of state if she wanted to. She holds all the aces. If you want to have a good fathering relationship with your kids, you have to smooth out the business relationship with your ex-wife. In light of all that, I want to suggest to you a little mind game that may be helpful in smoothing out the process of relating to your ex-wife so that you will have an easier time relating to your kids."

"A mind game?"

"Sort of a 'let's pretend' game. I want you to try to forget that Sophie is the woman you married, the woman you used to go to bed with, the woman you lived with and loved and fought with for nine years. From now on, Sophie is a stranger with whom you must conduct a business relationship. The reason you must conduct business with her is that she is the mother of your children."

"Gee, I dunno—"

"What do you do for a living, Oliver?"

"I'm in customer service."

"Ever have an unreasonable customer? Someone who bullied you, made outrageous demands, and generally set your teeth on edge?"

"Yeah."

"What did you do? Argue it out? Tell him how stupid and unfair he was being?"

"No. I placated the guy. The company doesn't care about winning the argument. The company cares about winning the customer. His money is just as green whether he's reasonable or a complete nut."

"Do you see a parallel here, Oliver?"

"Yeah. My goal isn't winning the argument or sitting in the first row at the school play. My goal is a good relationship with my kids. In order for this business relationship to function smoothly, I may have to placate Sophie. I may have to 'keep the customer happy,' so to speak."

"So to speak," agreed the therapist.

Oliver left the office with a new resolve. The next few months were not easy. He ate a lot of crow and bit his tongue till it bled. And he lost his cool more than once. But gradually his business relationship with Sophie improved. As his ex-wife noticed the "change" in Oliver, she began to loosen up and relate in a more cordial way. If Oliver needed a favor—an extra day with the kids or a few extra days to get the child support payment together, he called her and she was obliging.

We often give our clients the same advice Oliver's therapist gave him: if you want the system to work, if you want to enjoy a more effective fathering relationship with your children, you will have to find ways to get along with the mother of your children. In some divorces there is no problem at all. Mom is the soul of reason and cordiality, and she's just as focused on the needs of the children as Dad is. But even if that is not the case in your divorce, your ex is still the mother of your children, and, if you want to have access to them, you have to deal with her.

You cared enough about your children to walk into a bookstore, plunk down your hard-earned cash, and buy this book. You are taking your valuable time to read this book because you want to be the best father you can be, regardless of your divorce. It's not that you've been wrong, and you need to start doing things right. It's that you have demonstrated enough caring and character to come this far.

So we hope you feel good about this: you are committed to working within the system as it is to be the best, most effective father you can be. It's a tough job, but it's also one of the most important jobs any man can undertake. Your goal is not to be proved right, but to do what's right for your kids.

And we commend you for that.

In this chapter, we will examine the divorce process from your wife's perspective, then explore productive ways to respond to her so that you can achieve your goals.

HER PERSPECTIVE

In order to get along with the mother of your children, you need to understand what life is like from her point of view. This doesn't mean you have to sympathize with her or feel sorry for her, although that is certainly acceptable. It simply means you need to understand why she feels the ways she feels, thinks the way she thinks, and does the things she does. Once you understand her perspective, you will be able to operate more effectively in the interests of your children—and in your own long-term best interests.

First of all, it's important to understand that she is operating with a lot of unfinished business. No matter whose idea the breakup was, she may have a lot of anger, guilt, and sadness to deal with—and this unfinished business may drive a lot of her behavior at an unconscious level. These emotions will affect how she relates to you. If you have not dealt with your own unfinished business and if you are not aware of how her unfinished business may be driving her behavior toward you, then the two of you will be pushing each other's buttons, driving each other crazy, and butting heads from now until doomsday—

And your children will be the losers.

Let's look for a moment at what your ex-wife is going through in the wake of your divorce:

She is now the primary provider for her children. She has just inherited a lot of duties and obligations. She now has the sole responsibility for getting the children to school, for getting them home again, for getting them to the doctor and dentist, for making sure they do their homework, for having meals prepared. When the kids are sick, she is in charge—and she has no backup.

She may feel straightjacketed and trapped by all of these responsibilities. She may be wondering, "Can I do it? Can I be independent *and* meet the needs of my child?" At the same time she may feel a new sense of independence, which comes from not having to account to someone else. Both of these factors—her fears and her new sense of freedom—may affect how she relates to you.

HER BEHAVIOR

Something has happened in the life of this woman that you may find very hard to accept on an unconscious level: she has become single again.

You may be tempted to object, "No! You're wrong! I *do* accept that she's single again! That was the whole point of this divorce, to return her—and me—to a single status."

But hold on a moment. Look at her behavior. What kinds of actions does she engage in these days? She dresses differently. She goes out with girl friends. She goes out on *dates* with *men!* Regardless of all the conflict, the hurt, the separation, and the divorce, can you honestly say that her behavior doesn't have any affect on your emotions?

Let's face it. You spent a number of years building a family system with this woman. The image of that system is still resident in the core memory of your brain. And you can bet that on some unconscious level, that former system is going to try to re-assert itself from time to time. As you relate to her in this post-divorce situation, you may unwittingly find yourself attempting to relate to her on the basis of the old system and its rules. Old issues, old feelings, and unfinished business may surface inside you. Old resistances and patterns of behavior may re-emerge. You may find yourself trying to control her—as if you were still married to her—with questions such as, "Why are you dressed like that?" Or, "Where did you go last night?" Or, "Do you think it's a good idea to leave the kids with a babysitter all the time?"

Maybe you have made statements such as these in recent weeks. You didn't *consciously* intend to control your ex-wife with these kinds of remarks, but they are clearly designed *at an unconscious level* to re-assert the old system, to re-establish a measure of control over a situation that is beyond your control. This is nothing to be ashamed of. This is a natural dynamic in human relationships. But it creates a very serious problem.

At some level, your wife is aware that an old and unwelcome dynamic is coming into play. Perhaps one of the reasons she sought the divorce in the first place was that she didn't like feeling that she was being controlled by another person. If she feels you are "at it again," she is going to react in a way that will work against your goals and your interests. So it is very important that you learn *not* to relate from the same position that you did before.

If you are able to release this woman, to let her be single and independent again, to deal with her only as a person with whom you negotiate in a businesslike way for quality time with your children, then your behavior will ease her tensions and lower her resistance. You will be moving toward your goals.

As you relate to the mother of your children, remember that she is struggling with many issues, feelings, fears, and problems. She is dealing with her own pain as well as she can. Regardless of who initiated the separation, avoid getting pulled into an attempt to control her behavior—and don't let her "push your buttons" and control your behavior. If you find yourself bonded to this woman by your anger, then it may be that you have never gotten an "emotional divorce" from her. (For a more complete discussion of what it means to have an "emotional divorce," see Chapter 10: Look Before You Leap.)

In the next section, we will look at the differences in the way women think and communicate versus the way men think and communicate, and we will see how those differences can affect the business relationship between you and your ex-wife.

DOES SHE STILL CARE?

"Well, Fran, you take care of yourself," said Howard. It was just a polite phrase, something he habitually said to his ex-wife to signal he was getting ready to end the conversation and hang up the phone.

"I'm taking care of myself, Howie," Fran replied. "It's nice to hear the concern in your voice after—well, after everything that's happened. I hope you're taking care of yourself too. Are you eating right?"

Howard was speechless for a moment. "I—uh, yeah, Fran," he stammered, "I'm doing okay for myself."

"I hope so. 'Bye, Howie."

"Yeah. Uh, 'bye, Fran."

He settled the receiver on its cradle, and just stood there for a couple of minutes, looking at the phone and thinking: *What is she trying to say? Does she still care? Does she want to get back together again? She called me Howie! She hasn't called me Howie since before the divorce!*

If Howard is not careful, he may deal a serious set back to his emotional well-being, and to the businesslike relationship he is building with his ex-wife. Something has taken place here that is very common and which many divorced men fail to understand: Howard has misread what his ex-wife was saying to him.

This sort of communication often takes place in the aftermath of a divorce. The process has reached a point where anger and issues have calmed down, where matters are being handled on a fairly civilized plane. The woman wants to solidify the emotional gains that have been made. She wants good feelings to exist between herself and her ex-husband. Not a reconciliation. Just a cessation of hostilities, a little kindness between two people who have been at odds for a long time.

Remember your high school days when you were going steady with that girl in the cashmere sweater? Remember what she said when she broke up with you so she could date the football captain? She said, "Can't we still be friends?" When your ex-wife asks you if you are eating right and taking care of yourself, when she calls you

Howie (or whatever nickname you go by), when she says, "Thank you for caring," or offers some other expression of gratitude or kindness, understand this: she is not trying to get back together again. She's just saying, "Can't we still be friends?"

This is not a criticism of women. It's simply a fact of life that women think and communicate differently from men, and this is a woman's way of graciously extending the hand of—well, if not friendship, at least politeness and civility. To some extent, this may be a case of the old system unconsciously re-asserting itself within her. She is uncomfortable with conflict and hostility, so she is trying to restore an atmosphere of friendly cooperation. She wants things to be "nice." But it is very unlikely that she wants to marry you again. So simply accept the "niceness" she offers you, respond in kind, and then get on with your life.

Once you are living in separate households and occupying new roles, you may find it easier to communicate with your ex-wife in a cordial way. You'll be able to talk about day-to-day matters without every issue turning into a major conflict. Eventually, old marital problems and pain will recede into the background as you put your relationship with your ex-wife on a businesslike basis and focus on the common business between the two of you: child support, visitation schedules, children's activities, health matters, school, and so forth.

Occasionally, a man and woman divorce, then suffer years of indecision about whether they truly want to be divorced. They date, they spend time together, they fight, they make up—in short, they act almost as if they were still married. There are no clear-cut boundaries in their relationship. Sometimes they even continue an on-again, off-again sexual relationship or borrow money from each other. When boundaries in a divorce are blurred, the children become confused. Their parents' behavior drives the children's reconciliation fantasies wild.

It's amazing how some people who have had so much trouble making their marriage work are hardly more successful at making their divorce work. Our advice: if you are going to divorce, then divorce. If you are going to reconcile, get professional counseling and give it your best shot. But dithering back and forth just tortures your ex, your children, and yourself. If you are having trouble drawing clearly defined boundaries in your relationship, a therapist can help you. Some tips for making your divorce work:

- Set clear limits for your post-divorce relationship with your ex (write them out, if necessary).
- Openly discuss behavior that potentially signals a desire for reconciliation. If, for example, she gives you a hug or makes an affectionate remark, bring it out in the open. Ask her what she means, and tell her what you feel.
- Make a determined effort to let go, and to experience life in a positive way without your ex.
- Set limits on your ex-wife's intrusion into your life. If she calls you too often or asks you for too many favors, politely explain to her that for your sake and hers, you want to limit these contacts.

But what about the ex-wife who *doesn't* want things to be nice and cordial? How do you respond to an ex who insists on remaining hostile and combative?

"BUT MY EX-WIFE . . ."

Brett came out of a massively dysfunctional marriage, which lasted four years and produced one child, a daughter. Brett, an assistant manager of a drugstore, had a history of being physically abusive with his wife, Sandi. For her part, Sandi would continually set up situations to goad him into abusing her. She would get right in his face, insult his manhood, dare him to hit her—and sometimes he would. When he struck her, she would call the police and have Brett arrested for assault.

This pattern continued even after Brett and Sandi's divorce. She told all their friends that she had divorced him because he was impotent, even though he had divorced her because of her continual emotional cruelty. Every contact he had with her, every time he would come to the house to pick up his daughter for a visit, she would taunt him and verbally abuse him. Several times, she came to his place unannounced and yelled obscenities at him from the courtyard of his apartment. Usually, he held his anger in check, but sometimes she got to him. When that happened, he was always sorry later.

It may not be "politically correct" to suggest that some people actually put themselves in the position of inviting abuse, but psychotherapists who have practiced for any length of time know it is true. Does this relieve Brett of any responsibility for his actions? Absolutely not! If he lays one hand on his wife, he is guilty of abuse. Period. End of discussion. Brett is always 100 percent responsible for his actions. We are not excusing violence in any way. We are simply acknowledging that there are two participants to any dysfunctional relationship, and rarely is there a situation of absolute black and white, of pure villainy versus pure innocence.

To Brett's credit, he made a voluntary decision to see a psychotherapist about his abusive behavior. "My ex-wife is really difficult," he told the therapist, "but I don't want to hit her again. I asked Sandi to come in for counseling with me because I wanted to get these hostilities behind us."

"What was her response?" asked the therapist.

"She laughed. She thought it was real funny. 'I don't have a problem!' she said. 'I'm not the one who goes around hitting people! You're the one with the problem!'"

"It could be," said the therapist, "that the idea of looking inside herself scares her. She probably has a lot of unfinished business that she doesn't want to face—feelings and issues that go back long before you ever met her. We can't do anything about that."

"I know," Brett acknowledged. "I'll just have to do the best I can from my side of this thing."

So, as often happens in a dysfunctional situation, the counselor proceeded to work with the person who was accessible and available. In this case, that person happened to be Brett.

In the course of Brett's therapy, the therapist determined that a large part of his behavior problem was due to endogenous depression (that is, depression that was caused by inner emotional forces rather than external pressures). Some people become quiet and withdrawn when depressed, but Brett was one of those who became irritable and aggressive. Add to these internal issues a heavy case of external stress from his ex-wife, and you have the makings of an explosive situation.

So Brett's therapist prescribed a medication to help treat his depression, lower his stress level, and reduce his tendency for aggression. Brett's response: "But that's not fair! Why do I have to take medicine when she's the one who's always spoiling for a fight?"

"Because, Brett, you are the one who cared enough to come in to my office, look inside yourself, and try to find solutions. You don't have to take this medication if you don't want to. I hope you'll *choose* to take it because you are accepting some measure of responsibility for this situation and for your behavior. I'm not saying it's fair for you to have to live with a situation where Sandi is continually setting you up, but that's the situation that exists. Do you see any other way to deal with this problem?"

Brett shook his head. And he took his medicine. In time, Sandi got tired of goading a man who was too much in possession of himself to respond to her insults. It wasn't easy by any means, but life did get better for Brett because he made a tough choice in the face of circumstances that were grossly unfair.

Brett's situation is rare, but it does happen. We wanted you to know that the principles in this book can apply in even the most extreme cases. The key is to stay focused on your goal, which is not winning, not proving yourself right, not achieving "fairness," and not getting even. Rather, your goal is to be the best father you can be, for your kids' sake and your own. To succeed, you must be willing to do whatever it takes to get along with the mother of your children.

WHO GETS CUSTODY OF THE CHURCH?

Craig and Elaine have been members of the same church for twelve years. Craig has served on the church board, Elaine has been a Sunday school teacher, and both have sung in the choir. Everyone in the church knew them as a married couple, as Craig-and-Elaine—until they split up. Suddenly, both were attending the same church, glaring at each other across the aisle and making the rest of the congregation very uncomfortable.

Finally, Craig decided he had just about had enough of his ex-wife making him miserable during what should have been a meaningful worship experience. So he went to see his counselor.

"Every Sunday I go to church," Craig explained, "and there are my wife and kids sitting two rows down. She's just doing this to humiliate me! I grew up in this church, for crying out loud! Elaine only joined after we were married! How can I get her to leave?"

"I'm not convinced your wife *should* leave."

Craig's jaw worked up and down as he tried to find words. "I-I'm flabbergasted! How can you say that? Certainly, you're not suggesting *I* should leave!"

"Why not?"

"But I grew up in that church!"

"Well, maybe you're due for a change," said the counselor, "a breath of fresh air. Look at it this way: who else in your family has grown up in that church?"

"I don't— Oh! You mean Tarl and Kristin. The kids."

"Let's see," said the counselor. "Tarl is ten, and Kristin is eight. I imagine they've made a few friends in that church."

"Okay, okay," Craig grumped. "I get the message. Elaine wins again. She got the Audi, I got the Yugo. She got the house, I got an apartment. She got the kids, I got two Saturdays a month. It only makes sense that she gets custody of the church as well."

"I don't expect you to feel good about it."

"Well, fine, 'cause I don't. I mean, why do I have to make all the adjustments? Why am I being punished just because my marriage didn't work out?"

"No one's punishing you. No one's going to make you leave the church. Keep attending if you like. If you tough it out, maybe Elaine will get uncomfortable enough to leave and take the kids with her. That's entirely up to you. All I'm saying is that maybe you would like to consider a couple of *other* people who grew up in that church: your kids. You might want to think about their needs, then make whatever choice you want to. Also, since I can see that you are a man who cares about spiritual things, you might want to consider what God wants you to do in this situation. What do you think?"

Craig sighed. He was reluctant. He was unhappy. But he had made a decision. "I think that makes a lot of sense," he concluded.

Within a few weeks, Craig was attending a different church. He was surprised to find that, unlike his previous church, his new church had a support group for divorced men. He tried it, liked it, and found that there were other men dealing with the same issues that troubled him. He talked about these issues during a visit with his counselor.

"It's been great to hear other guys talking about the same feelings I've been going through," he said. "This divorce has been real hard on a lot of my core beliefs. I was raised to view divorce as unthinkable. It's 'till death do us part or nothing.' I was faithful to the church and to my wife. I prayed. I trusted God to keep my family together. I always believed that God didn't like divorce. He could have stopped it. He could have changed Elaine's mind. Why did He let this happen?"

"How do you feel toward God?" asked the counselor.

"I've had to redefine my perception of Him," Craig replied. "I've had to say to myself, 'A lot of bad things happen in this world to people who don't deserve it. Does that mean God has gone fishing? Or does it mean God lets people have their free will, even if it means letting them do things He doesn't approve of, such as divorce?'"

"What have you concluded?"

"I'm still in process. But I feel closer to God these days. I think the guys in my support group have helped me. Some of these men are a little farther down the road than I am in this divorce thing, and they're pulling out of it okay. Their faith is still intact. I figure I'll make it too."

On visitation weekends, Craig sometimes takes his children with him to his new church. He has decided they need to see the example of their father practicing his faith on a regular basis. He is careful not to disrupt the routine of his children any more than he has to.

Craig is glad he changed churches. It has given him a richer spiritual experience and the support he has needed through his divorce process. And it has given his children an added dimension in their spiritual experience as well.

The spiritual dimension of life is an enormously important part of recovery from divorce and of making wise, practical choices in the divorce process. The problem Craig had is the same problem most of us have at one time or another: in order to do the best thing for his kids and for himself, he needed to act *against his instincts*. We have found that there are essentially only two forces which can enable us to act against our instincts: (1) spiritual intervention and (2) learning new ways of thinking and feeling.

The divorce process is loaded with emotional issues and eventualities that tempt us to act in instinctual, counterproductive ways. We want to stand on our rights. We become territorial and aggressive. We are hurt, so we want to hurt back. We resent the stepfather who moves into our place and takes over our role. We are afraid of losing, so we try to win.

If we want to achieve our goals as effective fathers, we need to learn a more productive way and a more *spiritual* way of approaching the mother of our children. That means we must begin to operate on spiritual principles rather than on instinctive aggression.

Those spiritual principles include:

Practice the Golden Rule. Jesus said, "Whatever you want [others] to do to you, do also to them."[1] Don't wait for your ex-wife to be kind to you. Show kindness first. There is no guarantee that your kindness will produce a kind response in her. She may or may not respond the same way—but you'll never find out unless you make the first move.

Try to see every situation from the other person's point of view. "Let each of you look out not only for his own interests," says the Bible, "but also for the interests of others."[2] This is sound, practical advice for maintaining a good working relationship with the mother of your children. The better you understand her point of view, the more smoothly you will be able to work things out.

Forgive, don't get even. "Repay no one evil for evil," says the New Testament.[3] Bitterness and revenge work against the system and against your long-term goals. Forgiveness is good for you, for your children, and for your role as father.

Be a part of the solution, not part of the problem. "If it is possible," says the Bible, "as much as depends on you, live peaceably with all [people]."[4] *You are responsible for your half of the problem, not all of it.* So fix your half. As much as depends on you, get in there and make the system work.

Always make your children's welfare your goal. "And you, fathers, do not provoke your children to wrath, but bring them up in the training and admonition of the Lord."[5] Never lose sight of your true goal. It's a lot easier to swallow pride and bite your tongue when you know you are doing it for those precious little kids.

Do you see how the spiritual dimension affects the practical workings of the post-divorce system? Clearly, the principles we just cited are not mere pious platitudes about how to be "nice." They are practical solutions to real-life problems. And they are strong medicine.

In his book *The Seven Habits of Highly Effective People (New York: Simon and Schuster, 1989)*, Steven Covey lays out seven principles that are both profoundly spiritual and profoundly practical in their application. They are good habits for us to build into our lives and to call upon when dealing with the mothers of our children. We have adapted Covey's seven principles to the specific task of relating to your ex-wife:

1. Be pro-active. Don't just react to stimuli from your ex-wife; take positive action to create a better working relationship with her.

2. Begin with the end in mind. All behavior must be examined in terms of your goal, in terms of what matters to you most. Keep your goal—an effective fathering relationship with your children—in front of you at all times.

3. Put first things first. Prioritize. Don't get sidetracked on non-essentials such as proving yourself right or defending yourself. Your first priority is your kids. Never forget that.

4. Think win/win. A good negotiator leaves something on the other person's plate. A good negotiator lets the other side feel she has won something too. A poor negotiator tries to take it all, tries to be right all the time, and never swallows pride. You may be a billion-dollar negotiator in the business world, but if you can't negotiate on a win/win basis with your ex-wife, what have you got? When you negotiate issues such as quality time with your children, you are negotiating the biggest business deal of your life. *Don't blow it.* Think win/win.

5. Seek first to understand, then to be understood. You can't think win/win unless you know what her wants and needs are. Listen to her. *Really* listen. Empathize. Understand.

6. Synergize. Synergy is just a technical-sounding word for "creative cooperation." It was synergy between you and the mother of your children that brought those children into the world; neither of you could do it alone. Now, in a post-divorce context, you must creatively cooperate with this same woman to meet the needs of your children. Work for synergy, not dominance or control, in your new business relationship with this woman.

7. Seek balanced self-renewal. Covey suggests that we all need to experience renewal in the four dimensions of our being: Physical, Mental, Social/Emotional, and Spiritual. Of those four, we feel the dimension most often neglected is the spiritual. At this juncture, we submit to you that the spiritual dimension may well be the most crucial dimension of all. As you work at this new post-divorce system, don't neglect the all-important spiritual dimension. Seek to know God and His will for your life.

If you order your life by these principles, how can you go wrong?

GETTING ALONG

What it's all about is *getting along.*

To get along with the mother of your children, you have to have clear-cut boundaries. Respect your ex-wife's independence. Respect her "space." Some men hang around their ex-wife's house as if they still lived there. Some even keep a key and let themselves in unannounced.

One father, a fellow named Rich, had a habit of going to his ex-wife's house and mowing her lawn, even though he knew she had a gardener to do that. Rich claimed he was just trying to help, but what he was really doing was trying to create a sense of dependency, indebtedness, and even guilt in her. He was communicating that she couldn't handle things without him. These subtle, unspoken messages created enormous conflict, which only worked against Rich's relationship with his children.

Another man, Todd, had a habit of picking up the kids from school without telling his ex-wife. He might take them to a ball game or a movie—and his ex-wife would go frantic with worry. Todd was simply using his kids to harass his ex-wife out of spite. It got to the point where she had to threaten him with a court order to get him to stop.

To get along, keep promises and commitments. Be on time when you pick up the kids for visitation—and when you bring them back. Make child support payments on time. Be a man of your word.

To get along with your ex, build up your inner man. Obtain a source of emotional and spiritual support: a men's group, a group of absent fathers, a support group. Find a source of validation for all the issues and emotions you are going through—because it's a sure bet there will not be much validation coming out of the divorce situation itself! Contact your pastor or psychotherapist. If a support group doesn't already exist, consider starting a support group for absent fathers in your church or community. Contact your pastor or psychotherapist for advice on starting such a group. Many churches are willing to sponsor groups when there is a demonstrated need for them.

If you can get along with the mother of your children, you will be able to maintain a positive relationship with your children. Getting along is a long-term goal. It's the goal you keep before you as long as your children are in her custody.

Divorce doesn't end on the day the judge signs the decree. Divorce never ends. Your children may be small now, but they will grow up. They will graduate. They will get married. And at all these different intersections of life, you will encounter the mother of your children. Life has ripples and rhythms, which will repeatedly throw you together with the woman you once lived with. The two of you might as well decide to be friends, or if not friends, then at least agree to be cordial.

Don't ever forget what it's all about: your children and your role as their father. You will do whatever it takes to build your relationship with them. *Whatever it takes.* It doesn't matter whether their mother "deserves" any kindness and consideration from you. It doesn't matter what's fair. All that matters is what works and what moves you closer to your goal.

In the next chapter, we will examine what happens to your role as a visiting father when your ex-wife remarries.

Chapter 8

THE
STEPDAD'S
PERSPECTIVE

Christmas can be a logistical nightmare for any family, even a family that has never been through a divorce: "Do we spend Christmas Day with my folks or yours? But we already spent Thanksgiving Day with your side of the family! I don't care if Grandma Lewis gets her nose out of joint, we are not driving two hundred miles on Christmas Day!" And on and on.

But when families split and ex-husband and ex-wife remarry, the logistical complications can multiply beyond belief. The results: conflict, anger, hurt feelings, recriminations, and major disruptions in the family systems. Does divorce *have* to produce these kinds of disturbances?

"From my experience," says Ken Parker, "the answer is no. It really depends on the people in the system, and on their willingness to make the system work. If the key players in the system (absent father, mother, and stepfather) are willing to approach these logistical problems cooperatively and creatively, you can take an imperfect situation and turn it into warm family memories."

Ken's own story illustrates his point. "I'm a stepfather to two of my three children. We set up an arrangement with their biological father and his family that worked out really well. He lived in San

Antonio, and we lived in Austin, about eighty miles away. Every year, a few days before Christmas, the two kids would go to San Antonio for a visit. Then on Christmas Eve, my wife and I and our youngest would drive down to a little town called New Braunfels, midway between Austin and San Antonio. We'd meet the kids' father in the empty parking lot of this closed-down restaurant, and we'd make the switch. The kids would always have a lot of presents to bring back, so we'd load up the car, say our goodbyes, and head for home.

"A lot of people would say, 'What an inconvenience to have to do all that driving on Christmas Eve!' But that's not the way we looked at it. For us, Christmas Eve was one of our favorite days of the year! We were always in a festive mood, the two kids had already had the Christmas tree and presents at their father's house, and we would drive back to Austin singing Christmas carols. To me, we were living a scene right out of *Currier and Ives:* loading up the horse-drawn sleigh with presents, then heading home over the snow-blanketed hills with the sound of songs and jingling bells— only we didn't have horses, a sleigh, or snow!

"Once we got home, we would have supper together, and the kids would play with the presents they brought from their father's house. Then, right at midnight, we would watch a videocassette of Dicken's *A Christmas Carol*—which was real special because the events in the story all begin at midnight on Christmas Eve.

"That was our holiday tradition, and we have a lot of warm memories from those days. Now the two older kids are grown, and I miss those days. I miss the excitement of picking up the kids at that parking lot in New Braunfels. I miss the fun of the ride home.

"I give a lot of credit for those good memories to the kids' biological father, and I'd like to think my attitude and behavior had something to do with it also. I didn't try to deny the existence of the absent father in my kids' lives, and he didn't try to deny my role. He was part of our system, and I was part of his. That way, there was never any resentment or animosity.

"I think what really made it work," Ken concludes, "is the fact that we both were focused on what was best for the children."

Ken has described a situation that is attainable but all too rare in most divorce-and-remarriage situations: a spirit of cooperation. It's not hard to understand why this is so rare. For both the absent father and the stepfather, the art of relating to "the other father" is a learned skill. It goes against instinct. A lot of primal emotions are involved, such as, "This is the guy who is sleeping with my wife! This is the guy who's trying to take my place with my own kids!" It takes time and insight to unload this emotional baggage so you can be free to work with the stepfather for the sake of your own children.

Many of the dynamics of relating effectively to the stepfather are similar to those of relating to the children's mother. But there are also some very special emotional dynamics that need to be understood and addressed. One of these dynamics is *fear*.

WHY THE STEPFATHER SCARES US

The great fear that absent fathers face when a stepfather enters the picture is, "Will this man replace me? Will my children forget me?" These fears can vary, depending on the age of the child involved. The younger the child, the more acute these fears tend to be.

"It was hard to let go of my nine-year-old son and fifteen-year-old daughter," Van Jones recalls, "and let them be raised primarily by my former wife and her new husband. I wasn't emotionally ready to release them. Because my daughter was a teenager, that separation was made a little more bearable by the fact that she was already moving toward independence. But it was still very hard.

"The relationship between my children's stepfather and me had to evolve. It took time for me to reach a point where I could say, 'I raised my son for the first nine years of his life. Now this man will have an influence on him during his teenage years. The older my son gets, the more he becomes involved with friends, dating, and football—and the less important that he be with me.' Still, no matter how old our children are when we make this adjustment, we have to learn to let go."

How do we learn to let go of our children and let them be raised by our ex-wife and another man?

"It has a lot to do with attitude," says Van, "and with our self-talk, the inner messages we repeat to ourselves. We have to say in our minds, 'It's okay for my child to love both me and a stepfather. I'm not losing my child. I'm not losing his or her love.'"

Absent fathers tend to think, "If my ex-wife remarries, then this guy will be in and I'll be out." The fact is, that's never the way it works. The roles of biological father and stepfather are not interchangeable. The reason, from a systems point of view, is that the more this man tries to take over your role, the more resistance he will encounter. The saying that "blood is thicker than water" has a lot of meaning in this situation. That biological bond cannot be replaced or transferred. The system will not let this new man take over your role. If he tries, he will be treated as an intruder. Even if you have made a lot of mistakes as a biological parent, there will be an overwhelming tendency for your older children to remain loyal to you. *A stepfather can never step into the role of biological father.*

Once you truly begin to understand these truths, you realize that not only do the biological father and stepfather roles never replace each other, but they exist side by side and can actually complement each other in very positive ways. "In my case," says Van, "I recognized that my son and his stepdad could do things together that he and I couldn't do. For example, my son's stepdad likes to waterski and enjoys boating. So by living in this other household, my son is getting a dimension out of life that he wouldn't get from living with me. During visitation, I get to have an influence on him in ways his stepdad can't offer. Even though it's hard to give up that daily relationship with your child, there are positive aspects of this arrangement if you look for them."

"From my own experience," says Ken, "I can really agree with Van that there are potential advantages to a child having both a dad and a stepdad, especially if both men can cooperate with each other. I have been involved in raising both of my stepchildren since they were eight and ten years old. My stepson, who is in his twenties, has chosen to go into law enforcement, just as his father did. My stepdaughter, on the other hand, who has almost completed her degree in education, is aspiring to be a social worker! I think it's reasonable to conclude that both the biological father and I have had a strong influence on their lives. Not a competing influence, but a complementary one."

The cooperative working relationship between absent father and stepfather is not always easy to build. It usually takes time, and a lot of hurt has to be overcome in the process. Some of the biggest hurts emerge from some of the smallest matters, such as a simple introduction.

"Once I was at a social gathering with my children, their mother, and their stepfather," Van recalls. "My son was introducing his mother and stepfather to some friends of his. I was startled to hear him say, 'I'd like you to meet my parents.' I didn't say anything, but my first thought was, *Your parents! Who am I?*

"I don't blame my son. It wasn't his fault his parents divorced. He was just trying to make a simple social introduction without a long explanation of who was related to whom and why. But when it happens to you and you're not prepared for it, it hurts. You feel like a second-class father."

Situations like this can ambush an absent father from time to time. That's why it's important to change the messages we tell ourselves. We need to rid ourselves of the negative self-talk which says, "I'm losing my kids," or, "This guy's taking my place." Instead, the messages we should repeat to ourselves again and again until we have truly internalized them are:

- My child can love another adult.
- I'll always be his father.
- I can let go and still be loved.
- Time heals wounds.

THE STEPFATHER'S PERSPECTIVE

A stepfather enters the system. You don't like it. That's understandable. But you still want to make the system work for you and your children. So you need to have some idea of the way things look from the stepfather's perspective, in much the same way that you need to understand your ex-wife in order to get along with her.

Let's look at the perspective of the stepfather, as related by someone who has been there. "The absent father is often feeling so threatened by the arrival of the stepfather," Ken Parker observes, "that he may not realize that the stepfather is feeling just as insecure. When I married a divorcée with two children, I felt very much like an outsider treading on someone else's territory. Though Mary Jo had been divorced for several years, I still had a sense of her ex-husband's presence in that family. I remember wondering what he thought of me coming into this situation, whether he would accept me, and so forth. I knew we would meet someday, and I couldn't help speculating whether it would be a cordial meeting or an adversarial one.

"Very few stepfathers just move in and take over. They come in on tip-toe, and they feel their way around. They are entering a realm where Mom and the kids already have their roles carved out, where they have enjoyed a lot of autonomy and have practiced a large degree of self-reliance. In most cases, this guy doesn't have time to try to replace the absent father and impose his own style. He is too busy trying to establish his own role and win acceptance.

"Stepfathers who come on like gangbusters lay themselves wide open for rejection, not only by the kids, but by their mother. If he tries to discipline or dominate the children, those children will resist him all the way out the door, and so, very likely, will Mom. Even if she married this man because 'the kids need a man to keep them in line,' she will usually jump in and protect her children if he starts to assume a parental role with them. That's the way the system works."

Often the absent father who fears losing his kids to a stepfather is merely borrowing trouble where no trouble exists. "As a new stepfather," says Ken, "I came into that family fully wanting the kids to keep in close contact with their biological father. I supported and promoted that relationship. The last thing in the world I wanted was to move in and replace the kids' natural father. Why? First, because I felt it was best for the kids to maintain that relationship. Second, I felt it was in *my* best interests to encourage that relationship because it would keep things peaceful.

"I never asked the kids to call me 'Daddy.' In fact, my stepdaughter tried calling me 'Daddy' for one day—completely her own idea.

She found she was uncomfortable with it and quit. The kids always called me Ken, and that was the way I wanted it. Even though the absent father may *fear* being replaced by the stepfather, these fears are usually groundless.

"In the post-divorce system, there is plenty of room for the stepfather role and the biological father role to coexist, peacefully and productively. When stepdad and bio-dad are functioning well together, the kids are the winners. They will have not just one, but *two* male parental models to learn from; two sets of fatherly opinions to draw on; plus, *two* sets of gifts to open at Christmas!"

HOW TO RELATE TO THE STEPFATHER

"Some time ago," recalls Van, "I was sitting in the school auditorium, watching my son perform in a one-act school play. Seated near me was my ex-wife's husband and next to him was my ex-wife. And as I sat and watched my son deliver his lines, it dawned on me: 'Hey, we've come a long way! This would have been uncomfortable during the first year after the divorce or even the year after that. We've finally gotten to a place where we can cooperate and support our son together—and it feels good.'"

How do you reach a point where you can actually feel okay about relating to your ex-wife and her husband? How do you reach a place where you can truly focus on what is best for the children instead of focusing on blame and hurt and jealousy? Here are some practical, workable steps you can take that will enable you to work within the existing system for your own sake and for the sake of your children:

Approach the stepfather without defensiveness. There's an important psychological principle at work here: people take their cues from other people. If you walk up to a person, smile, and extend your hand, that person is likely to return the smile and shake your hand. But if you approach a person warily and defensively, that person will likely assume a defensive pose himself. Then what happens? Your mutual defensiveness becomes the issue instead of the issue being the issue.

So when you go to pick up the children for visitation and the stepfather is there, *greet* him. Talk to him. Include him. Avoid treating him as if he is invisible.

Communicate directly to him, man to man. Avoid communicating through your children or your ex-wife. That's called "triangulating," indirect three-cornered communication instead of straight person-to-person communication. Triangles are unhealthy, but direct communication is a sign of emotional health, strength, and maturity.

Consider what the stepfather is feeling. Understanding the other people in the system is the only way to make the system work for you. You don't have to like him. Just try to understand him.

Stay focused on your goal. Your objective is an enhanced relationship with your children. The purpose of being cordial with this fellow is not to build a warm relationship with him, but with your kids. Cordiality is an effective means to that end.

There's a natural tendency to say, "Why should I try to get along with this guy? He's over there with my wife and my kids, and I'm stuck in this little apartment! It's not fair!" As we have said before, the issue is not fairness. The issue is not who is right and who is wrong. The issue is *what works*. The question is, *What will it take to move you closer to your goal?*

Let the stepfather know that you are encouraging your children to have a good relationship with him. Right now, that piece of advice might stick in your throat. You may feel you'd rather swallow a bucket of hot coals than say such a thing to the man who is now living with your ex-wife. As you can see, we didn't set out to coddle you along with a lot of Pollyanna advice in this book. We're laying down some tough objectives because we want you to understand what is required of you, in no uncertain terms, in order to make the system work in your favor.

If you can let the stepfather know that you are encouraging your children to build a good relationship with him, that will go a long way toward tearing down barriers. Have a talk with your children and give them permission to be friends with their stepfather. Encourage them to accept him into their family system. Tell them you are not worried about losing their love and that you will always love them.

By doing this, you will clarify the loyalty dilemma for the kids— which is one of the biggest emotional issues they face in the divorce. When you show that you are not threatened and will not feel they are being disloyal to you, it completely removes the loyalty question as an issue.

Show respect and support for the stepfather. If you do, there is a good likelihood that respect and support will be returned. The stepfather has to feel secure in order to respond to you in a cordial and cooperative way. So it is in your best interest to help him feel secure. If you respect him in his role, he will be much more likely to respect you in yours and to make concessions in your favor where the children are concerned.

Use humor to get along. It's amazing how quickly you can defuse a tense situation with the injection of a little gentle humor. Humor doesn't just make a person smile or laugh. It sends a message. When you can joke about a tough situation, you say, "We're going to get through this," or "I don't feel threatened by this situation," or "I'm not afraid of these issues." Humor breaks the ice and creates a connection between people.

WHAT TO DO ABOUT NEGATIVE FEELINGS

Feelings of anger, hurt, betrayal, and jealousy are normal in the aftermath of a divorce. Those feelings may stay with you for months or years. There will be times when you feel you have purged all those poisonous emotions of the past—and suddenly they'll flood back into your life with a vengeance. That's unpleasant but normal.

To make the system work in your favor, however, you have to find a way to keep those negative emotions out of your relationship with the stepfather. No matter what you are feeling, you still have to con-

duct business with this fellow. That means there will be two processes going on inside you at the same time—and these processes
will be opposed and fighting each other. Process A: a belly-full of
negative emotions churning inside you. Process B: a desire to do
what's best for the kids. And Process B has to prevail.

In order to make sure that your goals and your children prevail
and not your negative emotions, make a positive effort to be aware
of your emotions. The more aware you are, the more control you
will have. Admit those emotions to yourself. Don't deny them. If
there is unfinished business in your life which is driving these emotions, then work on resolving that unfinished business. (For a complete discussion of unfinished business, see Chapter 4: Taking Care
of Business.)

Also, if you want to prevail over your negative emotions, we encourage you to seek a spiritual way of dealing with your emotions.
Before each interaction with the stepfather, ask God, "In this interaction, please help me to stay focused on what is best for the kids.
Give me Your strength and wisdom to know when to speak and
when to keep silent. Be my guiding force. Help me to put aside
feelings of hurt, jealousy, and anger."

Be as cordial as you can be. If the stepfather responds with rude-
ness or anger, avoid "returning evil for evil." No matter what he
does, stick to your commitment and your principles, praying as you
go.

When we counsel an absent father who is struggling with a stepfather who is abrasive, we often say, "Okay, let's agree that this guy
is a jerk. Gripe about him all you want. But ask yourself: What will
it take to get around this guy? What will he respond to? Anger,
confrontation, and blaming have all failed so far. What do you think
will work?"

Often, the father will think for a moment, then reply, "Well,
maybe if I put aside my grievances. Maybe if I walked over to him
and shook his hand. Maybe if I said, 'I want to get along.' That
might work."

"Can you do that?"

"I don't know."

"Why not?"

After a moment of reflection, he might say, "It'll feel unfair. I'll be giving in. I don't want to be a victim."

Our response: "You don't have to be a victim. You can do anything you want. You have the power to choose what you will do. You have options. By choosing one of those options, you can make it easier to have a positive relationship with your kids. Do you want to have a good relationship with your kids?"

"Yeah."

"Enough to eat some crow? Enough to put up with some unfairness?"

Hesitation. Then, "Yeah."

WHAT IF THE STEPFATHER IS HARMING THE CHILDREN?

Randy was faced with a judgment call. "For the first two years after my wife remarried," he said, "my children would come to me with stories about their stepfather. The guy was a heavy drinker and verbally abusive. He wasn't dangerous, but he wasn't very good to my three kids. There wasn't enough evidence for me to sue for custody or call in the authorities. He didn't hit the kids or abuse them sexually or push drugs on them. He just yelled at them a lot and made them feel miserable. What could I do about it?"

There was very little Randy could do under the circumstances. "I encouraged the kids to get along as much as possible," he said. "I kept in close contact with my ex-wife and her husband and tried to be cordial and supportive. I figured that anything I could do to reduce their stress level would work in the children's favor. Did I respect this guy? No way! But I just had to grit my teeth and be as supportive as I could.

"If I had gotten into bashing him, I would have lost in the long run. Even though this guy really deserved a good bashing, I would have lost more than I gained by getting into that."

In cases involving physical or sexual abuse, there is no question what must be done: call in the authorities—the police and the child protective services of the county—to safeguard the well-being of the children. But Randy's kids weren't suffering under a situation as clear-cut as that. Their stepfather was a wretched role-model with a borderline behavioral problem. In such situations, you have to tell yourself, "This guy is not doing what I would do. He's not the parent I would be. I don't respect him. I don't like the influence he has on my children. But I will keep my mind on my goal—the welfare of my children—as I try to have a positive and stabilizing influence on this man and this family system."

Sometimes the stepfather will change for the better, and sometimes there is just no happy ending. Sometimes a jerk is a jerk is a jerk, and there's nothing that can be done to change him. In Randy's case, however, there was a happy ending. "Eventually, the guy went to Alcoholics Anonymous and got his act together," says Randy. "Things are much better now. I don't know how much my influence had to do with it, but it sure didn't hurt. If I had charged in and stirred things up, it just would have made things worse."

ADVANTAGES OF THE STEPFATHER

There are probably not all that many *truly* friendly divorces. Divorce is frequently a very intense, knock-'em-down, drag-'em-out sort of business. It is hard to imagine any arena of human affairs which produces more hostility, more blaming, more bitterness, more irrationality, and more out-and-out hatred than a divorce.

And yet—

Let some time pass, let tempers cool, give emotions a chance to settle down, and maybe reason and common sense will have a chance to take over. It all depends on somebody making some constructive choices and being willing to make a few sacrifices. If one person in the system is willing to move off-center, relinquish the need to be right, and let go of some grudges, then everyone else in the system can relax a little and lower their defenses. Eventually, the participants who were once locked in a cold war may be able to achieve a truce. And when that happens, everyone benefits, adults and children alike.

We hope that you and your ex-wife have found a way to part as friends. But even if your divorce looked like a scene out of *The War of the Roses*, you can still negotiate a cease-fire and begin to work productively for the sake of the children. With the passage of time—perhaps even with the reading of this book—you may have begun to recognize that the mother of your children still has a very important and positive role to play in their lives. Perhaps a little healing is taking place in your feelings toward the woman you were once married to.

And what about the guy she married after she divorced you? No love lost there, right? Well, before you write this guy off, let's get practical. Have you ever considered how *useful* a stepfather can be? Oh, yes! Sometimes, stepfathers come in quite handy. Here are a few of the advantageous roles a stepfather can play:

Communication facilitator. Sometimes it's easier to communicate man-to-man than man-to-ex-wife. Men and women tend to use different communicating styles. Whereas, in some extreme cases, the ex-wife may be too hostile to deal with, the two men—despite their differences—can often communicate more clearly and calmly to each other.

Objective parent. A stepfather can lend some objectivity to the parenting process. While we respect and affirm those who must shoulder the burden of single parenting, it is clear that parenting is optimally a two-person job. When two people parent together, they not only share the work load, they also provide complementary perspectives and a reality check for each other. If Mom, being too close to the situation, is parenting either too leniently or too harshly, Stepdad can often provide some balance for her perspective. Having this kind of objectivity available to your ex-wife is clearly in your children's best interests.

Watchdog. Sometimes a stepfather can help keep an eye on things while you're away. A father named Stan told us why he was glad there was a stepfather on the scene. "Last summer," said Stan, "my fourteen-year-old daughter Hannah was spending a month with my wife and me. The two of us had to go out of town for a quick overnight trip, and we left Hannah at a friend's house to spend the night. As teenagers sometimes do, Hannah and her friend slipped out of the house in the middle of the night. Her friend's mother discovered the girls were missing and called us at the hotel. But what could we do? We were two hundred miles away!

"So I called up Hannah's stepfather, who lives in the same city we live in. 'Jack,' I said, 'I'm sorry to mess up your evening, but Hannah needs some structure. She obviously can't handle our being gone.'

"Well, the stepfather took it in stride, and he went out and found Hannah and her friend. She wasn't up to any serious mischief, but no fourteen-year-old girl has any business being out at two in the morning. He drove the other girl back to her house, then took Hannah back to his house and suspended a whole list of privileges.

"So everything worked out fine. But if the stepfather and I had been into an adversarial relationship, it would have been tough. We would have really been in a bind. Instead, we were a team. When you become a team with your ex and her husband, then you've got it made."

Here is an excellent example of what this book is all about: the divorce process is hard, it's painful, and it's frustrating—but when you are willing to focus on your goals and work through the issues, you *can* come to a place where the system will work in your favor.

These cooperative relationships rarely just happen. In most cases, *you* have to take the first step. So we offer you these words of encouragement: in dealing with Stepdad, always seek win/win solutions to problems. Put out your hand and say, "Let's work together for the good of the kids." Work to reduce the level of threat, tension, and insecurity. You don't have to like the man who married your ex-wife, but you can form an alliance with him to meet the needs of your children.

In the next section, we will delve deeper into the absent father experience and learn how to make your new fathering role work, including ways to:

- Communicate with your children at a meaningful level.
- Deal with your children's feelings.
- Get the most out of your visitation times.
- Make wise decisions and smooth transitions as you approach remarriage and other major changes in your life.

Part Three

MAKING YOUR NEW ROLE WORK

Chapter 9

THE EFFECTIVE ABSENT FATHER

Mike is a successful entrepreneur in his late fifties. About twenty years ago, he was a total workaholic, addicted to making money and running his business empire. His eighteen-hour-a-day schedule left him very little time for his family. When his wife divorced him, he didn't contest either the divorce or the custody arrangement she proposed. The divorce forced him to recognize that he had not made a priority of being either a husband or a father.

After taking stock of his life, it occurred to Mike that his greatest fear in life was that he might lose the respect, love, and friendship of his children. He promised himself that even though he had failed as a husband, he still wanted to succeed as a father. He didn't have a book like this one to turn to for advice, but he intuitively began to implement many of the principles we are exploring throughout this book.

Today, all three of Mike's children work with him in the various businesses he owns. They are his friends and partners. Not long ago, his oldest son said to him, "The divorce was hard on everyone in the family. But it could have been a lot worse. Dad, I'll never forget all the things you did to make it easier on us kids. You were always there for us. Even though we weren't together as a family anymore, we always knew we had both a mother *and* a father. We were never without a dad."

Our hope is that you will someday hear words like these from your children. We're sure that is your hope too. In this chapter, we will examine ways to make the absent father role work—despite the physical distance and the limited time you can spend with your children—so that you can keep the love and friendship of your children forever.

HOW TO TALK—AND LISTEN—TO YOUR KIDS

Ring. Ring.

"Hello?"

"Hi, Kevin, this is your father. How are things going, son?"

"Fine."

"Good, good. What have you been doing today?"

"Oh, you know. School and stuff."

"Good, good. How are your grades, Kev?"

"Okay, I guess."

"Good, good. How's it going in football?"

"Fine."

"Been dating some?"

"A little."

"How's your sister doing?"

"Fine."

Pause.

"Well, Kev, it's sure been good talking to you."

"Yeah. Same here."

"I'll see you, son."

"See ya, Dad."

Click. Dial tone.

In his book *Will They Love Me When I Leave?* (New York: Putnam, 1987), C. W. Smith calls these "Uncle Dad" questions. You go through your list of survey questions, the child answers in words of one syllable or less, and you hang up feeling more like a distant uncle than the child's father. You live on the periphery of their lives, and they can no longer relate to you. "I might as well send them a checklist in the mail," you think, "and they can mark it off, yes-no-yes-yes-no."

Effective communication is one of the key factors in effective fathering. The good news is you don't have to settle for an "Uncle Dad" level of communication with your kids. To have a *real* conversation with your children, keep the following principles in mind when you talk to them:

Model effective communication. Tell your children about the things in your life that you are truly enthusiastic about. Talk about shared interests. Look for common ground and for those things that you and your kids are really interested in: A favorite movie or TV show. Sports. Science. Computers. A hobby such as model railroading or collecting.

Ask relationship questions. Not just, "What have you been up to?" but, "How are you feeling? How have you been handling things? Tell me what this divorce thing has been like for you." Set the tone by sharing your own feelings.

Avoid questions that can be answered with "yes," "no," "okay," or "fine." Ask questions that require thought, feelings, or description: "Tell me all about your 4-H project." "How did you feel playing the piano in front of all those people?" "Oh, you want to be a marine biologist? What does a marine biologist do?"

Tune in to the things your child cares about most. Remember that what you care about and what your child cares about may be completely different. Your child is probably more interested in pets than grades. Stephen Covey says it best in his book *The Seven Habits of Highly Effective People* (New York: Simon and Schuster, 1989): "What is important to another person must be as important to you as the other person is to you."

Give some advance thought to some good questions you want to ask.
Think ahead about some subjects you want to talk about—not to be
over-programmed, but simply to have some good feelings-based
and reality-based questions. This will help you avoid the rut of the
superficial "checklist" questions.

HOW TO HANDLE FEELINGS IN YOUR CHILD

As you reach and maintain an in-depth level of communication
with your children, you will see them expressing emotions of anger,
resentment, sadness, apathy, or fear. You may become uncomfortable when they express such feelings. It will hurt, and you may be
tempted to try to shut out or repress their feelings.

All too often, instead of empowering our children, we *overpower*
them. Particularly when the child is acting in an angry, hostile, or
out-of-control way, we tend to try to control the child's behavior.
What we should be doing is uncovering the feelings which underlie
that behavior.

When your children express painful or unpleasant emotions,
make a conscious effort to *accept* and *absorb* their feelings. Let
them know that you hear and understand what they are going
through. Tell them that, even though it hurts now, they're going to
be okay. As you do this, you will give them a greater sense of control
over their lives and feelings. In other words, you will *empower*
them.

Here are some specific ways you can help empower your child:

When there is conflict, *lower* your voice. This goes against our instinctive tendency to *raise* our voices when we are angry. But try
lowering your voice and see what happens. Children often become
more cooperative when they feel less threatened and overwhelmed.

Practice active listening. Don't be too eager to jump in and counter
what the child is saying. Avoid interrupting. Listen for feelings:
hurt, grief, fear, powerlessness, a sense that nobody hears. Reflect
the child's feelings back so that he will feel he has been heard.

If the child is raging, say his name in a soft, affirming tone in order to calm him down. If his behavior is out of control, make it clear that you will not allow him to hurt himself or anyone else, nor will he be allowed to destroy property—but try to do so in a calm rather than threatening manner.

Pause. Don't feel you have to fill every silence with words.

Affirm feelings, deal with content later. Recognize that while the *content* of what the child is saying may be at times illogical, the child's *feelings* should not be disparaged or condemned. Help your child feel free to share feelings. Affirm the feelings, and deal with the content at a time when there is more calm and reason.

Inject humor. But keep all joking on a positive and good-natured level. Avoid insult humor. Be careful not to use joking to avoid being serious when you need to be.

Clarify expectations. State clearly what you expect of the child. Ask the child to state specifically what he or she expects of you. Say, "Okay, I've heard how you feel. Now, tell me exactly what you want me to do, and I'll tell you exactly what I can do and what I can't."

Tune in to your own feelings, and make sure you are not reacting to your own anger or to unfinished business from the past. If you are angry, avoid acting or speaking out of that anger. Take a break to recover your composure.

Empower the child by giving him some choices in life. When he visits, say, "Here are three things we can do. Which would you choose?"

Remind the child often that he is significant, he is okay, and his feelings and opinions count.

Divorce creates a sense of powerlessness in a child, which can lead to anger or despondency. He had no say in the divorce and no power to affect events. He may react to this sense of powerlessness by rebelling or withdrawing. If you practice these principles whenever you interact with your child, you can help him feel empowered. This will make your child a healthier, more positive person in the long run.

BEHAVIOR TO EXPECT IN YOUR CHILDREN

Children who have been through divorce will tend to engage in certain behaviors. If you're not prepared for these behaviors in your children, you might think your kids are spinning out of control. And this can be a scary experience for a divorced dad to deal with. These behaviors, however, are just passages that many children go through as they struggle to come to terms with the divorce process. Helping your children negotiate this passage in their lives is part of being an effective absent father.

Common behaviors in children who are going through the divorce process include:

Taking advantage of two-house rules. "I don't have to do that in Mom's house!" the child may say—and he may be telling the truth or pulling an outright scam. Regardless of the rules in the other house, you are the child's father, and you have a duty to set rules which conform to your values. Decide what the rules of your household should be, then stand firm. Tell the child, "Mom has certain rules in her house, and I have certain rules in mine. I have faith in you that you can make the adjustment to these rules when you're in this house."

Showing anger toward you by disregarding your rules. For example, your teenage daughter knows that her curfew is 11:00 P.M., but she doesn't get home until 12:30 A.M. How should you respond to this behavior? You will probably want to apply some corrective measure to her behavior. But don't stop merely at the behavior level.

Sit down with your daughter and talk about it. Find out if she is angry with you or with the divorce. This problem can be turned into an opportunity for better understanding and communication between you and your child. If she appears sullen and rebellious, ask what she is angry about. Ask her what life has been like for her. Ask her how she feels when she comes to visit you.

It may be that she has just begun to feel emotions she has denied in the first few months of the divorce. She may blame you for the breakdown in the marriage (don't be alarmed; she'll get over it, especially if she is allowed to talk through her feelings). She may be angry because she feels humiliated at school, because she has over-heard friends talking about her parents' divorce, because she doesn't know what to say. If she is using passive-aggressive behavior such as rule-breaking to express her anger, then you can help her by inviting her to express her feelings in words. (For a more thorough discussion of passive-aggressive forms of anger, see Chapter 3: How It Feels.) Keep in mind that Life is a process. This *can* change. In Van's case, his daughter Libby made a passage through the teen years and became more available as a young adult. Van says, "It's very satisfying to relate to your kids as adults after going through the teen years."

Complaining about the stepparent or custodial parent. Harry's thirteen-year-old son Joshua was unhappy with the living conditions at Mom's house. "Mom and Bob are ganging up on me," he griped. "It's really unfair."

"How are they ganging up on you?" asked Harry.

"They're like really strict and stuff," said Josh. "I was late to school last week, so they grounded me and won't let me watch TV for a whole week!"

"Why were you late to school, Josh?"

The boy shrugged.

"Well, that does seem like a lot of punishment for just being late to school—"

"Yeah, Dad, it's really unfair!"

"—so I wonder if there isn't more to this story than you're telling me."

Josh turned away and didn't say anything. There was a long pause—then the boy changed the subject.

Some time later, Harry called his ex-wife and, in a very polite and non-accusing way, mentioned that Josh had a concern about the punishment she and her new husband, Bob, had imposed on the boy.

"Did Josh tell you what he did?" asked Josh's mother. "He got caught stealing half a dozen packs of baseball cards from a convenience store on his way to school."

"He *what?*!"

"I would have told you about it sooner, but you were out of town all last week. He was picked up by the police and everything! You don't think we were too hard on him, do you?"

"Too hard on him! If I had imposed sentence on that kid, he'd be collecting Social Security before he got his privileges back!"

Harry wisely avoided taking sides or criticizing his ex-wife's decisions until he could get all the facts. He also was wise in maintaining good communication with his ex-wife and her husband so that he could make a cordial, non-accusatory call and keep from being "split" by his son. He carefully determined what was in his son's best interests, and in this case, it was clearly best to support his ex-wife's disciplinary action.

There may be times when a child has a legitimate concern about the way Mom and her husband are handling matters at home. If there are problems in the relationship between Mom and your child, you may want to cautiously consider whether it is wise to call her or not. Be careful not to get the child in trouble at home. Be careful not to violate the child's trust in you. If he comes to you with a legitimate problem and you call his home and make life hard for him, he may learn not to trust you.

You may want to ask the child, "Are you telling me this because you'd like me to make a call and intervene? What would you like me to do?" It may be that all he wants from you is someone sympathetic to talk to. Or he may want you to step in and help resolve the problem. Above all, you want to keep the lines of communication open between your child and you, and communication depends on trust.

MAKING VISITATION WORK

The vast majority of time you spend with your children must be compressed into a formal arrangement called "visitation." The access you have to your children is negotiated with your ex-wife, with the mediation of the court, and it is a very limited access compared to the relationship you used to enjoy as a live-in dad. So it's crucial that you find ways to make the visitation experience work as effectively as possible for you and for your children. Here are some visitation tips:

Give the new system time to develop. Allow your children to discover a different relationship and new roles. Build new memories in the new system. This is an ever-changing, fluid situation, so just let it unfold. Grow and change with it. You may find you are talking to your children in a different way, relating on a different level. If that's how it evolves, let it.

Stay loose. Avoid a rigid agenda. Give your children choices of things to do during visitation—including just hanging around, doing nothing. We've heard children say, "Gosh, I go to Dad's, and he's got the whole weekend planned out in his Day-Timer. Sometimes I just like to watch TV or play Monopoly or do nothing at all!"

If you are uncomfortable spending unprogrammed time with your children, ask yourself why you feel that way. Are you uncomfortable sitting in a quiet room with your children with nothing to do but chat? If so, perhaps there are some issues you need to talk through with them.

At first, you and your children may find visitation an awkward experience. You may wonder, "How do I keep these kids entertained for a whole weekend?" In the first few months, you will probably use commercial entertainment to fill up the time: movies, McDonald's, pizza parlors, video arcades, amusement parks, the zoo, and so on. But as you settle in to the visitation routine, you'll find you can relax and turn those all-too-short weekends with your children into warm, shared experiences.

In time, you and your children will probably spend less time going to Six Flags and Chuck E Cheese's and the Cineplex and more time camping, bicycling, beachcombing, watching TV, playing board games, and doing hobbies. Someday, you and your kids will look back fondly on the times you spent talking together about shared interests: hobbies, sports, pets, school subjects, and so forth. As you and your kids settle into the visitation routine, you will develop a natural, easy rhythm that will transform the artificiality of "fathering by appointment" into warm memories and strong family bonds.

Be flexible. Even though the court may have ordered that you can have the kids for visitation on the second and fourth weekend of every month, there's no reason you and your ex-wife can't vary that arrangement by mutual consent.

If, for example, your ex-wife wants to drop the kids off so she can go out on the town (making you her free babysitter) don't refuse to cooperate simply to spite her. If you feel okay about taking the kids, take them and have a great time with them.

By the same token, don't feel you *have* to be her free babysitter. The point is simply this: you can choose. It really is up to you. Never forget that you have the freedom to do whatever is best for your children and for you.

Don't force your values on your child. Share your values. Be open with your beliefs but accept the fact that your child is living in two homes. It's okay to have your own value system in your own home, but avoid making the child feel bad because he or she lives in a different system at his mother's home. Remember that the transition from home to home causes the child to feel an emotional "jet lag" anyway, and he or she needs time to decompress. So don't make it harder on the child by *imposing* or *forcing* a radically different value system on the child when he or she is in your home.

As much as possible, avoid confusing your child's values in such areas as entertainment (what TV shows or movies the child may watch, or what music the child may listen to); religious training (is it really a big deal if the child is raised Presbyterian or Lutheran?); bedtime, curfew, and other behavioral rules; holiday traditions; and so forth. The child has to make sense of the values and beliefs he or she is being taught, so the goal is to create as little confusion as possible. It's a delicate balancing act: you don't want to *inflict* your values on the child, but you do want to have an *influence* on your child. The key is to use good judgment and to focus on the needs of the child.

Reserve a special place in your home for your child. It helps the child feel more connected to you if he or she has a place in your house he can identify as *his* or *hers*. It can be a room, but if you live in a small apartment and don't have a whole room to spare, then a bed, a chest of drawers, or a bookcase will do. Set aside a special corner of the room and put up some posters that reflect the child's interests. Furnish that place with mementos that are special between you and your child—a model airplane you built together, a prize you won at the amusement park, pictures of you and your child together—anything that serves as a reminder of the bond between the two of you.

IF YOUR CHILD RESISTS VISITATION

"When my son was about fifteen," says Van, "he decided he didn't want to visit me as much as he used to. I had in my mind that he would come every other weekend because that's the way it was set up. The way I looked at it, if Ben didn't come every other weekend, I might lose him. It wasn't true, but that was the way I felt. That feeling of, 'What am I going to lose next?' is very pronounced when you live apart from your kids.

"One Saturday morning, I drove to his mother's house to pick him up. He came out to the car and said, 'I don't want to go this weekend, Dad.' I reacted emotionally when he said that. I tried to coax him into coming with me, but when it became clear he wasn't going to give in, I turned off the engine and said, 'Okay, let's talk.'

"We went in the house and sat down at the kitchen table. My ex-wife and her husband left us alone, and the two of us talked for an hour and a half. It was tough. When Ben said, 'I've got some things going on in my life, things I want to do this weekend,' I interpreted it as rejection. I tried to explain to him how I felt. It took a while for him to get through to me. He wasn't saying, 'I don't love you anymore.' He was simply saying, 'Could we be a little flexible?'

"After I calmed down and understood what Ben really wanted, I said 'Okay, so you just want a little more distance, a little more time. That's hard for me because we have so little time together as it is. But if that's what you want, I can live with that. I just want you to know that I need to stay connected with you. You're my son, and I want to be with you.' He said, 'I know, Dad. But can't you give me just a few more weekends to myself?' I said, 'Yeah. Why don't we agree to get together in a month?'

"So that's what we did. But it was too much for me to process in one ninety-minute conversation. So, I spent the next few weeks agonizing, mulling, stewing, and reading books on 'letting go.' Finally, I just decided to let it happen.

"Since that time, Ben doesn't come over as often as he used to, but when he does come, we have a great time together. The relationship is good. I still keep up with his life, I go to his football games, we talk on the phone—but I'm not as involved as I used to be."

Van's experience doesn't happen to every absent father, but it does happen. There are many reasons a child may resist visitation with the absent father. Studies show that as adolescent boys grow older, their relationships with their absent fathers tend to become more distant. Sometimes the child may resist because he doesn't like the woman you are dating or are married to or the new family you are living in. And sometimes, as in the case of Van's son Ben, the child may reach a developmental stage where friends, activities, and interests become so important he doesn't want to devote as much time to visitation.

You can't bribe, argue, or coerce your child into spending time with you. If the child objects to your new family or romantic interest, you may have to wait until the child is able to accept this change in your life. Whatever your child's reasons for resisting visitation, try to set aside your fears and insecurities. Be supportive, listen to your child, and accept his or her feelings. Also, make it clear that you have no hard feelings, that your door is always open, and that there is always a place for your child in your heart and in your home.

"In my case," says Van, "it is really just a matter of where my son was, socially and developmentally. What I was slow to realize is that it is *normal* for a fifteen-year-old boy to pull back from his family as he develops more and more interests and activities with his peers. This is true whether his parents are divorced or together. He's just becoming more independent. Of course, this transition is a lot more traumatic for a visiting father than a live-in, because the visiting father's time with his child is already so limited and tightly scheduled.

"Looking back, I realize that when I was that age, I didn't spend much time with my dad either. I had my own friends and my own interests, and I was trying to be independent. Once I realized this was just a normal stage in Ben's development, I could relax and go with the flow."

As your children grow toward young adulthood, here are some key truths to remember:

Your children are acquiring new interests and new priorities. It doesn't mean you are being replaced in their affections.

Don't listen to the self-talk that says, "I'm losing my children." Instead, tell yourself again and again, "To let go is to love."

Your children are your number one concern. Their growth, maturity, and emotional well-being are *your* top priority.

Never use guilt or manipulation. If they seem to be distancing themselves from you a bit as they grow older, try to accept it gracefully and support them from afar.

Keep the lines of honest communication open. If you feel that the increasing distance between you and your teenage child is a real problem, talk openly with your child about it. It may be that your child is just thinking about other things and doesn't realize how you feel.

No matter how old your child is, when he or she resists visitation, it hurts. But the hurt will pass. It doesn't mean you're losing your child. It's just one more part of the divorce process you have to get through. And you will get through it.

THE ABSENT FATHER AND DISCIPLINE

Ted is a classic "Disneyland Dad." When his kids come over to visit, everything is fun, fun, fun. They can stay up late, even all night if they want. If they want him to buy something—whether a roll of Lifesavers or a new stereo—he says, "Sure! Why not!" He *almost* lost his temper when he walked into the living room and found a water-balloon fight in progress, but hey, he only gets to see them every other weekend, right? Why spoil their visit with a nasty thing like discipline?

Ted thinks that by being a "Disneyland Dad," he can keep their love and respect. He would know better if he had heard what his oldest son said to a friend at school last week: "My old man is such a chump, a real pushover. I can get anything out of him."

Does that sound like *respect* to you?

Many absent fathers hesitate to discipline their children out of fear they will lose favor with them or mar the limited time they have with them. The fact is, an absent father is still the *father*, and he has a responsibility to assume the parenting role. Children need structure, limits, and rules.

Discipline doesn't mean punishment (although penalties and correction are a necessary part of discipline). Discipline means guidance so that the children will grow to become the kind of people you hope they will be.

Effective discipline and guidance for your children requires coordination and communication with the children's mother. You may not be eager to communicate with her, but you can cooperate on guidance issues with your ex-wife *if* you keep your conversation focused on your children's needs. Reassure her that you will be supportive of her efforts to raise the children, that you will discipline the children when they are with you, and that you will tell the children you are acting in cooperation with their mother.

If there are discipline issues you can't agree on, talk about those differences. Agree to disagree, but don't condemn the parental choices your wife makes. She has her home and her rules, and you have yours. Calmly tell her, "I won't undermine your parenting style, and I won't criticize the way you discipline, but I will choose to do it this way." Then reaffirm that message to your children, "Your mother and I have somewhat different discipline styles and expectations, and that's okay. We're each raising you the best way we know how. We try to work things out so the rules aren't too different between her house and mine, but there will always be a few differences. So try to respect your mother's rules when you're with her and my rules when you're with me."

The Ineffectual Disciplinarian

Jeff adored his kids, but he came close to having his visitation rights severely restricted. It all could have been avoided *if* he had shouldered his share of the parenting responsibility.

Divorced for two years, Jeff saw his children every other weekend. He is passive by nature and was never an involved disciplinarian, even during the marriage. When the kids came to visit, he let them run riot: eating whatever they wanted, watching all the cable shows their mother never let them see at home, staying up all hours of the night. They threw fits if he even suggested any curbs on their behavior. They bullied him into doing whatever they wanted and taking them anywhere they pleased.

On returning to their mother's home, it took three days for the kids to return to any semblance of manageable behavior. The temper tantrums, selfishness, and irrational demands of the children left their mother and stepfather frustrated and frazzled—and resentful toward Jeff. In desperation, Jeff's ex-wife called him.

"Jeff, you've got to give the kids some limits!" she told him. "Every time they come home, they are totally out of control!"

"Come on, Louise," Jeff replied defensively, "you're just being too hard on the kids. When they come to visit me, I want them to have a good time. It's good for them to get a little freedom now and then."

"You're idea of 'freedom' is turning the sweetest kids in the world into terrorists, and I won't stand for it!"

"Well, what are you going to do about it?"

"If you don't start acting like a real father, you'll find out what I can do about it!"

Well, Jeff had no intention of changing his style. So a few weeks later, when the kids came home from a visit in typical bonkers fashion, Louise decided to show Jeff exactly what she could do about it. After she and her husband finally managed to get the kids in bed and quieted down, she declared, "That's it! No more of this! I'm going back to court and get Jeff's visitation rights reduced!"

So the scene was set for a nasty court battle. The prospect of having contact with his kids reduced even further forced Jeff to face reality and seek counseling. Just in the nick of time, Jeff came to understand that his lax approach to parenting grew out of his own fear of losing his kids and his own sense of inadequacy. With the help of his counselor, Jeff was enabled to support the discipline in the other home and communicate with Louise so that there would be a consistent approach to discipline and guidance.

He became an effective disciplinarian.

Jeff now knows what we all need to understand: you can't be an effective father and an ineffectual disciplinarian. You can't win a child's love without winning his respect. You don't do your children any favors by being a permissive father. If you love your children, give them the limits and structure they really need.

SHOULD YOUR CHILDREN LIVE WITH YOU?

There are many children of divorce who, for one reason or another, decide they want to come live with Dad. Some have a fantasy of Dad's house as an endless visitation, filled with pizza, movies, and trips to the amusement park. Other children may see their father's residence as a haven from rules and constraints they feel are too harsh. Still other children may express a desire to live with Dad because they have unresolved inner conflict regarding the divorce, and this is their way to resolve that conflict. Saying "I want to live with Dad" may be an expression of the child's wish to have himself and both parents all living together again.

When your child says, "Dad, I want to live with you," look at the situation from every angle. This is the perfect setup for some disastrous decision-making on your part. Here are some questions to consider:

- "How do I feel about having my child live with me?"
- "What are the child's motives for wanting to live with me?
- "What are my ex-wife's feelings about this situation?

Let's examine each of these questions individually:

"How Do I Feel About Having My Child Live with Me?"

Examining our own feelings and motivations can be a tricky business. The pitfalls of denial and self-deception are easy to fall into. It can be a very gratifying, ego-boosting experience to hear the words, "I want to live with you, Dad." It makes you feel appreciated, affirmed, and validated. You may experience a sneaky satisfaction in the fact that your child now prefers you over your ex-wife (a subtle sense of triumph that she is getting what she deserves). None of these feelings, of course, are valid reasons to have your child move in with you.

Don't make a hasty, emotion-based decision that you will regret later. In order to make the best decision possible, try to clear away all the emotional reasons for wanting your child to live with you. Boil it all down to one essential consideration: "Is this the best thing for the well-being of my children? Who can provide the best overall home environment for my children—their mother or me?" Here, your feelings don't matter. Triumphing over your ex-wife doesn't matter. The only thing that matters in this decision is the children and their best interests.

"What Are the Child's Motives for Wanting to Live with Me?"

This is a key question. Early in the process, sit down with the child and gently probe for the answer. Some of the questions to be asked include:

- "*Why* do you want to move in with me?"
- "What is happening in your life *right now* that makes you want to live with me?"
- "How is the relationship between you and your mother?"
- "Has something happened at home that causes you to want to move out of her home?"

Take time to fully investigate the reasons for your child's desire to leave Mom and live with you. As you talk to your child, be encouraging, supportive, empathetic—*but be certain that you don't make any commitments to the child at this point.* Make it clear you are just exploring the options and you are not making any promises.

After investigating the child's reasons for wanting to change households, you may find the child is simply trying to escape the consequences of something he did at home. If so, your response may be, "I know you're unhappy right now, but you really need to go home and work this problem out with your mother and stepfather." Avoid any suggestion you are even considering allowing the child to switch homes. The child has to learn to work through problems instead of running from them.

At the same time, make it clear that you are not rejecting the child but making a decision in his or her best interests. "It's not that I don't love you, or that I don't want you to live with me," you might say "but right now you have to face this problem and solve it. This isn't easy for me to say because I like being with you. But this is what's best for you."

You may find there is validity to the child's request. If, after talking and thinking it through with the child, it seems the right thing to do, the next step is to talk to the child's mother and stepfather. Continue to be careful, however, not to make any commitments to the child at this point.

"What Are My Ex-Wife's Feelings About this Situation?"

Arrange a meeting with your ex-wife and her husband, *without* the child. Tell them what the child has told you, and ask them how they would feel about letting the child move in with you. Be open to new information. You may discover that the child has been exploiting an opportunity to "split" his parents, to play one against the other. He may have threatened, "If you do such-and-such, I'll go live with Dad."

The next step is to bring the child into the decision-making process. If everyone is agreed that the child's wishes should be carried out, then the new arrangement can be discussed with the child. If the adults feel a move would not be in the child's interests, then the child needs to understand the reasons for the decision. A meeting of all the parties may or may not lead to a change in the living arrangement, but everyone affected should be part of the process. Having everyone present will minimize any chance of the child "splitting" the parents. If the child knows that problems and issues are discussed by *all* the parties together, he will learn that "splitting" doesn't work.

We recommend that a counselor be involved in the decision-making process. He or she can help you avoid the emotional pitfalls of such a decision and help everyone make the transition as smoothly as possible. A professional counselor can also objectively help you assess whether this move is best for everyone and whether there are hidden issues or unfinished business involved.

Sometimes, a decision to have the child move in with Dad can be a bad decision, even if all the adults and the child are in agreement. For example, Mom may want Dad to take her child because the child is acting up and becoming difficult to handle. She may call absent Dad and say, "Mary's becoming impossible to deal with. I think it's time for her to live with you. See what you can do with her."

If this happens to you, *proceed with caution!* Experience shows that when Mom "dumps" a "problem child" on Dad, the situation rarely improves. Moving a child from one household to another doesn't resolve the root problems that caused the behavior. In fact, the child may perceive he is being punished—banished to live as an outcast with Dad!—and his behavior may actually worsen. Avoid being cast in the role of Dungeon Master to your child. Instead, suggest to the other parties that the entire family system work through these issues in counseling with a professional therapist.

MAKING THE ABSENT FATHER ROLE WORK AT SCHOOL EVENTS

"Divorce puts geographical distance between two people," says Van Jones. "But, like it or not, school events—the games, the plays, the programs, the commencements—keep throwing those people back together again. School events test whether or not the absent father can make his role work."

For many divorced fathers, school events can be full of dread. You want to be there for your child—but your ex will be there too. And so will her husband (boyfriend, whatever). There may be icy stares, the cold shoulder, silence, tension, maybe an uncivil word or two; and maybe worse.

But does it *have* to be that way?

No. The system *can* work. Parents *can* focus on what's best for the children, not on the emotional debris of the past. Your goal, as you attend the event, is to be supportive of your son or daughter. *Nothing else matters.* With that as your focus, you are free to respect the position of every other person there, including your ex-wife and the stepfather. Just find your place (even if it's in the back of the auditorium), and be there for your child.

Are we asking you to demonstrate the selflessness of a saint? No, not selflessness. *Enlightened self-respect.* You are not stuffing your pride for the sake of your ex. You are doing it for your kids' sake and your own. When you are secure in your own selfhood, without having to prove anything to anyone, then you can do whatever it takes to be an effective, supportive, involved father to your children.

THE VIEW FROM THE BALCONY

"When my stepdaughter got married several years ago," Ken Parker recalls, "one of the big questions was, 'Who gives the bride away?' I joked to Laurie, 'How about if we do it the way we did it in real life? Your dad can walk you halfway down the aisle, and I'll walk you the other half?' Well, she didn't go for that. As it ended up, Laurie's biological father walked her down the aisle, and I sang at the wedding.

"During Laurie's wedding, as in all weddings, there was a lot of chaos. The last thing I wanted was to add to it. I thought, 'This is her day, and my feelings don't matter a hill of beans compared to what is best for her.' So I didn't walk her down the aisle. Her other dad did that. And I didn't stand in the receiving line. Her other dad did that. On one level, I wasn't crazy about my role, but on another level I counted it a privilege to do anything to make Laurie happy.

"Now, Laurie didn't make those decisions lightly; she carefully checked out how I felt about it. And to be honest, I think her dad was almost as uncomfortable with his role at times as I was. The point is this: it doesn't matter whether I am Laurie's stepfather or her biological father. The principle is the same: if we focus on what's best for the children, we will never go wrong. The system will work. We will create happy memories instead of regrets and bad feelings.

"There's a term for the kind of person who will bow out, step aside, and make way in order to make the system work. He's called a 'Balcony Person.' He's the person who doesn't get to sit in the front row, doesn't get to share the limelight. It's the person who sits in the balcony, applauding and supporting and cheering. Our kids need Balcony People as much or more than they need 'Front Row People,' and 'Limelight People.'"

YOUR KIDS NEED YOU—AND YOU NEED THEM

Absent fathering is hard work. You have to sort out a lot of feelings, you have to make a lot of adjustments, you have to schedule your time with your children. At times, you may wonder, "Is it worth all this trouble? Do the kids really need to spend time with me every other weekend? Am I helping them by maintaining a regular visitation routine, or am I intruding on their lives?" Some fathers fall into the trap of thinking, "The kids need their mother, but they don't really need me all that much. An absent father is just a useless appendage."

Wrong! Your fathering role *is* worth every ounce of effort you put into it. Cherish and preserve that role, because your kids really *do* need you. And what's more, you need them.

Even an infant needs a father. Babies grow and learn from the physical contact they receive. The touch and look and sound of a father is different from that of a mother. Mom cradles and cuddles a child, but it is Dad who rides the child on his back and teaches him the meaning of the word "Da-Da." A father provides a variety of experience and stimulation to a learning, growing infant that a mother can't supply.

As the child grows, his or her need for a father increases. A father is a model of strength, wisdom, and masculine identity to a young child. His big, strong hand is the perfect enclosure for the tiny, tentative hand of a toddler. He is the one the preschooler goes to for answers about his world: Why is the sky blue? If God made me, who made God? Why did my goldfish die? Am I going to die too? A child relies on Dad to tell him what is right, what is wrong, and how to feel safe and secure.

The school-age or adolescent child needs a father to help him or her become aware of feelings and values. When a father is open about what he feels, his children learn how to accept their own feelings by observing his example. They watch how he responds to life, and they learn how a man of mature character deals with problems, pain, and difficult issues. As they watch, they absorb his values and spiritual strength.

Boys need fathers to model healthy masculine self-esteem and to instruct them in what it means to be a man. Girls need fathers to affirm their femininity and their self-worth. Fathers give counsel, protection, and support to children who are going through the turbulent, erratic stage of adolescence. They give experienced advice on matters ranging from money, dating, and car repair to such weighty matters as choosing a career and the meaning of life.

A child even needs a father when childhood is past, when he or she is ready to launch into full-fledged adulthood. That adult child will always want a father's friendship. He or she will always want to hear a father's stories and memories and counsel. A father's arm around the shoulders, a word of affirmation, an expression such as, "I'm so proud of you," can mean so much when that grown child graduates or earns that doctorate or launches a new business or makes that father a grandfather.

Your child will always need you.

And you will always need that child.

Fathers give so much to their children, but they also get so much back in return. Children enhance a father's inner being, making him more of a man, more of a human *soul* than he would be if he were alone in the world. Watching your child—your own flesh and blood—come into the world, watching that child grow, seeing his or her potential unfold, encouraging that child to compete and do well in the world, sharing that child's joys, wiping that child's tears, giving love and receiving love in return: these are the experiences which give richness and scope and meaning to a man's life.

Do your children need you? Do they want you to be a part of their lives, even after the divorce? Yes! They definitely need you.

And you need them.

It's hard being an absent father. It's harder than you ever imagined. But it's worth it. And you can do it. Even though you are a visiting father, you can still be an effective and involved father. It may be the toughest job you'll ever have—but it's also the most rewarding.

In the next chapter, we will look at ways to keep your life on an even keel while you are recovering from the trauma of divorce.

Chapter/10

LOOK
BEFORE
YOU LEAP

T hey called him "Steady Eddie." He was an accountant, a family man, and he drove a sensible Ford sedan. His other car was a station wagon.

But after his divorce, "Steady Eddie" began to wobble—big time. It started with his new wardrobe—loud sport coats and even louder ties—and he topped it all off with a very bad, very obvious toupee. He sold his sensible Ford and bought a cherry-red Porsche 911 Targa (and racked up two speeding tickets within a week). The first time he picked up the kids in the new car, he laid rubber in the driveway. Amanda, age 8, thought it was fun. Marc, age 14, sank down in the bucket seat, hoping none of his friends saw.

Eddie took his kids to his apartment (he called it his "bachelor pad") and unveiled his new lifestyle. It took a while for the kids to accept what they saw.

"Is that really a lava lamp, Dad?" asked his son Marc.

"Yeah, isn't it great? And look at this."

Eddie strode to the chrome and black monster stereo that covered one wall. He pressed a button labeled POWER, and the face of the stereo lit up like a Christmas tree. A bass hum rattled the windows.

"What do you guys want to hear?" asked Eddie, picking up a stack of compact discs. "I've got rock, rap, heavy-metal—"

"But, Dad," said Marc, "you like John Denver and Barry Manilow."

"That was the *old* Eddie. The *new* Eddie grooves to Michael Jackson and Madonna and—"

"'Grooves'?" Amanda asked quizzically.

"—and Paula Abdul and Hammer."

"What does 'grooves' mean?" Amanda asked again.

"Just listen to this." Eddie put on a CD and began bobbing his head to the music. "Isn't that cool?"

Amanda giggled. She thought her daddy was being funny. Marc shook his head. He knew old Dad was just plain pathetic. He had never been more embarrassed in his life.

Whatever happened to "Steady Eddie"?

SUDDEN LIFE CHANGES

When a man gets hit by a major emotional trauma such as divorce, he will sometimes try to cope with it by making sweeping changes in his life. He may:

- Change his lifestyle or image.
- Change the way he dresses.
- Trade the old clunker for a red-hot sports car.
- Leave the city or the state for another job.
- Buy a new, high-powered video or stereo system.
- Become sexually promiscuous.
- Jump into a new romantic relationship.

The reason a recently divorced man sometimes makes sudden, often foolish life changes is that he is trying to short-circuit the healing process by inventing a "new self," separate from the "old self" who was wounded by the trauma of divorce. In his desperation to leave his pain behind, he attempts to redefine himself, to deny the person he used to be. The people around this poor guy will often shake their heads and talk behind his back about how he's going through "mid-life crisis."

Why do we men often fall into the trap of making sudden, unwise changes in our lives? Part of the problem is the male mind-set, which says, "Got a problem? Just fix it." If we're unhappy, we grab something that will make us happy again: a new relationship, a new lifestyle, a new "toy" (car, stereo, casual romance). Got a crisis? No problem. Grab a quick solution and feel better fast!

THE PERFECT SETUP FOR GUILT

A surprising number of men will, after a separation or divorce, suddenly stop being involved with their kids. Why would any father do that? Perhaps because he feels guilty about the divorce and can't face his kids. Or perhaps he is trying to redefine himself in a new "bachelor" role, and children are just not part of the "bachelor" lifestyle. Whatever his reason, the man who abandons his kids is doing harm to them—and to himself.

Divorce provides the perfect setup for a lifetime of guilt. Many men, to put it mildly, don't do their best thinking during the breakup of a marriage. Some make choices that they later regret. We have counseled numerous men in their forties, fifties, or sixties who look back with intense remorse on the way they treated their children in the wake of separation and divorce. "I abandoned my kids years ago," they say, "and all those years are lost. Now the kids hate me. All the pleadings and apologies in the world won't change that."

If you abandon your kids now, you can count on one thing: You will have a burden of unfinished business on your back for years to come. You can move to the other side of the planet, remarry a dozen times, change your career a hundred times, but there is one thing you can't change: the knowledge that there are kids out there somewhere, and you have cut them right out of your life.

So what do you do if your pain is so intense you simply have to put some distance between yourself and the old family system? You do it in such a way that you can allow the relationship with your children to continue at some level. Write letters. Make phone calls.

Don't leave your children to wonder why you don't love them anymore. Don't make them think you have divorced them as well as their mother. Find some way to maintain contact with your kids—for your sake as well as theirs.

REMARRY IN HASTE, REPENT IN LEISURE

Burt was married for nine years and was the father of two children. Throughout his marriage to Eileen, he often caught her flirting with other men. Eileen was an active church-goer, a member of the choir, and she absolutely adored her little children—but she was also a terrible flirt. Because his job often took him away from home for days at a time, Burt suspected she was having an affair behind his back, but he never had any proof.

One day, Burt arrived home a day early from a business trip. Suddenly, he had proof. Boy, did he ever have proof!

Burt divorced his wife and went into a deep depression for about two months.

Then Burt met Candy. Candy had been divorced numerous times before. "I guess I just never met the right man," was her explanation. Warning bells should have been screaming inside Burt's brain—but if they did, he just turned them off. Burt was in love.

It was a whirlwind courtship. Two months after they met, Burt and Candy were married. It was a lavish wedding (Burt took out a personal loan to pay for it).

In Burt's mind, the relationship couldn't have been more perfect. Candy was a sweet, charming, petite blonde (much like Eileen, in fact). She was also a church-goer who enjoyed singing in the choir (Burt admired spiritual sensitivity in a woman). Sure, Candy had a tendency to be sweet and charming around other men, but Burt knew that this time he had found the woman he was destined to marry all along. It was just meant to be!

The marriage lasted eleven months (considerably less time than the fifteen years he's going to spend paying off the wedding). The fact is, he's paying for that wedding in more ways than one.

As it turns out, this divorce, like all of Candy's previous divorces, was the result of her infidelity. Burt was left stunned and bewildered and wondering how he could have been so wrong—*twice!*

One of the most common and disastrous mistakes we see men make is the mistake Burt made: jumping right into a second relationship before completely grieving the first. In the process, they not only make themselves miserable, but they usually make some poor woman miserable as well! What causes so many men to take the plunge again, while their heads are still reeling from the previous marriage?

Here again, systems theory offers some profound insights. A man who has just gone through a divorce is hurting, in large part because he has just exited from his family system. To "fix" the situation and to erase the memory of his ex-wife, he may try to install a new romantic interest as soon as possible. But installing a woman in your life is not like installing a new light bulb. There is no "quick fix" to the hurt of divorce. And jumping into a new relationship while you're still "on the rebound" is worse than a "quick fix." It's usually an outright disaster.

On a conscious level, the man who leaps into a new relationship probably thinks he is looking for a "change." On an unconscious level, however, he doesn't want real change at all. The "change" he is reaching for in the form of a new woman to love is actually an attempt to restore the old system. Deep down, he is not looking for a *new* and *different* wife, but a *replacement* wife. He is operating on the basis of an unconscious compulsion to put things back the way they were, and this poor guy is going to get himself into a world of trouble!

It is not uncommon for a remarried husband to tell his new wife how to dress, how to act, and how to color and style her hair—all so that she will more closely resemble his ex-wife. He doesn't realize what he's doing, but on an unconscious level, he is trying to "fix" the new system so it conforms to the old system. Obviously, no woman is going to appreciate being cast in the role of "stand-in" for Wife Number One.

We have also seen the opposite (and equally destructive) situation: husband becomes phobic toward anything that reminds him of his ex-wife. If his new love interest happens to wear a dress or make a remark that reminds him of his first wife, he goes ballistic. When Wife Number Two gets fed up with having to wrestle with the ghost of Wife Number One, the relationship tends to dissolve very quickly.

The moral of the story of Burt, Elaine, and Candy is the same moral we could attach to story after story we have heard in our counseling practices: remarry in haste, repent in leisure.

GETTING AN EMOTIONAL DIVORCE

You may have already made Burt's mistake: You jumped out of one relationship and right into another. Now you're thinking, "What have I done?!"

Just sit tight. You may have gotten off to a rocky start by remarrying before you were emotionally ready, but you can still make the new relationship work. Listen to the story of one of the authors, Van Jones, and you'll see how:

"The Rookie"

"I can speak to the problem of making big life changes early in the divorce process," says Van. "I remarried eleven months after the breakup of a seventeen-year marriage. I started dating Ibby (that's short for Elizabeth) the same month the divorce became final. I felt ready, but the fact is—and an army of psychologists and marriage counselors will attest to this—a guy who's freshly divorced is at least two years from being ready for a new relationship. I had grieved my loss; I had gotten support and counseling. But there was one thing I didn't have: an emotional divorce.

"A legal divorce is one thing. The judge bangs a gavel and issues a decree, you get a piece of paper, and the marriage is over, right? Wrong! That's just the beginning of the divorce process. It takes time and work to get an emotional divorce. I hadn't taken the time, and I hadn't done the work."

How do you know when you've gotten an emotional divorce from your first wife? You'll know you're emotionally divorced from her when you can think about her without feeling anger. You'll know you're emotionally divorced when you no longer try to get back at her or when you no longer try to please her. You'll know you're emotionally divorced when you no longer care who she's going out with or even who she's marrying. You'll know you're emotionally divorced when your behavior is no longer triggered by her behavior, when her behavior loses the power to affect you emotionally. You'll know you're emotionally divorced when you don't think about her on a regular basis.

"An emotional divorce doesn't take place in a few months," says Van. "That's just not enough time to clear your head from the emotional turmoil of the divorce. In my case, there was still a lot of denial going on, plus a lot of anger, hurt, and other emotions.

"When Ibby and I were dating, she jokingly called me 'The Rookie,' because I was so new to this divorce thing. She had been divorced for three years and had made a lot of emotional progress that I hadn't even started yet. She told me, 'I shouldn't get involved with a rookie, but this feels right.' In this case, we got lucky.

"I was lucky, first of all, that Ibby has the kind of character she has. She's patient, understanding, courageous, and calm in a crisis. There were a lot of external stresses on our relationship in the first few years, stresses that are normal in any second marriage, yet which test the durability of a relationship. That's why the divorce rate among remarriages is greater than 60 percent. Some couples crumble under stress. Others pull together. Fortunately, Ibby and I pulled together through the stresses instead of pulling apart. We were happy together, but there were a lot of tough times, times when we just felt our lives were out of control. After a few years, things settled down, and we were able to relax and enjoy our relationship a lot more.

"It took time to work through my emotional divorce. I would recommend that people work through their divorce issues for at least a year or two before getting into a new relationship—and some marriage and divorce experts, such as Jim Smoke, recommend a minimum of three years. I didn't wait that long, so it took me longer than it should have to resolve my issues and get an emotional divorce. I was much more absorbed in building my new relationship than in resolving past issues. Jumping into a new relationship too soon almost always hinders the process of divorce recovery, of grieving your losses, of putting your life back in order.

"Still, once you are in that situation, you don't have to despair. There are things you can do to make the relationship work. The first and most obvious step is for both of you, husband and wife, to get some good marital counseling, or better yet, *pre*marital counseling if you haven't already tied the knot.

"Some friends of mine who had been through divorce and remarriage encouraged Ibby and me to get counseling—but we didn't take their advice. After all, I'm a professional counselor, so I should see all the pitfalls before we fall into them, right? No, it doesn't work that way. After all, who has a better view of the lay of the land: the guy who's flying over the terrain in an airplane or the guy who's picking his way over the rocks at the bottom of the ravine? The guy with the aerial view, of course. Remarriage is one of those situations where the people who are down in the depths of it can't see their way as well as somebody who is outside it and can be more objective. That's why counselors can be so helpful.

"But I didn't think Ibby and the kids and I needed counseling. I figured, 'Hey, I'm in the field, I understand these issues.' As it turned out, the fact that I am a trained family counselor doesn't mean that I didn't need a counselor myself. It means that I, of all people, should have known better than to try to do this without professional help. Ibby and I could have saved a lot of time and grief if we had spent some time with a therapist, sorting out our feelings and our issues.

"The second step toward making the relationship work: communicate. Be very honest and open about your feelings. Now, to a lot of people, honesty means blowing out your anger right in someone's face. But no, you can be honest and open without destroying the other person. If you have trouble communicating with your new wife, then see a counselor. That's the counselor's job: to help you acquire the skills so that you and your wife can communicate with each other in a way that is both honest and mutually supportive.

"Third: make a commitment to treat stresses and problems as an external threat, not an issue between you and your wife. When life gets tough, don't turn on your wife and treat her as the enemy. Don't take out your frustration on her. Join forces with her, pull together, agree to beat those problems together.

"Fourth: make your new relationship your Number One priority. Your job, your kids, your leisure pursuits, your church, everything has to be secondary. Your focus must be on making your marriage work. Don't think of it as an either/or proposition—'Either I have to focus on my relationship with my kids, or I have to focus on my relationship with my wife.' If you make a go of your marriage, then your kids, your work, your church, and every other facet of your life will ultimately benefit."

How Dad's Sudden New Romance Affects the Children

When absent Dad falls in love, he rarely takes into account the profound effect his dating and remarriage are likely to have on his children. After all, the children are still on an emotional roller coaster too.

Van talks about the effect his remarriage had on his own son and daughter. "After my divorce," he recalls, "I was living in an apartment, and my children would come to visit every other weekend. I was dating Ibby fairly exclusively from January until we married in October, and, though I didn't fully comprehend it at the time, that was hard on my children, who were still reeling from the divorce. Their world was torn in two, and they had to deal with some very confusing loyalty issues. The pain my kids were going through showed in their behavior, in their anger, and in their schoolwork. But I didn't read the signs very well.

"On one level, my transition into a new marriage went fairly smoothly. I was getting my needs met in the new relationship, and that was where my focus tended to be. I was happy, and I thought we were all happy, including my children.

"Both of them seemed to be handling it just fine. They took part in the wedding. My daughter gave a toast at our rehearsal dinner that was absolutely beautiful. I'll never forget that. I realize now that it must have been very difficult for her.

"As I look back at the wedding pictures and study the faces of my children in those pictures, they look more like they are going to a funeral than a wedding. It was hard for them, and I didn't appreciate how hard it must have been until several years later."

What would Van do differently if he had it to do over again? "I would marry Ibby again in a New York minute! But, you see, that's the dilemma of stepfamily life: what is a positive event for one member of the family may not be a positive event for another. If you can't live in that kind of ambiguity, don't try it.

"If I had it to do over again, I would be more solicitous of my children's feelings. I would open the subject of divided loyalties and ask them how they would feel if I married again. And I would bring my children into at least one session with a counselor, so that we could explore the special issues a child has to deal with when a parent remarries.

"Being more open with the kids would not have changed my decision to remarry, but it probably would have been helpful to them to have talked more about it. As it worked out, both of my children have been supportive of the new relationship and quickly grew to appreciate Ibby as I did.

"I might also slow down, move the wedding plans back a bit, just to give my kids and Ibby's kids time to get used to the idea, time to work through some issues. And I would slow down to give myself enough time to get my own emotional divorce, to get my emotional life in order before I make such an important commitment to another person."

And that's our counsel to you, if you are about to jump from a "just divorced" to "just remarried" status: slow down. Look—take a good hard look—before you leap into a new relationship. Give yourself, and your children, a chance to work through your issues and clean out any residue from your divorce. Pray and ask God for wisdom, discernment, and clear insight into your own feelings and motivations. Ask yourself some crucial questions: Are you unconsciously trying to restore the old system and replace your ex-wife? Are you trying to turn off the pain and loneliness of your divorce? Or have you, like Van, really found someone who is a positive complement to your personality, your interests, your values, and your goals?

The reasons we *think* we do what we do are often not the *real* motivations behind our behavior. The power of denial is strong. So is the power of the old system, which continually tries to reassert itself through our unconscious drives and motivations. There is probably no single area of our lives where we are more prone to self-deception than the area of love and marriage.

"LOOK BEFORE YOU LEAP": THREE KEY PRINCIPLES

Here are some suggestions to guide you through the process of getting an emotional divorce. The following principles relate not only to "leaping" into remarriage, but to "leaping" into any sudden life change.

Make a Commitment

Make an agreement with yourself not to make any sudden changes in your life. Commit to setting aside a predetermined period of your life, preferably a year or more, during which you will grieve the breakup of your marriage and go through the stages of loss. Remind yourself that you are vulnerable right now, and make a pact with yourself that you will not trust any impulses to make major changes in your life. Ask a close, trusted friend or counselor to hold you accountable to keep this commitment. Then ask that person to check in with you on a regular basis to make sure you are keeping your commitment to yourself. If you really feel that a major change, such as a relocation, a lifestyle change, or a new relationship, is in your best interests, then get the counsel of several honest, objective friends and a therapist before jumping into such changes.

Cultivate Friendships

In the aftermath of divorce, one of our greatest enemies is isolation. Many of the factors which compel us to make sudden, unwise changes in our lives are the direct result of isolation: feelings of loneliness, feelings of impatience.

The best way to break the grip of isolation is to cultivate a network of friendships, especially friendships with other men who understand what we are going through. We all need friends we can talk to and be honest with. We all need someone we can go to and say, "Give it to me straight. Am I making a mistake? Am I making a fool of myself?"

Don't hesitate to initiate contact with friends, "What are you doing tonight? Why don't we get together for a movie or just to kick back and talk?" This advice probably goes against the natural tendency of a man who is going through a divorce. It's easy to withdraw from friends at a time like this—and, unfortunately, it's not unusual for friends to withdraw from us. They may not know what to say or what to do. They may not understand how we are hurting. That's why, in a crisis like divorce, the very support systems we need most often fall away.

Harrison was raised in the church and had always been a very involved church member. But after his divorce, he was amazed at how the people he had been in fellowship with for years suddenly disappeared. "If I had been dealing with death or an illness," he told us, "my church friends would have been right there. But church people often don't know how to respond to a divorce. After my divorce, none of my friends from church called. The minister called just once and that was to try to talk Melanie and me out of the divorce. My friends at work helped me get through the divorce process more than my church friends."

When friends withdraw from you, it reinforces the notion that divorce must be an unforgivable sin. It makes the divorced person feel embarrassed and humiliated. But the truth is that most people don't really view you as "bad" because you are divorced. They simply don't know how to respond to you, so they stay away, they say nothing. That's why you may need to initiate contact with people in order to punch through this period of isolation. You don't need a lot of friends right now—just a few dependable friends who will affirm you and buoy you up through the divorce process.

"I found I had to learn to let people be supportive," Harrison told us. "Even though I felt like dropping down a hole and pulling the hole in after me, I had to learn to let people into my life.

"My friends from the office made the whole transition go a lot easier for me. They knew how hard it was for me to move out of my big house in the 'burbs and into a little apartment. They threw a party for me and brought me gifts like food, furnishings, and decorations. They were available for me even after the first few weeks. If I had some decisions or changes to make, I could go to these guys and take a reality check. They saved me from some really dumb mistakes during a time I wasn't thinking too clearly.

"If there is one thing I would do over again about my divorce, I would spend more time with my friends and less time alone in my apartment, feeling sorry for myself."

Good friends are like mirrors. They reflect reality back to us: the reality of our circumstances and the reality of ourselves. Good friends guard us against loneliness, which is one of the chief causes of hasty, disastrous decision-making. A good friend may be just what we need to show us how stupid we look driving that red Porsche.

Friends don't let friends go off the deep end.

Maintain Contact with God

God never intended that a man's behavior should be driven by guilt, shame, or any other negative emotion. Behavior that is motivated by such emotions is unhealthy behavior. Negative emotions often drive men to make sudden, unwise life changes. A man feels guilty, so he withdraws from his children. He feels ashamed, so he tries to re-invent himself as an entirely new person. He feels lonely and anxious, so he jumps right into a new relationship.

There is a spiritual reason why some men leap—without looking—into major life changes. "If I can just make a big enough change on the outside," he thinks, "maybe I can be absolved of the guilt, or the disgrace, or the pain I carry from the divorce." In some ways, it's as if he is trying to create an artificial "born again" experience. He is trying to redefine himself on the outside instead of transforming himself from within.

The fact is, we all need a *real* "born again" experience, not just an artificial one. We need an authentic change from within, not just a cosmetic makeover. We need to become what the Bible calls "a new creation."[1] When we experience an authentic inner change and commit ourselves to God through Jesus Christ, we no longer have to re-invent ourselves. We can simply accept ourselves as God has accepted us. Instead of making artificial, external changes in our image, we become wiser, stronger, more mature human beings through and through.

We would encourage you to make contact with God through prayer, asking Him to make you a new creation through His Son, Jesus Christ. Ask Him to forgive you for the things you may have done that have contributed to your sense of guilt and shame. Ask Him to enable you to forgive yourself. Pray for the ability to forgive your ex-wife. Ask for wisdom to know what aspects of your life need changing and for patience to endure those aspects of your life that cannot be changed right now.

A helpful prayer for those who are tempted to make sudden and unwise life changes following a divorce or separation is "The Serenity Prayer" of Reinhold Niebuhr:

> God, grant me the serenity
> to accept the things I cannot change,
> the courage to change the things I can,
> and the wisdom to know the difference.
>
> Living one day at a time,
> enjoying one moment at a time,
> accepting hardship as a pathway to peace;
> taking, as Jesus did, this sinful world as it is;
> not as I would have it,
> trusting that You will make all things right
> if I surrender to Your will;
> so that I may be reasonably happy in this life
> and supremely happy with You
> forever in the next.
>
> Amen.

Focus on the Needs of Your Children

The first year or so after the divorce is a time when fathers need to be especially sensitive and attentive to their children. If you devote yourself to developing your relationship with your children in the aftermath of your divorce, you will be less likely to devote yourself to developing romantic relationships.

It is in your children's best interests, and ultimately, it is in your best interest that you concentrate your attention and devotion on your children. When you jump into a new romantic relationship, you may well be running from the feelings and issues that have been stirred up by your divorce. Romantic entanglements often hinder clear thinking. But when you move deeper into the relationship with your children, you get in touch with the true feelings and issues within yourself and your children, and your thinking becomes more coherent and reality-based.

TAKE YOUR TIME

You've got the rest of your life ahead of you—and it can be a great life if you don't blow it by jumping into another disastrous relationship.

Take as much time as you need to clear your head and get your life back together. Get an emotional divorce. Get a handle on the issues that drive your behavior. Finish your unfinished business.

Talk to your closest friends. Talk to your pastor. Talk to a therapist. Get some good objective insight into the directions you are contemplating.

Why rush things?

You're going to do just fine if you take a good hard look at your life—

And take your time.

Someday, love may come around again and you may remarry. In the next chapter, we will examine the ways remarriage affects your role as a visiting father to your biological children.

Chapter/11

WHEN YOU REMARRY

Second marriages," says Ken Parker, "are filled with all kinds of surprises. When I entered my second marriage, I had been divorced for about three years. I was used to living the bachelor life, accounting to no one, ordering my life and home exactly as I pleased. When I married Mary Jo, I gave up my apartment and moved into the home she and her two children were already living in. I didn't understand that I was entering a system that was already up and running—and many of the customs, rules, and eccentricities of that system were the exact opposite of what I was used to. Some examples:

"Shortly after I moved in, I tried to use the phone. It was an old rotary phone, the kind where you stick your finger in the holes and spin the dial around. Well, Mary Jo's phone didn't have a finger stop (the little metal piece that stops your finger so the number can be entered). The first time I used it, I spun that dial like the 'Wheel of Fortune.' I asked her, 'Where's the whatchamacallit?' She said, 'Oh, that broke off years ago. Just stop your finger where the whatcha-macallit's supposed to be and it'll work fine.' I said, 'Well, why don't you get the phone fixed? Or junk it and get a touch-tone phone?' She said, 'It's a perfectly good phone. You can make calls on it. You can receive calls on it. It does exactly what a phone is supposed to do. You just have to learn how to use it.'

"Mornings were another big adjustment. I was used to having the bathroom whenever I wanted, having a quiet cup of coffee with breakfast, having a nice orderly morning. When I became part of Mary Jo's family system, I couldn't get into the bathroom in the morning, and the kids were rushing around and getting ready for school, yelling, 'Where's my stuff?' It was just the normal routine most families go through every day, but for me it was total chaos!

"Another adjustment: Years before I moved in (probably around the time the phone broke) someone had put salt in the pepper shaker and pepper in the salt shaker. And every time the shakers needed filling, they just added more salt to the pepper shaker and vice versa. I tried to change that, but I eventually just gave up.

"And then there was the car. I had a little VW, Mary Jo had a big Plymouth. The first time I took her car on the highway and got it up to around 55, the car started shimmying and shaking all over the road. I said, 'Ohmigosh, we've got trouble!' Mary Jo said, 'What do you mean?' I said, 'Don't you feel that? This car's about to rattle apart!' And she said, 'Oh, that! It always does that. You just have to get used to it.' Well, the next week I took the car into the shop and spent five hundred dollars on a front-end job.

"Mary Jo and I had to make a lot of adjustments to keep our marriage working. I tend to be an obsessive-compulsive neatness nut. I like to have everything scheduled, put in its place, and in perfect working order. The four of us went through a period of getting used to each other, a period of settling in. We clashed and hashed things out, and we made our adjustments.

"I learned to get used to a certain amount of happy chaos, a couple of noisy kids, and a phone without a whatchamacallit. It could be frustrating at times, but mostly it was an adventure. Learning to fit into a new family system is a challenge, and if you approach it as a challenge, you can have a lot of fun along the way."

THE THREE LEVELS OF ASSIMILATION

In this chapter, we will explore the adventure of remarriage in three distinct but interlocking dimensions. First, we will look at the three levels you must negotiate in order to be fully assimilated into the new family system. Second, we will look at the effect your remarriage has on your children and on your role as their absent father. Third, we will put these first two dimensions together and show you how you can successfully juggle these two roles: effective biological father to the children of your first marriage and (assuming you marry a woman with children of her own) effective stepfather in your second marriage.

Most people entering a second marriage have no idea what they're getting into. We're not saying remarriage is a disaster, but it is a different experience from a first marriage, especially when one or both spouses has children from a former marriage. Remarriage involves dynamics, issues, and stresses that never arose the first time around.

The first thing to understand about remarriage is that the Brady Bunch scenario is a myth. This fantasy of Mom and Dad coming together with their respective broods and instantly becoming one big happy family just doesn't happen in real life. There is a three-level process by which Dad becomes included in the new family system:

Level 1: Being Tested;
Level 2: Making Adjustments; and
Level 3: Achieving Acceptance.

If Dad thinks he can move right in and skip Levels 1 and 2, he will probably never get to Level 3. Let's look at each level in turn:

Level 1: Being Tested

When you remarry, it is common to find yourself being tested by the children of your new family system. This can be a very frustrating and bewildering experience. "Hey, I'm a nice guy," you may say, "I've gone out of my way to be friendly to these kids, yet they still won't accept me! What am I doing wrong?"

You may not be doing anything wrong. From a systems perspective, it is perfectly natural that you will be tested by the new system before you are accepted by it. Here's how it works:

Before you even entered the picture, your new wife and her children were a family system. Together, they have gone through the trauma of either divorce or bereavement, and they have formed their own family system without their original dad. They have been functioning for months or years without a man around the house. Everyone knows his or her role and operates on a common set of rules, values, and expectations.

Suddenly Mom remarries, and now the system must accommodate another person—you. And there is great resistance to that. It's to be expected that you will be treated as an intruder, at least at first, because from a systems perspective that is exactly what you are. The natural inclination of the system is to right itself, to restore itself as it was, and this means the system will seek to expel, not embrace, the newcomer. The unspoken question that will continually arise in the first weeks and months after the wedding is this: *Where does this new guy fit in?*

"Early in my second marriage," recalls Van Jones, "I *really* felt like an intruder. I took some of Mom's time away from the kids, especially the youngest, who was eight at the time. She resented that, and she also struggled with loyalty to her father. It's a very common situation: in her mind, if she liked me, she was being disloyal to her dad. So for the testing period of our relationship, she gave me the cold shoulder a lot.

"The two older kids were adolescents, so they had their own business, their own friends, and fewer problems accepting me than the youngest did. Still, they put me to the test as well. With them, I was the 'Invisible Stepfather'—a very common syndrome. They didn't quite know what to do with me, so they treated me as if I wasn't there. I would walk into the room and there was no acknowledgment, no hello, not even a glance in my direction. They directed all conversation to their mother.

"Should I resent it? No, this is a normal reaction. It felt awkward at the time, but I understood. There I was, coming into their system. They didn't ask me to be their stepfather. They didn't necessarily want their mother remarried. It was a very cozy, familiar arrangement before I came in. When I entered, it was very threatening and unfamiliar. I was like a houseguest who wouldn't go home. They didn't know what to do or how to include me because I had not been part of their system before."

Even your new wife, who is romantically attached to you, may at times find herself unconsciously torn between wanting to incorporate you into the system and wanting to resist your "intrusion" into the system. Why? Well, just look at what she has gone through in the past few years as a single mom: she has learned that she can parent on her own, and she may take justifiable pride in her autonomy. She has gained inner strength and confidence from being on her own—and now *you* come along! She loves you, but you are upsetting the self-contained little world she has been building with her children. She may not *consciously* resent you, but at an unconscious level she may sense that you are encroaching on her selfhood and on her turf—and this unconscious resentment may come out in unexpected behavior and conflict.

You will feel like an intruder when you look at the photo album and see the Christmas and vacation pictures of your wife, her kids, and *him*. You'll see all kinds of reminders, *ghosts* of the man who preceded you in that family system. At times, you'll be reminded you weren't there when your stepchildren were born, when a tradition was started, or when the events in that funny story took place.

Until you have built some history in this family system, you will feel like an outsider. It will take time before that feeling goes away. It's a testing period, a time when your stepchildren, and to a lesser degree, your wife, will tend to place you on probation. But give it time, and eventually the testing period will give way to a new level of relating to the other members of your new family system.

Level 2: Making Adjustments

In time, the system settles down. Your stepchildren have figured out that you are here to stay and that they have to deal with you. You have persisted in being patient, cordial, and interested in their needs. You have begun to penetrate the icy protective shell they have encased themselves in. They haven't quite accepted you, but at least you are no longer the "Invisible Stepfather." You have begun the task of making adjustments and working through issues with your new wife and her children. Issues such as:

Negotiation of Roles and Relationships. Having passed the testing stage, you are figuring out where you fit in and what's expected of you. You've discovered that becoming an instant family is hard work. Roles have to be sorted out and relationships have to be negotiated. You find yourself weighing each situation in the light of such questions as, "How much parenting should I do? Should I step in? Should I step back? Will my actions be received as the involvement of a parent—or the intrusion of an outsider?"

"In the 'Making Adjustments' level of my present marriage," says Van, "we didn't have a lot of open conflict—just the usual stressors and friction. The fact is, a little more open conflict might have been helpful because everyone in the family tended not to talk about what was going on. A couple who had gone through it all before gave us some good advice, but we didn't take it. They said, 'If you don't do anything else, go to counseling with the entire family. There are so many issues involved in bringing a family together that you really need to work it through with an objective third party.'

"Well, my wife and I were so much in love that we figured we didn't need counseling. We were lucky. It all turned out okay. We have a great family, but we could have made the adjustments faster, and more effectively, with the help of a counselor."

Some tips for successfully negotiating roles and relationships in the new system:

Give the system—Mom and stepkids—time to adjust to you. Your entrance into their world will almost certainly stir up old insecurities and feelings of loss in the children. Go slowly, and give them time to get used to you. Give them reassurances, and try to disturb the functioning of their system as little as possible. Make changes slowly and gradually.

Tune in to your stepchildren's feelings. Be aware that they may not be ready to accept their mother's remarriage. Your entrance into their system may be a shattering disruption to their reconciliation fantasies. Sometimes a child uses obnoxious behavior in an attempt to break up your marriage and restore biological father to the picture. Try to understand that this behavior is rooted in the child's emotional pain, not in true hatred for you.

Talk openly with your new wife about what your role should be. Keep the lines of communication humming. Avoid burying issues. Listen carefully and sympathetically to her feelings and issues. If necessary, draw her out. Find out what she expects of you, then either try to accommodate yourself to those expectations or negotiate with her to modify her expectations.

Keep the romance alive. Carefully guard and nurture your role as your wife's husband and lover. If your stepchildren seem to resent open affection between you and their mother, then be discreet at first—but be sure to find special ways to keep the honeymoon going on a day-by-day basis: behind the bedroom door, on dates, and in all the private moments you share together. A good marriage enrichment group is a wonderful place to get ideas on making your relationship even better!

Don't let conflict throw you. Most people think that relationships are built out of Kodak moments and warm fuzzies—and there is certainly something to be said for the value of fond memories. Yet some of the most valuable times of relationship-building come out of the conflict and crises of the "settling in" process. If those scraps, skirmishes, and scrimmages are faced honestly and with a genuine concern for the best interests of everyone in the system, they can actually be the catalyst to bring you and your new family closer together.

For the first year or two, the people in the system live together but often do not relate to each other on a real basis. Conflict and crises drive people in the system to deal with each other and to be honest with each other—and that's a basis upon which you can build a relationship.

Family rules, traditions, and customs. For the first year or two, you will find yourself continually stubbing your toe on a lot of rites and rules of your new family system. These unspoken traditions have been in place so long that they are just assumed to be understood by all the members of the system. Your wife and stepchildren may forget that you weren't around when the "rule book" was written.

Children (being the outspoken and tactless critics that they are) will not hesitate to say, "That's not the way my daddy did it," or, "You're doing it all wrong," or, "You're not my daddy. I don't want *you* to do it." Until you learn the ropes, you will be continually reminded that you're the new kid on the block.

Take time to familarize yourself with the unwritten "rule book" of the family. Be observant, and try to accommodate yourself to the unspoken rules of the house. Notice the small things: Does the toilet paper go over the roll or under? Is everyone expected to put their own plate in the dishwasher after dinner? When putting away the groceries, do all the cereal boxes go on the top shelf and all the cans on the second shelf?

Don't be too quick to write your own rules into that "rule book" by imposing a new curfew, dictating the amount and kinds of entertainment the children may watch, criticizing their dress and hairstyle, correcting their behavior, or tinkering with their traditions.

"The first year of my present marriage," says Van, "I was constantly having to say to myself, 'Van, you're on different turf now. You have to adjust.' Sometimes our different ways of doing things clashed. Ultimately the burden was on me to be patient, to respect their traditions, and to gradually build some new traditions with my new family.

"For example, the first time we put up a Christmas tree as a new family, I brought a box of ornaments into the living room. These ornaments had been part of my Christmas tradition. But Ibby and her kids had their ornaments and traditions too. There wasn't room on that tree for everybody's ornaments, so somebody had to give a little. I wanted to respect the feelings and traditions of Ibby and the children, so that somebody was me. Family traditions run deep, and it's hard for people to give up or change those traditions. So it was awkward at first as we made these and other adjustments, but over the years we have built our own history and our own traditions together. If you are patient and give it time, it will happen."

Feelings. One of the most difficult adjustments to be made in your new family is in the area of feelings. Divorce tends to generate continual periods of emotional upheaval that persist on into the new marriage. You may continue to experience conflict with your ex-wife, while simultaneously becoming embroiled in conflicts with your wife's ex-husband. Your biological children and your stepchildren may not get along well. All of these issues pull and tug at your new family system at a time when you are trying to settle in and build a normal life together.

It's not uncommon for you, as a new husband, to take on your wife's anger toward her ex. In fact, this anger is one of the bonds you share with your wife. You may not know her ex from Adam, yet you may have a built-in dislike for him because of her interpretation of the divorce. Even if her divorce was amicable, you may still encounter some remnants of her unfinished emotional business.

Of course, if you look at this situation objectively, you'll realize the irony of being angry with this guy: if he and your wife had experienced a great relationship, she'd still be married to him instead of to you! Part of your anger toward her ex is the old male territorial response: "This is my mate, and I'm going to take care of her!"

During the first year or two, you may experience so many frustrating encounters with exes, in-laws, and children that you'll begin to wonder if it was really worth it. But after a while, your relationship with your ex-spouse improves (as does your wife's relationship with her ex-spouse), in-laws learn to accept the situation, and kids begin to settle in. Hang in there. You're going to make it.

Another set of feelings you may experience at this time is a sense of divided loyalties. You may feel guilty when you interact with your stepchildren. Understand that it is okay to love your stepchildren. If your involvement with your stepchildren becomes a problem for your own kids, raise the issue, and talk it through with them. Reassure your children that while you can love other people, no one can ever replace them in your affections. And, if necessary, reassure *yourself* of that same fact.

"My own sense of divided loyalties was an issue I had to deal with in my second marriage," says Van. "Part of the problem was that I had not fully grieved the loss of my first family and all that meant to me. I felt such a sense of loss, and even guilt, toward my biological kids that I didn't feel worthy to build a new relationship with my stepkids. It was an issue I had to actively, intentionally work on in the first year or so of my marriage."

Discipline. Here's another tricky area to negotiate during the adjustment period. Your new wife may be eager to unload all the parenting responsibility on you: "I can't handle them! Come in and save my kids before they end up in Juvenile Hall!" She may be completely frazzled from years of single parenting, and her unspoken agenda is to bring in a stepfather who can take over and make everything okay.

Or the reverse situation may be the case: your new wife may be dead-set against letting you share the parenting role: "Just one cross word to my kids and you're dead meat!"

Even the mother who initially wanted you to come in and rule her kids with an iron hand may suddenly transform into a lioness defending her cubs the moment you move to discipline her kids. Does that make sense? Actually, it does—once you understand the emotional dynamics.

Even though you are an *invited* intruder, on your way to becoming a full-fledged member of the family system, you are still likely to be unconsciously viewed as an intruder. When Mom sees you disciplining her kids, the first thought that leaps to her mind is not, "It's so nice to have a man around the house," but, "He's not their father! Who does he think he is, passing judgment on my kids!" The mother-child bond is strong—and any man who inserts himself in the middle of that relationship by assuming the role of disciplinarian should proceed with extreme caution.

Moreover, the children themselves may resist you on the basis that you are not their father. You have not had a chance to establish yourself in that role. It takes time to earn the respect of your stepchildren so that they will accept your authority.

"I've seen men come into a family," says Van, "and really damage relationships. They try to be forceful right away because that's what their wives want, but it just doesn't work.

"In my own case, I tried to establish a solid relationship with the children by being cordial and friendly, by just letting the parenting role grow and evolve over time. I found that the best way to ease into the parenting role was by backing my wife. Instead of trying to discipline the kids myself, I supported her and encouraged the children to respect their mom. Gradually—over a period of about two years—I became more assertive with the children. I need to restate, however, that I was lucky. My stepchildren are quality kids who focused their energy on productive ways to achieve independence.

"To sum up my advice to a newly remarried dad, I would say: Be flexible. Be patient. Respect the family system you have just entered. Don't try to change it, or impose your own style on it. The existing system has purpose and validity. It will incorporate you and include you—but it will do so slowly and on its own terms. If you storm in like you own the place, odds are you're going to bite into a hurricane."

Level 3: Achieving Acceptance

Slowly, over a period of at least a year or two, the adjustments are made. The major issues are worked through. One day it just dawns on you: you have been accepted into the system. You are a member of the family.

Acceptance is a two-way street. You want to be accepted by the system. But you must also accept the system and not just the cozy little system of your wife and her children. The system also consists of grandparents, exes, and in-laws. If you want to be accepted by the system, you have to embrace the system yourself.

"My biggest mistake," Van recalls, "was not understanding how important it was for me to accept the entire system. I tended to build a little fence around our family and say, 'This is our family now.' But Ibby's kids needed grandparents, aunts, and uncles. Intellectually, I understood these people had to be involved, but emotionally it took a while for it to sink in.

"Being a family counselor, you'd think all of this would have come easy for me. But there is a big difference between knowing these principles intellectually and being able to work it through on an emotional level. Counselors are still human beings, and when our own emotions and issues are on the line, it's easy for our book-learning and our counseling experience to go right out the window.

"I was trying to re-create the system from my first family. Unconsciously, I was trying to get my sense of 'family' back by re-creating the familiar little family enclosure I had known in my first family.

"Once I decided to intentionally, aggressively include the extended family in my concept of 'our family,' my relationship with my stepchildren improved dramatically. I would ask them, 'How's your dad doing?' or, 'Tell me about your visit with your grandparents.' Emotionally, that was a big step for me to take.

"Some men take that step sooner than I did. But a lot of men either can't, or won't, take that step. They keep the war going, and that makes life miserable for everyone, including the children. Once you get to acceptance in your own mind, the struggle ceases. Relationships become easier to negotiate. You accept the system, and soon the system accepts you. And that's a great feeling."

HOW YOUR NEW MARRIAGE AFFECTS YOUR CHILDREN

In the first part of this chapter, we talked about what happens when you marry into a new family system. Now we shift focus back to your biological children. Let's consider what your new marriage means to your children:

Your children see you dating and marrying a woman who is not their mother. This woman may also have children of her own. As you move into that new family system, your children see it taking more and more of your time and attention. They worry that this new family system is taking priority over the old family system, that is, *their* family system. Your children will almost certainly find this a threatening development, and more so if your children are harboring any reconciliation fantasies.

The relationship between you and your children is taking a new turn. Roles will have to be re-negotiated. Expectations will have to change. Adjustments will have to be made on both sides.

Ever since the divorce, your children's access to you has been limited to every other weekend or so, but at least it was unimpeded. During visitation, they had your undivided attention. You could spend the whole weekend with them. They didn't have to share you with anyone.

Now, however, your children have to share you with your wife and perhaps with her children. Your children have to redefine their roles. They may feel abandoned, threatened, and jealous. Their world was shaken once in the divorce, and now it is being shaken again, so they may feel a keen sense of loss. Their place in the family system, in the birth order, and in your affections now seems uncertain. Your youngest child, for example, may no longer be the baby in your life, and this may be threatening to that child.

You may see many new and unexpected behaviors emerging in your children: rebellion, attention-getting, angry outbursts, accusations, or withdrawal. The child is hurting and thinking, "Daddy used to be part of my world, my family. He paid attention to me; he affirmed me; I derived a lot of my sense of self-worth and importance from his involvement and affection. Now he's become part of another family. I still see him, but I'm not Number One with him anymore. All the things he did with me he is doing with other children. I've been replaced and abandoned. I'm losing my daddy. I'm losing his love."

Van recalls the first couple of years of his own second marriage. "As I was building a relationship with my stepchildren," he says, "I wondered, 'Is this a problem for my own kids?' Every time I interacted with my stepkids, even when my own children weren't around, I felt like there were two sets of eyes watching me. I sensed that it was an issue with my kids."

Even if your child doesn't articulate all these feelings, these emotions will drive a lot of the child's behavior during the first year or

more of your transition into a new marriage. Though you repeatedly reassure your children that you will always be their Dad and
you will always love them, the first time they see you playing
or demonstrating affection with your stepchildren, they will probably feel threatened. The abandonment fear will rear up like a
monster—and this can create strains not only in your relationship
with your children, but in your new family as well.

Dave learned this the hard way.

"I'm in Your Place Now"

Lanie, Dave's wife, came into her counselor's office feeling emotionally wiped out. "It's my husband's daughter," she said. "Megan
was at our house for the weekend. By the time she left, I was a
wreck. This happens every two weeks, and I'm getting to the point
where I just can't take it anymore!" Lanie proceeded to pour out
her story to the counselor.

It seems that whenever fifteen-year-old Megan comes to visit, she
immediately starts playing manipulative games with Dave, her
father. She occupies all his time. She suggests activities that she and
Dave can do together that exclude Lanie. Whenever Dave's around,
Megan is sweet and gracious to Lanie, offering to help with the
dishes or the cleaning—but when Dave walks away, she turns nasty
and rude to her stepmother.

"Saturday night, the three of us were watching TV together," Lanie told her counselor. "I was sitting next to Dave on the love seat,
and Megan was on the floor. She said, 'Do we have any popcorn?' I
said, 'Sure, I'll go make some.' So I got up and put some popcorn in
the microwave. I came back with the popcorn and found Megan
sitting in *my* place on the loveseat, snuggled up against Dave! And
she was grinning at me, as if to say, 'Too bad for you, I'm in your
place now.'

"Megan knows I like to go to bed around ten, so she just sat there
and waited me out. Finally, I got tired and got up to go to bed.
Dave started to get up to go with me, but Megan tugged on him and
started a conversation—anything to keep him from going to bed
with me. It was so obvious what she was doing, yet Dave didn't

seem to notice. When I tried to talk to him about it later, he acted like I was paranoid, like it was all in my mind.

"Whenever it's just the two of us, Dave is very affectionate. We have a good sex life. But when Megan is in the house—even though her bedroom is downstairs and ours is upstairs, Dave freezes up. He never shows me any affection when Megan is in the house.

"Sunday after church, I was fixing lunch. I had put a roast in the oven before church and it was almost done. I had vegetables on the stove, bread warming in the oven, and I was making the salad. Then, from the next room, I heard Megan say, 'Dad, why don't we go out for pizza!' I groaned. Though I was sure Dave would scotch the idea, it still made me mad. But then Dave walked in and *really* floored me.

"'Megan had a great idea,' he said. 'Let's go out for pizza.' I couldn't believe my ears! I said, 'You're joking! Lunch is almost ready!' He said, 'I know, but Megan doesn't like roast. Pizza's her favorite, and she'll be leaving in a couple of hours. We can reheat the roast for supper. I like it better reheated anyway.' I argued with him, but I lost. The two of them had pizza, and I ate crow.

"I'm tired of competing with Megan for Dave's affection. I've told him repeatedly that he has to give me his allegiance, he has to set limits with his daughter. But he just keeps getting twisted around her little finger. If it doesn't stop soon, I'm going to leave him."

Dave's got big trouble on his hands. Lanie has a right to feel unfairly treated by Megan—and by Dave. He sees Megan as his own flesh-and-blood, and there is a parent-child bond there that causes him to neglect his allegiance to his wife whenever his daughter is around. But Lanie feels no such parent-child bond with Megan. To her, Dave's daughter is the other woman—and a scheming, manipulative other woman at that! So she feels jealous and threatened whenever Megan is around.

Dave is the key to resolving this situation. He may feel he's in the middle, with two women pulling on him, wanting him to dance on a string. He may have a parenting history with Megan, but he owes his allegiance to his new wife. He has to live with her after his daughter goes home.

What's more, it is in his *daughter's* best interests that she resolve the feelings that are causing her to use such destructive tactics. Her behavior is rooted in feelings of insecurity and hurt. If he will take the step of communicating openly with Megan, drawing out her fears and anger, and helping her to feel more secure and loved, then her behavior may settle down, and both Megan and Lanie will feel less threatened.

If not—well, Lanie has made her position clear: "If it doesn't stop soon, I'm going to leave him."

Our advice to Dave: stop indulging and coddling your daughter. Don't let Megan manipulate you. Instead, reassure her of your love. Tell her, "I am your father, and I will always have plenty of room in my heart to love you, no matter who else I choose to love." Remind her that you can love her at the same time you love your new wife. Directly answer and disarm her fear of loss—a fear which many children experience, but few dare to express. Let her know how happy you are to have her visit, but she must understand that her role and your wife's role are not competing relationships, and she should stop trying to compete.

In the next section, Van Jones explains how he dealt with the tension between his role as biological father from the old system and his new roles as husband and stepfather in the system of his second marriage:

Replace Tension and Friction with Understanding

"It's understandable," says Van, "that a father would want to devote his visiting weekends to his biological children. They don't see each other often, so that visitation time is very precious.

"After I remarried, my kids would come to visit and I really tried to make it an inclusive experience. I tried to be with everybody— Ibby, my children, my stepchildren. But the reality is that I still ended up spending most of my time with my biological children. Ibby was very understanding of that and never complained or interfered. There were never any problems or conflicts because of it. But about two years after we were married she told me she sometimes felt twinges of jealousy. It's an issue that naturally arises whenever a remarried father has to juggle these different roles: parent, husband, and stepparent."

This is a common complaint among wives in second marriages. "My husband's children come," they say, "and he's gone. Physically he's there, but he's gone, he's not available to me or my kids. He's completely absorbed in his biological children. He says, 'I've got to get this quality time in! I've got to make the most of every minute!' Okay, I understand that—but can't he include us in his quality time? Aren't we his family too?"

This tension can't be avoided, but it can be disarmed as an issue if you bring it out in the open and talk about it. Talk to your wife. Talk to your stepchildren. Talk to your visiting children. Build understanding around the issue so that there is less tension and friction surrounding it.

CALMING THE FEAR OF LOSS

When you enter a new family system, you will come in under a cloud of fear. Your biological children will be afraid. Your stepchildren will be afraid. Your new wife will be afraid. And you will be feeling some trepidation and anxiety too. What is everybody afraid of? *Loss.* The unspoken question in everyone's mind is, "What am I giving up? What am I going to lose?"

What does your wife have to lose? She's gaining a husband and a stepfather for her children, isn't she? What is she losing? The fact is, she stands to lose a lot. She is losing "the way things used to be." Change is coming into her life, and change can be very threatening.

For example, your children come over for visitation and your new wife fixes sloppy joes for dinner. Her kids always raved about her sloppy joes and never ate less than three helpings. But *your* kids pick at it and shove it around their plates without eating a bit. They're polite, but they simply won't eat it.

"Don't you kids like sloppy joes?" your wife asks.

"Oh, yes, ma'am, we love sloppy joes," your kids reply—then add, "the way our mom makes 'em."

Well, *that* comment scores a big hit with your wife! She may become frustrated and upset—and she may not even understand what it is about a few uneaten platefuls of sloppy joes that makes her so upset. It's not that big a deal, yet it *feels* like a big deal. Why is that?

The answer is found in a systems perspective. She is upset because this new system doesn't function like the *old* system. *Her* kids liked her sloppy joes. *These* kids should like them too. When they don't, it symbolizes to her unconscious mind that the system isn't working the way it's supposed to. The pattern is changed and unfamiliar. She has lost "the way things used to be."

Your remarriage also stirs up a great deal of fear within the children in both systems. Your biological children fear losing your time and affection. Your stepchildren fear losing the comfort and security of the old system and access to their mother.

When you remarry, everybody loses something or fears losing something. These fears and losses have to be dealt with on a continual basis. Here are some tips for dealing with the fear of loss in your children, stepchildren, and new wife:

Be sensitive to behavior and words which indicate this fear. Reassure the people in your life that even though changes are taking place, you are committed to maintaining as many features and traditions of the past as possible. Make it clear that the addition of new relationships does not mean the loss of old relationships. Tell the people in your life that the old customs and traditions will go on, and new and equally meaningful traditions will be added.

One way the fear of loss often shows itself is through the old line, "You love _____ [fill in the blank] more than you love me." You may hear that from your child, your stepchild, or your wife. Just understand that the person saying that is testing your response.

"There was only one time my stepdaughter ever accused me of favoring my biological daughter," says Ken Parker. "She was upset with the way I handled some parenting issue, so she said, 'You love Mandi more than me!' Well, I've always been a little off the wall, so the way I handled it was to say, 'Yeah, you're right.'

"Well, she was really shocked when I said that. She had been expecting me to deny it. 'What do you mean?' she said.

"I replied, 'Well, she's my real kid and you're just my stepkid. Of course I love her more.' She was speechless for a few moments, then it hit her that I was ribbing her. And she got the point. I was using a therapy technique called 'paradoxing,' going along with her statement just to show how absurd it was. I have never played favorites between my stepchildren and my biological daughter, and all my kids know that. In fact, I never even refer to any of my kids as 'stepchildren' except in a clinical discussion like I'm having right now, where I use the term for the sake of clarity. All three of my kids are just 'my kids,' period.

"Sometimes people, both children and adults, will use that line, 'You love so-and-so more than me.' It's a manipulative ploy. Just don't be taken in by it. Don't respond to it by overcorrecting in your parenting style or your marriage relationship. Just give that person the reassurance he or she is looking for. Let that person know that your love for him or her does not hinge on your love for anyone else."

PRACTICAL WAYS TO JUGGLE THE ROLES

Remarriage is not for the fainthearted. It's a juggling act—but instead of keeping a bunch of dishes, ninepins, or carving knives in the air, you are juggling roles, relationships, emotions, and human lives. If you're thinking, "Whoa! Remarriage is a lot tougher than I thought!"—well, you've got that right! A lot of people are taking their cues from you and looking to you to make it work. It's a big responsibility.

But relax. We've got some ideas and suggestions that can help you make this complex, confusing system called "remarriage" work. These are not just theories. They are proven, road-tested principles which come out of our own lives and experience as remarried men and from our clinical experience as counselors. Here are some practical ways you can effectively, successfully juggle the roles of husband, father, and stepfather:

Get major problems resolved *before* marriage. If you don't, you will go into your new marriage with two strikes against you and a fastball coming right at your nose.

Rob was having nothing but trouble with Linda's two adolescent sons, but he figured, "I don't get along with them, but that'll change. They'll have to accept me. I'm marrying their mother, so they're stuck with me." Rob was not being realistic. If he doesn't get along with the kids before marriage, there is nothing magical about a wedding ceremony that will change that. Often, children who were troublesome before the wedding will intensify their efforts to sabotage the relationship after the wedding.

There are counselors who have specialized experience working with blending families. We strongly encourage premarital counseling for couples in this situation so that issues can be sorted out and communication can be improved before the marriage begins.

Find out everything you can about stepfamilies (also called "blended families," though that's a misnomer; stepfamilies are always blend*ing*, not blend*ed*). Read books on stepfamilies. Get counseling from therapists who specialize in stepfamilies. Contact the Stepfamily Association of America, Inc. (215 Centennial Mall South, Suite 212, Lincoln, Nebraska 68508-1834). This is a book for absent fathers, not a book on stepfamilies. We've just scratched the surface on the subject of stepfamilies and stepparenting. There is an enormous body of stepfamily information available that we just don't have room to squeeze into this chapter.

We recommend starting your new marriage in a neutral setting. Move out of your apartment, sell her house, and get a brand new house in which to start fresh. This will give everyone in the system a sense of starting something new—a new system with all new rules and all new relationships. This helps to level the playing field for the father coming into the system, so he can be assimilated more easily. If you move into the house Mom and her kids have been living in for ten years, the kids will look at you and say, "Who is this guy moving in on our turf?" If you all move into a new house together, there is no turf to protect.

Focus on your new marriage relationship. Make that relationship primary. You may think, "If I make my marriage relationship primary, won't I be slighting my kids?" No. The best thing you can do for your kids is to model what a healthy marriage looks like. Your first marriage didn't work out. But why compound the problem with another unsuccessful marriage? Do everything in your power to make this one work. You'll still have plenty of time and energy left for relating to your children. Your relationship with them will be more positive when they know their place is secure because you have a stable marriage.

Encourage all players in the system to talk openly with each other about feelings. Set an example by being honest about your own emotions. Remember that the feelings we describe throughout this book are normal and will occur throughout your new marriage.

When conflicts arise between your wife and your children, work to settle that conflict with all members present. Encourage honest communication, and practice conflict resolution skills. First, schedule a time for everyone involved to discuss the issue. Then openly discuss the issue at hand. Allow everyone to brainstorm possible solutions to the problem. Agree to change, compromise, or simply agree to disagree. And finally, follow up on your progress in a few weeks, making any needed adjustments to your original solution.

Don't be afraid of the feelings that may come out. Remember that these crises can be opportunities for building greater understanding and deeper long-term relationships.

Don't worry if you don't immediately feel the same love for your stepchildren as you do for your biological children. Some fathers feel guilty about this, but it's really only natural. Be patient and the love will come. If you understand and accept that fact, it will free you up to gradually build a relationship with your stepchildren.

"I wasn't around for the first eight or ten years of my kids' lives," says Ken, "so my relationship with them will be different from their biological father's relationship with them. It doesn't mean I love my biological daughter more than my stepchildren. It just means the relationship is different. I have never tried to replace the kids' original father. I've always just enjoyed the role of stepfather."

Meet the loyalty issue head-on. Tell your own children that no one can replace their mother in their own lives, and that's the way it should be. Tell them you don't expect them to immediately have warm feelings for your new wife, and you don't expect them to call her Mom. But let them know that, as an adult and as your wife, she deserves their respect and courtesy. Tell them that anything they do to be kind to her is a kindness to you.

During visitations, plan fun activities that include everyone. It's good to plan some activities that only include you and your biological children. But also plan some activities that include your new wife and her children. For example, on Saturday you can take your children to the ball game or a movie, followed by dinner at a restaurant or a fast-food place. On Sunday, the whole family can go to church, followed by a picnic or a trip to an amusement park. Anytime is a good time for all-inclusive outdoor fun—boating, driveway one-on-one, a backyard scrimmage, or a Frisbee toss. Another good activity which involves the whole family is playing board games or card games.

These kinds of inclusive activities are fun for everyone, but there is something even more profound at stake. When people play together and laugh together, they come to know and like each other. It is in these relaxed and unguarded moments that relationships and warm memories are built. Don't neglect the serious business of play.

GETTING TO ACCEPTANCE

It's a great feeling to get to the acceptance level in your new family. The testing is over. Most of the settling-in adjustments have been worked through (although there will always be at least a few minor adjustments to be made now and then, as long as your family *is* a family).

At Christmastime 1991, about six years after his remarriage, Van wrote a letter that expresses where he feels he and his new family have come on their journey of *becoming* a family. In some ways, this letter was more of a page from his own personal journal because until now he has only shown this letter to his wife. But here, in this

book, he shares it with his entire family—and with you. If you are
remarried or considering remarriage, the perspective Van shares in
this letter could well serve as your goal:

> I see this as an important year in our stepfamily journey. I
> think it's because my definition of *family* has finally caught up
> with the times and with who we are as a family. You see, we have
> attempted over the last six years to become a stepfamily, to
> feel like a family, and to be comfortable with each other.
>
> Our new family is very different from our first family or our
> family of origin. The traditional postcard pictures of family gath-
> erings don't really fit the shape of our new family, a family of the
> 1990s. Our Christmas gathering this year will be in stages. Our
> children—all five of them—will share their time with us at odd
> intervals, making sure they give their parents, grandparents,
> stepparents, and stepgrandparents as close to an equal share as
> possible.
>
> Our family is larger now, much larger than six years ago
> when we married. Somehow, through the years, we have all al-
> lowed our vision of family to grow. This was a big step for all of
> us. We have to honestly admit that, in the past, some of us have
> felt strong resentment, hurt, or anger toward others in this big
> family of ours. Yet time has healed old wounds, and each of us has
> made room in his or her mind and heart for the ones with whom
> we were once angry. This has been the most difficult part of our
> journey—more difficult than paying bills or child support,
> more difficult than making grades or moving, more difficult
> than acquiring larger cars or houses, or more dogs.
>
> We've let go of hurts. And in letting go, we have let others in.
> We've let in stepkids, stepparents, stepgrandparents, stepbrothers
> and stepsisters, friends, and yes, exes and the spouses of exes.
>
> It feels so much better. Acceptance feels better than rejection,
> welcoming feels better than exclusion, warmth feels better than
> cold.
>
> The journey is not over. There is more welcoming to do.
> There are more milestones to pass. But looking back over the last
> six years gives me confidence that our family is going to be just
> fine.
>
> Welcome everyone.

Chapter 12

BEGINNING THE JOURNEY

My concept of family," says Van, "was ingrained at an early age, and that concept did not include divorce. I grew up in a small, conservative town in Texas during the 1950s. My family attended a Southern Baptist church, and we were a secure, intact, close-knit family. My parents have remained married to each other all their adult lives.

"Divorce was not even mentioned in my upbringing. I strongly believed that when you marry, you marry for life, and the first family you have must be the family you will have for life. I tended to see divorce as an unthinkable, immoral catastrophe. So when it happened to me, it was absolutely horrible—even shameful. I thought, 'This can't happen to me! What will people think? And what about my kids? They need a family to grow up in! This isn't supposed to happen!'

"I fought hard against the divorce because of my kids and because of my feelings about divorce in general. The entire idea of divorce was like the end of the world. And yet, there it was. It was going to happen, and there wasn't a thing I could do about it.

"After the divorce, I realized that the problems in the marriage had been there a long time. I had time to reflect and to realize that

I could turn this painful experience into a fresh start. I could still have a rewarding relationship with someone else, and I could take the lessons from my past mistakes and benefit from them."

Like Van, you may have been raised to believe that divorce is wrong and shameful. Certainly, the authors of this book do not endorse divorce as a solution to marriage problems. In this book, we simply acknowledge that divorce happens, and we try to help people cope with its effects.

The authors of this book have been through divorce and so have you. Regardless of who initiated the divorce, it is now a fact, and the question is: how do we respond to divorce so that we can continue to be effective fathers? Throughout this book, we have offered guidance and perspective to those who have made the decision to divorce or who find themselves the unwilling participants in a divorce. Our goal has been to help absent fathers maintain relationships and move toward wholeness.

Our desire to help divorced fathers is based on the example we see in the life of Jesus Christ, who reached out to and befriended and healed all people, regardless of their circumstances, regardless of their hurts, regardless even of the moral choices they had made. While He didn't excuse sin or immorality, He never turned anyone away.

THE SPIRITUAL DIMENSION

One of the most destructive by-products of divorce is the sense of guilt, inadequacy, and shame it creates in so many people. We have seen it again and again in our counseling practices. We know the feeling ourselves. "After my divorce," Van recalls, "I struggled with the question of what God would think of me if I became divorced. I was thinking in black and white terms, and of course, that kind of rigid, absolute thinking can get you in a lot of trouble in crisis situations."

If you have had a relationship with God in the past, you may feel, as Van did, that your divorce is a barrier in that relationship. You may fear that God will punish you or reject you because of the divorce or that your divorce is itself a punishment from God. We want you to know that the God we believe in doesn't work that way. Your divorce does not affect His love for you.

Throughout the Bible, God is described as a Father—a loving, forgiving Father. One of the best pictures of the fatherhood of God is found in Luke 15, the story of the Prodigal Son and the Loving Father. It's the story about a son who strays, who makes a complete mess of his life, then comes crawling back home. He doesn't feel worthy to be a son anymore, so he just begs his father to take him back as one of the hired hands. But this boy's father still loves him. This father not only forgives the boy but restores him to his position as a son and an heir. The point of the story is that God is just like this loving, forgiving father.

You're a father yourself. Just think about it: if your three-year-old disobeyed you and ran into the street in front of a car, would you stop loving him? Would you shut him up in an orphanage and say, "If that's the way you're gonna behave, then you're no kid of mine!"? Of course not. You don't stop loving your children because they make mistakes or get into trouble. And neither does God.

We're weak. We fall short. We make a mess of our lives. That's why we need God. He's our Father, the One in charge of putting us back on our feet again. He may lovingly admonish us when we blow it, just as you would correct and admonish your three-year-old when he runs into the street. But He will keep on loving us. He will forgive us. That's what He promises in the Bible. "If we confess our sins," says 1 John 1:9, "He is faithful and just to forgive us our sins and to cleanse us from all unrighteousness."

It doesn't matter if you initiated the divorce, or if your wife initiated the divorce, or if the two of you mutually decided to part as friends. The causes of your divorce are irrelevant at this point to God. He wants to meet you where you are right now. He is ready to receive your hurt and your confession and to give you His forgiveness. He is ready to help you rebuild your life and your relationship with your children.

You may say, "Well, I know all this stuff; at least, I know it intellectually. But I still feel guilty all the time. I feel guilty when I relate to my wife. I feel guilty whenever I'm around my kids. I feel guilty whenever I'm alone with my thoughts or praying. I just can't get rid of these feelings of guilt."

If you continually struggle with feelings of guilt and unworthiness, you may have a problem distinguishing authentic guilt from imaginary guilt.

Authentic guilt (also called "conscience") is the spiritual and emotional twinge we feel as a result of some specific wrong act we have committed. Authentic guilt is a short-term issue, not a chronic condition. We deal with authentic guilt by confessing it to God and to the person we have injured, by repenting (that is, making a commitment to turn away from that kind of behavior in the future), and by receiving forgiveness. Then we continue on with our lives, free of guilt.

Imaginary guilt, however, is a chronic problem which arises from a sense of worthlessness, shame, and inadequacy. Imagined guilt is often difficult for people to let go of, because it is manufactured in our unconscious mind and often derives from the "critical parent" image in our minds—the image of a punishing parent standing over us with a big stick. These generalized feelings of guilt and shame are often rooted in negative childhood experiences, such as growing up with a parent who was physically or psychologically abusive or controlling.

God never intended that a man's behavior should be motivated by guilt, shame, or any other negative emotion. These emotions hinder our relationship with—and our enjoyment of—our children. These emotions can also drive us to make poor decisions, such as distancing ourselves from our children and others or jumping into new romantic relationships too soon. If you are unable to let go of chronic, generalized, imaginary guilt, then we would urge you to consult a therapist who can help you resolve those deep-rooted emotional issues.

Remember, no book of general principles and advice can substitute for professional psychotherapy, focused on your specific needs and issues. If you need help from a professional counselor, don't hesitate to seek that help. Don't let anything stop you—not even finances. Many health insurance plans provide coverage for psychotherapy. Also, many churches have funds available to help their members with counseling expenses.

If you are dealing with authentic guilt, which is directly related to specific issues in your life and your behavior toward your family and others, we would encourage you to deal with that guilt and make those relationships right. The best place to begin is with your relationship to God. Make a commitment of yourself to Jesus Christ and receive his forgiveness. Strengthen the spiritual dimension of your inner man. Talk to God daily. Read the Bible. We also suggest you read the book written by our colleague, Dr. Larry Stephens: *Please Let Me Know You, God* (Thomas Nelson Publishers, 1992).

THE "SECRET INGREDIENT"

Ken Parker remembers his own journey to God. "As a child," he says, "my parents took me to church. But to me, church attendance was about waiting for it to be over. Church was an ordeal, a lot of boredom.

"Prior to that, I got a lot of my early religious training from my grandmother, my biological father's mother. I listened to her talk about how Jesus loves me, but I never considered myself a Christian. In fact, I never had any interest in spiritual things throughout my childhood and adolescence.

"When I was in the Navy, however, I began to think about the possibility that God might actually be relevant to the way I live my life. I began to wonder what happens to you when you die. I was dissatisfied with the self-centered way I was living my life. I began talking to base chaplains, trying to get a fix on who God is and if He is real, but I didn't really get very far in that search.

"It wasn't until years after I got out of the Navy, after I had gone through one brief marriage, then married again, that I really got serious about making a connection with God. I guess I had to get some of the wildness behind me; I had to get my drinking over with. When my wife confronted me about my alcoholism, I was ready to give my life over to a Power beyond myself.

"I started reading the *Big Book of Alcoholics Anonymous*, and I started talking to God—the God which the Twelve Steps of A.A.

call 'God as we understood Him.' I started attending church and taking our daughter, Mandi, to Sunday school. I just picked the closest church to our house (probably not the best way to choose a church, but in this case I got lucky). It was a good church, and I felt right at home there.

"Over the years, my spiritual journey has taken me closer to God. I've read the Bible from cover to cover, and I talk to God on a regular basis. I believe my spiritual journey has had a profound impact on my marital relationship and my relationship with my three kids. I'm convinced that a connection to God is the 'secret ingredient' to a man's effectiveness as a father, whether he lives at home with his kids or whether he is an absent father."

As you move deeper into your own experience with God, you will find that many of the concepts we have explored in this book will take on new meaning. You will find it easier to face and resolve unfinished business. You will find it easier to forgive others—and yourself. You will have a greater motivation to swallow your pride and set aside your anger, to cooperate with your ex and her new husband, and to do whatever it takes to make the system work. You will find it easier to include everyone in your family system: children, stepchildren, stepfathers, mothers, exes, grandparents and others. All this will happen because we are all children of God, created in the image of God, loved by God, accepted by God, endowed with value by God.

You will be a happier man.

And you will be a better father.

PARTING THOUGHTS

As we close this book, we want to leave you with a few parting thoughts.

First, as you finish the last page and close the cover, we hope you will not say, "Well, I'm done with that book," but rather, "I've taken the first step on a long journey." In fact, we hope you will return to this book and dip into it again and again. In the preceding eleven chapters, we have dealt with various stages of the divorce process, and we have no way of knowing where you, as an individual reader, find yourself in that process. Some of the issues we talked about may not mean much to you right now, but six months or a year from now you might open this book again and say, "Oh! So that's what those guys were talking about! Now it makes sense!"

Second, we would encourage you to find a group of men you can talk to and be honest with. It could be as informal as a few friends from your church or office. Or it could be as structured as a support group or a therapy group formed by a professional counselor. Few experiences are more encouraging and therapeutic in life than finding and talking with other people who have walked in your shoes and know how you feel.

Contact your pastor and see if there is a support group for divorced men at your church. If you don't have a church home, then phone around and find a church which offers support groups— especially a group for divorced men. If you can't find a group, talk to your pastor or therapist about starting one. Consider using this book as a twelve-week discussion guide (one chapter per week) to jump-start a lively, freewheeling discussion.

Third, take advantage of this opportunity you now have as a divorced father to enhance your relationship with your kids. We have counseled many men who have simply turned over all parental responsibility to their wives—and they miss out on the joys of parenthood. Right now, you have a golden opportunity to improve your relationship with your children. Don't blow it.

Just think: You can see your children, you can spend quality time with them, you can be their friend—*and then you can send them home to their mother's house!* Seriously, this is a time for finding new dimensions to your relationship with your children. Take this time and use it. Please understand, we're not recommending divorce so you can have a better relationship with your children. We're saying that since you are divorced, take up the challenge to grow your relationship with your kids in new, exciting, and positive ways. Divorce is not an ideal situation by any means, but it is a situation that allows plenty of opportunities for a father to continue to build his relationship with his children.

Fourth, determine to be a good example to your children. There are a multitude of emotional ramifications to separation, divorce, remarriage, and parenting from afar. Your children are watching you and learning from you. How you deal with the divorce process will have an enormous impact on how they view you and how they approach their own lives. Right now, you are laying a foundation in their lives that will carry them into adulthood and into their own married lives. The behavior and attitudes you model for your children *right now* will determine how they view relationships for many years to come.

Fifth and finally, make a commitment to do *whatever it takes* to maintain a good relationship with your children. If it means setting aside your anger and being nice to your ex, *do it*. If it means sitting in the back row at your daughter's play or your son's basketball game, *do it*. If it means swallowing pride until you choke, *do it*. Tell yourself, "Whatever it takes, I'll do it."

Your children are more important than your pride. Your children are more important than your anger. Your children are more important than any grudge you've got against your ex-wife or her new husband. Always think of the impact of your behavior on their lives. Never take your eyes off the goal: *your relationship with your kids*.

You've gone through an ordeal—a legal and emotional nightmare that no one can understand until they have been through it themselves. And there are still tough times ahead. But there are also good times ahead—a good relationship with your children and a good life for yourself. Our prayers and our thoughts are with you. Don't give up. You're going to make it.

We wish you peace and a bright future together with the most important people in your life—the ones who call you "Dad."

Notes

Chapter 4: Taking Care of Business
1. See Mark 11:15–16.
2. See Ephesians 4:26–27, 31–32.

Chapter 7: The Mother's Perspective
1. Matthew 7:12; see also Luke 6:31.
2. Philippians 2:4.
3. Romans 12:17; see also Matthew 18:21–22; Colossians 3:13.
4. Romans 12:18.
5. Ephesians 6:4; see also Colossians 3:21.

Chapter 10: Look Before You Leap
1. 2 Corinthians 5:17.

About The Authors

Ken Parker maintains a full time practice at the Minirth-Meier Tunnell and Wilson Clinic of Austin, Texas. He is a licensed marriage and family therapist and holds a master's degree in social work from the University of Texas at Austin. He is the author of *Reclaiming Your Inner Child*. He is remarried with three children.

Van Jones works as Director of Treatment Services at Methodist Home Family Services and Counseling Center in Waco, Texas. He maintains a private practice in counseling, specializing in working with families in transition—divorce, remarriage, and stepfamilies. He is remarried with five children.